T0209576

# PREVAILING PRAYER LIFESTYLE

Ovo Imoedemhe

WESTBOW
PRESS®
A DIVISION OF THOMAS NELSON
& ZONDERVAN

WestBow Press books may be ordered through booksellers or by contacting:

WestBow Press
A Division of Thomas Nelson & Zondervan
1663 Liberty Drive
Bloomington, IN 47403
www.westbowpress.com
1 (866) 928-1240

ISBN: 978-1-9736-5349-3 (sc)
ISBN: 978-1-9736-5350-9 (e)

Print information available on the last page.

WestBow Press rev. date: 3/11/2019

# Contents

# Acknowledgements

Saying 'thank you' is a virtue I relish and at the same time I shy away from most times because of the fear of missing out important people that should be mentioned. I solicit the forgiveness of everyone in advance in case I omit any name. I appreciate my in-dwelling partner; the Holy Spirit who keeps teaching, instructing, guiding and supplying me with all that I need, spiritually, materially, physically, emotionally and mentally, without Whose inspiration, this book wouldn't have been a reality. Thank You Lord! Thank You Dear Holy Spirit.

Special thank you to the General Overseer of The Redeemed Christian Church of God (The RCCG) worldwide, Pastor E.A Adeboye and his lovely wife Pastor Mrs Folu Adeboye. Although I do not have a personal relationship with you both, I am grateful to have been part of the millions of people your lives have impacted. Thank God for your obedience in yielding to the call of God. Thank you for your exemplary lifestyle of prayer, holiness and obedience as typified in your *posture, precision* and *persistence* in prayers.

A special thank you to my Pastors, Ministers and the entire family of the Amazing Grace Parish (AGP) of The RCCG Queens Road Leicester United Kingdom, where I have been mightily blessed by everyone for the past seven years. You all are indeed AMAZING!!! Thank you all.

Specifically, I want to thank Professor Stephen and Mumsie Rufina Odusanya for being my pillar of strength, but for you both I couldn't even thing of keeping my sanity, having a shelter over my head, and strength to carry on, let alone be able to complete this book. God bless you mightily for being my Mum and Dad in every way. I am immensely grateful. Thank you.

Thank you to my Pastor and Pastor Mrs Demola Obembe for all your support. Thank you to Pastor Emmanuel Baba Isiaka for your huge support. Million thanks to Mr and Mrs David Adebayo. Special thank you to Pastor and Mrs Olushola Subair. I am also immensely grateful to Mr and Mrs Kehinde (Kay) Odude, Mr and Mrs Taiwo (Tee) Odude, Mr and Mrs Shehu Ibrahim. Huge thank you to Bola Ogunkoya, Jude Bwire, the Adeguns, the Babajides, the Popoolas, the Gittaos, the Bejides, the Ajiehs, the Akandes, and Grandma Maureen... Together with the entire AGP family, you all played very crucial roles in my life, the completion of this book in this season of my life is a testimony of how amazing you all are. Thank you all.

I like to extend my deep appreciation to my friends who though far away but had very compelling positive impact in my life while writing this book. Chinyere Onwuchekwa, Marie David, Mena Ajakpovi, Maxwell Kadiri, Edokpolor Ighodaro, Oseme Adesuyi, Isabelle Ejikeme, Lola Duroshola, Patrick Udeh, Olumide Solake, Bunmi Iyere, Valentina Asagba, Mary Abamwa... The list is endless. Also, my profound gratitude goes to Eddie and Gesi Eddie-Imishue, and to Pastor and Pastor Mrs Akpo Onduku all of the 'Bradford Family'. You all had and continue to have profuse impact in my life. Thank you all.

I would also like to thank my pastors for the past years since I became a member of God's family, notably Rev Cyril Yerifor, Pastors Duke Okosun, Matthew Arowolo, Omo Gbinigie, Tayo Bamgbose, and Evangelist Chuks all of the Redeeming Love Chapel, Lagos. Thank you all. Thank you to Pastor Professor I.O Omoruyi of Dominion Life International Ministries, Pastor Dr Bright Obasuyi, Pastors Demola Akinbami, Johnson Erahor, Dr. Dave Oseyemwen, IZ Omoruyi as well as Pastor Wallace Lodge and Rev Chuks Okonyia of blessed memories. You all have made significant impact in my life over the years. Thank you.

Although I have several instructors, teachers and pastors who have been and continue to be of immense blessing to me, and to whom I am eternally grateful, my foundation in the Lord stems from my spiritual Dad who is also the founder of the Pneuma Force Foundation Ministries Glory Pavilion Church Rev Dr Efe Obuke and his lovely wife Priscilla Efe-Obuke. Despite being in Louisiana, United States of America, your continued support and prayers for me are very highly treasured. Thank you both.

My profound gratitude to Pastor Funmi Obembe. Thanks so much for your love, patience and painstaking proofreading of my manuscript. You did not only support with the editing and providing very insightful and useful suggestions, you also supported me financially to ensure that this book is a reality. Thanks so much for your immense support and encouragement in every way. May the Lord God bless and reward your labour of love towards me. Thank you.

I am indebted to my husband Walter and my lovely children Oyarelemi, Oghenakogie and Aghunopua (Lemmy, Ogie and Ono). Without your support, this book wouldn't have been a reality. Thank you for being my support and strength! Thank you for making me cups of tea when I stayed up late at night, thank you for parting me on my back and saying 'Mum, you will be fine'. Thank you for the hugs and thank you for praying for me. Thank you all.

# Foreword

Every Christian has been given the wonderful privilege of a relationship with God as Father. A relationship they can deepen by communicating with Him and staying connected and close to Him. Every Christian has the opportunity to draw closer and closer to God, and to get to know His will and in the place of prayer enforce it and His purposes in our world. However, unfortunately many do not take advantage of this great opportunity for various reasons ranging from ignorance about prayer, complacency, a lack of discipline, an unawareness of the urgency to pray, all the way down to a lack of consistency and intentionality in prayer. In this book 'Prevailing Prayer Lifestyle', Ovo addresses these issues, helping by God's grace to dispel ignorance about the importance of not just prayer but of having prevailing prayer as a lifestyle.

It is very easy to discount this piece because of the assumption that we are already praying and therefore, any literature on prayer may be repetitive. However, reading through this book did not only highlight some important points that we sometimes take for granted but it also fuelled the urgency to pray more. Some of the highlighted points include praying with discernment, understanding the spirit realm as being superior to the earth realm and our position of authority in that realm, the need to prioritise prayer, to have the right posture, persistence and proportionality in prayers. In addressing these points, the book brings to my mind the need to be strategic and intentional in our prayers because the days are evil, and the opposition is not relenting. There are several other dimensions to prayer that this book brings to the fore. Specifically, the book talks about a blend of praise and prayer thereby saying that prevailing prayer has no end because we do not only make spiritual deposit in our spiritual bank account when we pray, our prayers are actually safely banked in heaven.

Therefore, regardless of where you are at, whether about to give up because of a protracted situation you have been praying about and with no apparent answers, whether you have everything going rosy for you, I recommend this book to everyone. In reading it, I pray that like I did, you will find bubbling up within you a new and strong desire to pray more but not just pray more but to also pray well (i.e. in line with God's will). I also pray that you will not be casual with prayers, you will not miss a prayer meeting, but above all, I pray that we will be consistent and persistent as we cultivate prevailing prayer as a lifestyle all our days.

**Pastor Funmi Obembe**
The Redeemed Christian Church of God
Amazing Grace Parish
Leicester UK.

# Glossaries

| | | |
|---|---|---|
| AMPC | - | Amplified Bible Classic Edition |
| ECHR | - | European Convention on Human Rights |
| IJMN | - | In Jesus's Mighty Name |
| IJN | - | In Jesus's Name |
| KICCTV | - | Kingsway International Christian Centre Television |
| KJV | - | King James Version |
| NIV | - | New International Version |
| NKJV | - | New King James Version |
| NT | - | New Testament |
| OT | - | Old Testament |
| TV | - | Television |

# Introduction: Prevailing Prayer Lifestyle

Prevailing prayer is the prayer that prevails over any negative atmosphere or circumstances in our lives, in our families and in our world. However, there can be no prevailing except there is first a travailing. It is seen in the Bible that when Prophet Isaiah questioned whether a nation could be born in a moment he concluded by saying; '...as soon as Zion travailed she brought forth her children' **(Isaiah 66:8; KJV)**. Although like others, this scripture has deeper connotations and interpretations, and admittedly, there is danger in reading scriptures in isolation or taking them out of context, Zion represents the Church. Isaiah uses the birthing process to describe prayer. Therefore, the Church can prevail only when we have travailed in prayers. I perceive the Lord impressing in my heart; *'Awake Church and realise the season you are in, discern and understand the times that you might prioritise the place of prayer'*. Like a pregnant woman about to give birth, we must begin to take the appropriate posture in prayers, we must be precise, purposeful, persistent and proportionate in our prayers. For the time is coming and now is that time when people will kill you and think they are doing God a service **(John 16:2; NKJV)**.

Simultaneously, it is a time when seven women will take hold of one man and say we will eat our food and provide ourselves clothes but only let us be called by your name **(Isaiah 4:1; NKJV)**. This speaks of people running to the Lord and His Church, because there is only one NAME by which all men must be saved. And nations, principalities, powers and people everywhere will run to the Church to ask to be taught the ways of the Lord.

> Now it shall come to pass in the latter days *That* the mountain of the LORD's house Shall be established on the

top of the mountains, And shall be exalted above the hills; And all nations shall flow to it. [3] Many people shall come and say, "Come, and let us go up to the mountain of the LORD, To the house of the God of Jacob; He will teach us His ways, And we shall walk in His paths." For out of Zion shall go forth the law, And the word of the LORD from Jerusalem.
**(Isaiah 2:2-3; Micah 4:1-3; NKJV)**

The precursor to these coming to pass is the Church taking the place of travail to give birth.

This book was prompted by my 'senior brother' David Adebayo who is the Minister in charge of the Prayer Department in my local Church Amazing Grace Parish (AGP) of The Redeemed Christian Church of God (The RCCG) Queens Road Leicester United Kingdom. Sometime in February 2017, AGP held its usual 'Prayer Weekend'. Customarily, AGP holds about three prayer weekends in the year, one for every quarter of the year save the last quarter. February 2017 Prayer Weekend was an in-house programme and David Adebayo approached me and asked if I could be one of the speakers for the weekend. 'Yes, it's always an honour and a great privilege to serve in any capacity in God's house...' I responded.

With that, Adebayo said he would come back to me on the theme for the prayer weekend and on which of the days I would speak. In fact, he asked me right there what day I would like to speak; Friday or Saturday, as Sunday was reserved for our Senior Pastor, Pastor Demola Obembe. I initially said any day would be fine with me but he insisted that I choose between the two so I decided on Saturday so that our 'Big Daddy' Pastor Emmanuel Baba Isiaka would have opened the programme on Friday and I would be able to build on the foundation he would have laid. Soon after this conversation, I began to panic, and several questions ran through my head, 'what do you think you're doing accepting to speak at a programme and in this congregation where almost everyone is a Bible Scholar?' However, I pushed the thoughts and fears aside and began to pray and ask God what He would have me say and do on the day.

Not too long, the day came and I couldn't even go through half of what the Lord had laid in my heart. This is not the first time. Everyone knows me for my inability to 'finish', whether in writing critical examinations, or presentations at seminars and conferences. Specifically, I recall one of the examinations I wrote during my undergraduate days, where I inadvertently made my friend Chinyere Onyekwere Onwuchekwa to panic because she usually sits beside me in every exam. In fact, on this occasion, it was 'Jurisprudence and Legal Theory', and about an hour into the exams, I had requested for extra answer booklet because I had exhausted the one I was given, curiously, everyone had similar answer booklet. My friend panicked and thought to herself that she may have performed poorly in the exams because she had not as much as gone half way into her own booklet let alone finish it to ask for another one. (Of course Chichi performed excellently well in all her/our exams together both at the undergraduate level and at law school. She is a perfect blend of beauty and brilliance. She is a New York Attorney and currently at the University of Arkansas Law School for her JD.)

What annoyed my friend most was that after the exam, I came out feeling and looking miserable and she couldn't get it. 'Ovo what's the matter with you?' She asked, 'I didn't finish' I answered weeping. 'Ah! Ovo when will you ever finish, when?' Chichi quizzed. 'You collected two extra booklets meaning you submitted three whilst I managed to finish one…what were you writing?' 'Did you answer five as against the four questions we were asked to answer? Or did you set extra questions for yourself? What was it that you didn't finish…?' Chichi's questions seemed endless. This became a recurrent situation, but with time my friend understood me and left me alone, so anytime I complained that I didn't finish a particular exam, she just kept quiet, and walked away. Somehow, this 'I couldn't finish' syndrome has been a major highlight of my life. *It is well with me! I pray that in my life time I am able to finish my ministry and the specific assignment that God has for me. It is well with me in the Mighty Name of our Lord Jesus Christ. Amen!*

Coming back to the story of this prayer weekend, Saturday 18 February 2017 came and the Lord helped me to deliver the message, which most people commended as very detailed and really incisive and that they were really mightily blessed, but I was full of tears and guess why? '… I didn't finish'!

It began to dawn on me that there is no other way 'to finish' than to put my thoughts and the things God is teaching me into writing. This became apparent because I am not a Pastor in the sense of having a congregation and so I do not and will never have the opportunity to teach every Sunday. I think if God called me to pastor, I might just be the only congregation because even my children and my husband will probably leave me in church and go home, because 'I must finish', and everyone has a concentration span. My husband is not a Pastor either and I thank God for that because I am sure I would have made his life really miserable by hijacking the pulpit all the time.

This is the way I think I have been able to discover that there is something locked inside of me and since everything in the earth realm is time-bound, the option I am left with to pour out what is in my heart is by writing. Thank you Lord for creating us and putting us in the realm of time. Time constraints with everything on earth helped me to find this channel through which to ventilate and pour out what God is teaching me daily by the Holy Ghost. I thought deeply that if I must realise my potentials, then this avenue of writing a book and probably books must be explored. This would be my first Christian literature and I owe it all to God Almighty and the Holy Spirit who is my helper, teacher and guide. Again, thanks to my Pastors Demola and Funmi Obembe, and the entire leadership of Amazing Grace Parish (AGP). Specifically, I want to thank David Adebayo for giving me the opportunity to be one of the speakers at that prayer weekend.

The theme for the AGP Prayer Weekend 17-19 February 2017 was '**The Lifestyle of Prayer**' coined from **Daniel 6:10**. However, while I prepared for my speaking session the Lord dropped in my heart the word '**Prevailing**' and hence the title '**Prevailing Prayer Lifestyle**'.

Again, special thanks to my spiritual Dad Efe Obuke. The foundation of the word and the life in the Spirit he taught me in those early years have very specific and profound impact in my life and the insights in this book.

## Structure of the Book

The book is structured into three parts.

**Part one consists of four chapters as follows:**

**Chapter One** provides different and general definitions of prayers. It also provides the specific definition the Lord impressed in my heart as I prepared for the Prayer Weekend and that is that prayer is spiritual communication that connects us with God, grants us access to the spirit realm to enforce heaven's agenda on earth. A working definition of 'Prevailing Prayer' is also provided as spiritual communication orchestrated by God or in line with God's divine mandate and fervently enforced on earth on a continuous basis. Some components of this definition which includes 'spiritual communication', 'orchestrated by God' and 'fervently enforced on earth on a continuous basis' are explained in the chapter. The chapter also discusses the specific definition of 'prevailing' and two instances where the word was used in scriptures.

**Chapter Two** deals with prayer primarily as access to God, access to the spirit realm and access to the supernatural. The chapter provides detailed explanation of a few facts about the 'spirit realm'. These include that the spirit realm is real and tangible even though not to our physical senses. The spirit realm is more powerful and superior to the earth realm, everything on earth stems from the spiritual i.e. everything including our blessings are in the spirit realm. There is order and ranking in the spirit realm and we have authority and a higher ranking than Satan and his fallen demons. These explanations are considered important because when we engage in prevailing prayers, we need to understand our identity; who we are, our ranking and spiritual authority in the realm of the spirit.

**Chapter Three** includes a discussion of the different types of prayers. There could be more and admittedly, most of the eight types of prayers discussed do overlap. Nevertheless, it is important to understand these different types of prayer so we can be better equipped to pray more intelligently by engaging the right type per time. The types of prayers identified and discussed include the prayer of salvation/redemption, the prayer of consecration, the prayer of faith, the prayer of agreement and the prayer of thanksgiving. Others include the prayer of dedication, the prayer of intercession/supplication/petition and the prayer of praise/worship.

**Chapter Four** includes a discussion of two broad classifications of prayer, namely private/individual and public/corporate. For all kinds of prayers discussed in the previous chapter and whether prayers are privately or publicly offered, two main ingredients are discussed. They are the ingredients of agreement and faith. Prayer is therefore predicated on these two elements. First, we have to agree with God and agreeing with God means being in alignment with His word. Second, we need to have faith in God that He is able to do what He promised.

**Part two of the book consists of Chapters five, six and seven.**

**Chapter Five**, is the nucleus of the book. It provides a case study of Daniel with an exposition of **Daniel 6:10,** which says *'Now when Daniel knew that the writing was signed, he went home. And in his upper room, with his windows open toward Jerusalem, he knelt down on his knees three times that day, and prayed and gave thanks before his God, as was his custom since early days'* (**NKJV**). From this scripture, I got the impression of 7 'P' words in relation to prevailing prayers. They include the need to have a *place* of prayer. Although several issues may arise in our daily lives that may provoke us to anger, but rather than being provoked we should be propelled to *prioritise* prayer. There is an appropriate *posture* when we pray, and that posture is kneeling down, which reflects our humility, total submission and surrender to our God. Others include the need to be *precise, purposeful* and *persistent* in prayer. Lastly, there is need for *proportionality* in prayer. These 7 'P' words were reflected in Daniel's prayer and for us to engage in prevailing prayer these 7 P words should be understood and observed.

**Chapter Six** analyses how Daniel's lifestyle of prayer mirrors the early Church and by extension, it reflects the Church in contemporary times. The early Church was hated and persecuted the same way Daniel was persecuted. Obnoxious laws were promulgated which were essentially targeted at Daniel, again, this did not only occur with the early Church, it is also happening in contemporary times'. A few instances of the enactment of obnoxious laws in Scriptures are enumerated in this chapter and in all instances, such laws were passed with the sole intention of annihilating God's people. Despite all, through Daniel's *dedication, diligence* and *determination* he gained the benefits of a strong intimate *relationship* with God. Daniel's relationship with God resulted in ***revelation,*** as God ***revealed*** deep secrets to him that made him to remain ***relevant*** throughout his time in Babylon, under four different kings spanning several decades. Therefore, for the Church to remain relevant in contemporary times, we must prioritise our relationship with God so we can receive revelation relevant to the questions and puzzles in this dark and dying world.

The thrust of **Chapter Seven** is the biblical fast and prevailing prayer because prayer and fasting go hand in hand. In His teaching the Lord Jesus Christ admonished believers to fast. He said; 'Moreover, ***when*** (not 'if') you fast...' **(Matthew 6:16; NKJV)**, which means fasting is not an option. He also said that certain things cannot be dealt with except by prayer and fasting. It is important to note that merely abstaining from food is only the first limb of the biblical fast. The second limb which entails having an intimate relationship with God by studying, meditating His word and praying is what makes the biblical fast distinct from every other kind of fast. Different impacts and blessings of the biblical fast, which include both spiritual and physical benefits are also discussed.

**Part three of the book consists of Chapters eight, nine and ten.**

**Chapter Eight** discusses the question of whether God hears and answers us when we pray. Although the answer to the question is an overwhelming obvious YES, I decided to examine ten pre-requisites that guarantee answers to our prayers. The list is not exhaustive. Therefore, there could be more but these are primarily very important pre-conditions to answers to our prayers. Are there reasons for seeming delays in answers to our prayers and is God silent to our prayers sometimes? Yes and yes. At times we have no explanations but in hindsight we are grateful to God for delays and for unanswered prayers.

**Chapter Nine** includes the discussion of the mix or the blend of prayer and praise. It highlights that when there is a mix of both prayer and praise, the prophetic is inevitable; the prophetic being the open declaration of God's mind to us per time. The importance of listening to and hearing God when we pray cannot be overemphasised. Prayer is not talking to God alone. What completes the communication is when God speaks back to us. Significantly, this is a strong distinguishing factor to other 'prayers' (spiritual communications) that other people engage in; our God speaks back to us. Indeed, in some cases, prayers start with Him. Therefore, the importance of watching in prayer, includes listening to and hearing God speak to us.

**Chapter Ten** provides further exposition of the 7 P words in prevailing prayers. Although an explanation of these words was provided in Chapter Five, this last chapter offers a more detailed discussion.

In conclusion, I discussed the lifestyle that is required namely the lifestyle of love, being full of the word, and a life in the spirit. Love will always drive us to the place of intimacy with God in prayer, as well as propel us to pray for other people, cities and the nations of the world. The same way the Lord Jesus Christ had compassion for people during his earthly ministry is the exact same way love should make us selfless and sacrificial in praying for others. Whilst sin-free living, and obedience are equally important, I believe these could be subsumed under love. The book concludes with the ***proof*** of prevailing prayers. Whilst admittedly, the proof of prevailing prayer may be answers and physical manifestations of the things we pray about, I conclude that prevailing prayer is 'unfinished business', *ad-infinitum*.

# CHAPTER ONE

# What is Prayer?

## Introduction

It may seem pointless to attempt a definition or explanation of prayer because everyone knows what it is. However, I think we need to explain this a little bit for the sake of those who are not yet in Christ and who may be wondering what this means. What I have come to realise is that everyone engages in one form of prayer or the other whether subconsciously or consciously. But not everyone really knows what prayer is and who they address when they pray. As we would see in subsequent chapters, in our context prayer is primarily a relationship with God. In prayer we partner with God with the understanding that He made the whole universe and He has His divine will and purpose for creation. Therefore, His mandate should be enforced on earth. So regardless of what understanding we had previously of prayer, we still need to know or be reminded of what it is.

## 1.1 What is Prayer?

There are several definitions of prayers. The most common definition is that *prayer is talking to God and God talking back to us*. Prayer has also been defined as the means by which heaven's agenda is accessed and enforced on earth, '...Your Kingdom come, Your will be done on earth as it is in heaven...' (**Matthew 6:10; NKJV**). Other definitions include:

1

Prayer is the act of talking with God. It is an action, not merely an attitude. Prayer is the practice of the presence of God. It is the place where pride is abandoned, hope is lifted and supplication is made. Prayer is the place of admitting our need of God who is our source-Father, prayer is adopting humility and claiming dependence upon God. Prayer is the needful practice of the Christian. Prayer is our exercise of faith and hope. Prayer is the privilege of touching the heart of the Father through the son of God, Jesus Christ our Lord.[1]

Prayer is access, it is the privilege to connect with our source our Heavenly Father through our Lord Jesus Christ. Prayer is enforcing Heaven's mandate here on earth. Prayer is superimposing God's will on every negative situation. Prayer is the opportunity to access the will of God and His power to accomplish the five-fold assignment on earth namely to be fruitful, to multiply, to replenish, to subdue and to have dominion over all of God's creation. Prayer is giving God permission or licence to interfere and intervene in the affairs of the world. Prayer is spiritual warfare.

A few of these definitions will be referred to later, but while preparing for the prayer weekend, the understanding of prayer that was brought to my mind by the Holy Spirit was that **Prayer is Spiritual Communication...**

As you will agree, this is a very broad and incomplete definition, but that made me to prod further with questions; spiritual communication by who, to who, in what manner, in what place and how... and several other questions came up. The first understanding I got was that every human being on earth is a spirit being and every human being on earth prays. In other words, every human being on earth communicates with something or some deity, every human being on earth petitions and requests something from someone higher and superior than them. In this context, the Hindus, the Muslims,

---

[1] Marie David 'Does God Answer Prayers?' Being message preached at Liberty Square Ministries (LSM) Church Gwarinpa, Abuja Nigeria on Sunday 18 June 2017.

the Sikh, the Buddhists and everyone that belongs to one form of religion or the other prays. Even the Atheists who don't believe in God and Satanists pray. They all engage in one form of spiritual communication with some invisible god.[2]

As a sports lady, the Lord also brought to my mind my active days in sports, playing field hockey how I used to lead the prayer before every hockey tournament and 'surprisingly' then I used to wonder why the opposite team prayed and who they prayed to, because I thought that I belong to the one true and living God and it is only prayer by God's people to the only true God that can be regarded as prayer. With the help of the Holy Spirit and in hindsight, I realised that every human being prays, and if every human being is asking some superior being or superior spirit for something, why won't we who belong to God and are the children of God ask God for what we want, why do we leave everything to chance, why are we so casual when it comes to prayers…?

Therefore, there is a call to the place of prayer, because if everyone prays to some invisible spirit being, then much more should the Church, believers in Christ who are called to pray. God has instructed us to pray without ceasing (**1st Thessalonians 5:17; NKJV**). In other words, prayer ought to be our lifeline and therefore a lifestyle. Prayer connects us to our source. God is Spirit and He can only give birth to spirit beings therefore we who are God's children are spirit beings and prayer is one means by which we connect with our source. With time the fullness of what prayer is came to me as; **Prayer is spiritual communication… that connects us with God, grants us access to the spirit realm to enforce heaven's mandate on earth.**

---

[2] I can almost hear someone say what about agnostics (those who doubt the existence of God) and humanists (non-religious people who advocate human welfare and happiness)? People who don't believe in anything but themselves and the spread of the humanistic gospel and individualism are real. However, what I believe is that deep down in every human being is the craving for their source and therefore those who propagate secular humanism are in delusion and self-denial. God loves them, Jesus died for them and so we must love and pray for them for their eyes to be opened to the glorious gospel of the Lord Jesus Christ.

## 1.2 What is Prevailing Prayer?

Prevailing Prayer is *spiritual communication orchestrated by God or in line with God's divine mandate* and *fervently enforced on earth* on a *continuous basis.* The different components of this definition (i) spiritual communication, (ii) orchestrated by God or in line with God's divine mandate and (iii) fervently enforced on earth on a continuous basis, will be discussed in the next chapter, but here we will explain the word 'prevailing' and the meaning of the phrase 'spiritual communication' within the context of this book. The question may be asked; "why 'prevailing' prayer?" Everyone will agree that prayer is prayer and the only way we can prevail or triumph over the enemy is through prayer. It therefore seems superfluous to add 'prevailing'. Nevertheless, the word was prompted in my heart by the Holy Spirit.

## 1.3 What does 'Prevailing' mean?

'Prevailing' is the present continuous tense of the word 'prevail'. According to the English Oxford living Dictionaries, 'prevail' has its origin in the Latin word *Praevalere,* which is made up of two words; *prae,* which means **'before'** and *valere,* which means **'have power'**. Cumulatively 'prevail' means to **'have greater power'**.[3] It means to prove more powerful or superior. It means to win, to win out, to win through, to triumph and to be victorious. To prevail means to carry the day, to finish first, to come out ahead, to come out on top, to succeed, to prove superior, to conquer, to overcome and to gain mastery or ascendancy. Other meanings of 'prevail' include to get control or influence over.[4] To prevail means to be widespread or current in a particular area or at a particular time.[5] To prevail on/upon means to succeed in persuading someone to do something, or to persuade someone to change their mind.

---

[3] See the English Oxford Living Dictionaries. Available at https://en.oxforddictionaries.com/definition/prevail> (Assessed 7 October 2017)

[4] See Cambridge Dictionary available at http://dictionary.cambridge.org/dictionary/english/prevail> (Assessed 7 October 2017)

[5] See the English Oxford Living Dictionaries.

From the above, 'prevailing' connotes a continuous state of having greater power, of winning and triumphing, a continuous state of being more powerful and superior and a continuous state of constantly gaining ascendancy over something, a situation or an opponent. It also means constantly persuading and getting someone to change their mind about a situation.

## 1.3.1 Instances of the word 'Prevail' in Scriptures

Reference to **Isaiah 66:8** '…for as soon as Zion travailed, she brought forth her children' (KJV), shows that we must travail in order to prevail. Travail means labour, struggle, effort, and toil. In fact the New King James Version uses the word 'labour', which describes a pregnant woman about to give birth. This implies that there is appropriate posture and like a woman about to give birth, we must position properly for a smooth delivery process. Posture in prevailing prayer includes the physical and heart postures, which means that both what goes on within us and our expressed or outward attitudes are important. These would be discussed in detail subsequently, for now let us examine the word 'prevail'. There could be more, but as I prayed the Lord impressed in my heart two specific instances in scriptures where 'prevail' was used. The first was with Jacob and the second relates to Apostle Paul's ministry in Ephesus.

## 1.3.1.1 Jacob *Prevailed* over the Angel of the Lord

> And He said, "Your name shall no longer be called Jacob, but Israel; for you have struggled with God and with men, and have **prevailed. (Genesis 32:28; NKJV)**

Jacob is the son of Isaac and grandson of Abraham. He was the younger of the twin children that struggled in their mother Rebekah's womb. The senior of the twin was Esau. However, by reason of his struggle, Jacob became the senior and the first grandchild of Abraham, even though he was meant to be second. Admittedly, there are different perspectives on the life of Jacob, but I truly identify with Jacob's life because for some of us, even though we are in the dispensation of grace, 'struggles' seem to trail our lives, nothing just come on a platter. Thank God for the Lord Jesus who has paid fully for all things to be freely ours, yet it appears we still have to 'struggle' for somethings?

Jacob's struggles were both physical and spiritual. In fact, because he began struggling right from his mother's womb, struggle trailed his life. The conclusion was that although his name Jacob meant grabber, deceiver, cheat, manipulator, liar, trickster, supplanter, he was changed to Israel which means 'Prince with God', 'God persists' or 'God perseveres'.[6] Thus, despite all odds, Jacob struggled and wrestled himself out of the negativities that accompanied his name and life. Jacob's life mirrors some of our lives because in contemporary times, it appears that our lives are full of both physical and spiritual struggles. Therefore, if we have the example of a man who struggled physically and spiritually both with men and with God and prevailed, then, we must follow that example and not give up.

## A. Make a switch from the physical to the spiritual.

The things we are confronted with are only symptoms, the root of all problems lies in the spirit realm and it is by engaging in that realm that we get the problems decisively dealt with. It must be noted that the defining moment for Jacob, was not with his physical struggles. Rather, it was the spiritual struggle that brought him a change of name and fame. No wonder, the Bible says 'For we do not wrestle against flesh and blood...' (**Ephesians 6:12; NKJV**). In other words, we do wrestle but our wrestle is not against anything in the physical but against wicked spirits in the spirit realm.

Interestingly, although Jacob began struggling right from his mother's womb, his main struggle and troubles began after he received the blessing from his father Isaac. No sooner had Jacob received the blessing from his father than his trouble started. Could it be that the reason we are faced with several struggles and challenges is because of the blessing that we carry? Jacob fled to a foreign place; Paddan-aram to live with an uncle, Laban,

---

[6] **'Israel'** consists of two components, namely **'Isra'** which means struggle, persevere or contend and **'El' (Elohim),** which means God. See 'Israel Meaning' *Abarim Publications.* Available at http://www.abarim-publications.com/Meaning/Israel. html#.WeCYGz93GUk>

whom he served for 20 years, out of which 14 was for Rachel because he was deceived to have Leah after the first 7 years **(Genesis 29:15-30; NKJV).** His physical struggles continued.

Although Jacob had accumulated enormous wealth by the wisdom of 'incubation',[7] which I believe God gave him, his struggle continued as he had to confront Esau from whom he ran all these years. It was at this point that he made the switch from the physical to the spiritual. While the physical struggles trailed his life the spiritual struggle was for a night and yet that one night of encounter brought a change of name, the birth of a nation Israel and marked the beginning of a journey into divine purpose and destiny **(Genesis 32:22-32; NKJV).**

---

[7] Incubation is the process of keeping or maintaining something at the most favourable temperature and under the right condition so it can develop. It means sitting on eggs so as to hatch them by the warmth of the body. The method Jacob used to 'out-con' his uncle Laban and to get wealth has been discussed by different theologians. Most of the views are embedded in what is called a 'Theology of Divine Deception' in which the narratives of Abraham Isaac and Jacob including Joseph are portrayed as divine deception by God to bring about His promises. However, I see the specific story of Jacob especially relating to the wisdom to use peeled poles, and to get the animals to look at them while mating to have some kind of prenatal influence on the flocks as a divine wisdom of incubation. It is divine wisdom because previously no one had used that method to increase productivity. The idea was that if the flocks had a visual impression of stripes while they were mating and conceiving, the offspring would assume this same form. Jacob placed these peeled poles in front of the animals for the resulting offspring to become exactly like them **streaked, speckled, or spotted (see Genesis 30:37-39).** There are about three stages of this incubated strategy up to the last verse of **Genesis 30**, which I will encourage us to read because the result was that although Laban had tricked Jacob and made Jacob to serve him for 20 years, with one divine idea, the wealth of Laban was transferred to Jacob. How does this relate to prayer? This is very strategic because prayer is likened to the process of birthing and therefore incubation is important. While we pray and wait for the physical manifestation of what we pray about what do we see? We cannot pray for healing and yet what we see is sickness, we cannot pray for peace and yet all we see is violence, killing, disaster and calamity, we cannot pray for abundance and yet all we see is lack and depravity, we cannot pray for freedom and liberty and yet all we see is slavery, servitude and bondage. Prevailing prayer includes changing our perspectives, we must see what and how God sees because it is what we see that we can possess. **(see Genesis 13:15)**

## B. Confront your fears

Despite his wealth both in cattle and substance, there was a void in Jacob's life. The only way to fill that void was to confront his fears, namely, face his brother whom he had seemingly defrauded of his birth right and blessing. It was on his way to face his brother that he wrestle with the Lord and that spiritual struggle changed not only his life but it also marked the birth of the nation of Israel. We must realise that most times, our prayers aren't about us, but about generations yet unborn. Also, at some points in our lives, we will all have to confront our fears and the very things we had hitherto run so far away from. However, when we engage in the spiritual by travailing in prayer, we are sure to prevail, the same way Jacob did. As mentioned earlier whilst the first impression of 'Prevail' relates to Jacob, the second was with Apostle Paul during his missionary work.

# 1.3.1.2 Paul Prevailed in Ephesus

So the word of the Lord grew mightily and **prevailed** – **Acts 19:20**

Apostle Paul was in the **City of Ephesus** cumulatively for three years (**Acts 20:31; NKJV**). During his missionary journeys, it appears that Paul spent more time in Ephesus than he did in other cities probably because of the widespread practice of magic and the worship of a 'goddess Diana' (**Acts 19:19, 23-27; NKJV**). In fact, at a point, one Demetrius who was the leader of silversmiths that made the graven images for the worship of Diana, instigated a riot amongst the 'union' of silversmiths and worshippers of Diana that if they did not drive Paul away, his preaching of Jesus will stop them from securing their only means of livelihood. However, with the persistence and perseverance of Paul, applying proportionate force in that City, Bible says the word grew and it prevailed over the practice of magic and the darkness brought about by the popular worship of goddess Diana. Similarly, the Lord impressed in my heart that when we engage in prevailing prayer we should expect some confrontations, but we will certainly overcome and prevail over the darkness in our lives, families, cities, and the nations of the world both in our day and in the next generation if we persist and persevere.

Prevailing prayer relates to the mandate that God has given to believers to enforce heaven's agenda here on earth on a ***continuous basis***. The phrase '… Your kingdom come, Your will be done on earth as it is in heaven' (**Matthew 6:10; NKJV**), sums up the essence of prevailing prayer. This phrase in the 'Lord's Prayer' is the core of all prayers, i.e. getting God's original intent and purpose for the earth and all of His creation to be enthroned and enforced. Therefore, the understanding is that we must have a constant and continuous consciousness of the fact that we have not only won, but that we continue to win whenever we pray. A consciousness that we enforce and superimpose heaven's agenda on earth whenever we pray. The 'win', 'victorious' or 'triumph' consciousness comes by meditating the word, recognising that all that we desire have already been made possible and available in Christ. Isn't it an honour that God's rule and influence on earth is totally dependent on us and our prayers? This is an awesome privilege! Therefore, prayer is not meant to regurgitate our problems or the precarious circumstances we find ourselves, rather, we are meant to discover the mind of God concerning the issues and bring God's rule to bear in those areas and circumstances.

## 1.4 Prayer: A Spiritual communication

Prayer is simply talking. So when we say prayer is spiritual communication, we mean prayer is 'spirits talking'. This is so because every human being is made with the ability to talk and relate with his environment, even people with speech impairment, deaf and dumb find a means of expression. In its broad sense, communication goes beyond speaking. In fact, the most powerful communications are those not verbalised in words, i.e. communications that are incapable of being crafted in words or expressed in particular language. Therefore, in the broadest sense, even silence is communication and we communicate with every part of our body, we communicate when we cry, when we stare, we communicate when we wear particular clothes or when we dress-up in a particular way, there are also the non-verbal cues and gesticulations in communication.

Due to space constraints and the need to focus, we will not discuss the different forms of communication here. However, I'd like to quickly mention that sometime ago, in my quiet moments with the Lord in prayer, I sensed the

Lord smiling over me. This may be a very strange or familiar experience with some people but in my case, it was strange, as I had not experienced it prior to this time and it went on for a long time. It was a season in which I couldn't verbalise a word in prayer, all I could do was cry. I had lost a loved one and it was a season in which all around me were very negative and unsavoury situations. It was a season in which I sincerely desired to worship and pray but anytime I tried, all I could do was cry a river of tears before the Lord and it was in that season that I experienced the smile of the Lord over me. Initially, I was upset because I didn't and couldn't understand why the Lord would smile when I was in such a devastating condition. Honestly words can't explain the feeling I got from the Lord's smile over me in that season. Although I didn't hear the Lord speak to me, that smile was so reassuring that after a while I began to smile back with the feeling that I wasn't alone and that He is with me. Thus, communication is not only in words.

As is common knowledge, feedback completes the communication process. This means that communication is a dialogue not a monologue. A dialogue entails two or more people engaged in a conversation. In this broad sense, spiritual communication could be between the believer and God, between the believer and an angel, between the believer and a demon spirit, between the believer and other spirit beings. Therefore, it is not in all prayers that the believer is actually communing with God. There are times when believers pray and the prayer is enforcing God's will on earth so for example if a believer is plagued with a disease or illness, it will be correct to pray and ask for the healing power of God for that condition, as well as pray to enforce the divine healing that God has made available in Christ Jesus.

On the contrary, if a believer is being oppressed by a demonic force for example, it will be wrong to pray to God to remove that demon spirit, because God has given us the authority to trample upon all the powers of the enemy and to enforce our victory in Christ. So, the right prayer would be for the believer to exercise the authority we have been given in Christ Jesus in the place of prayer and by spiritual communication command that demon spirit to leave.

I recall one of Kenneth Hagin's teaching, which I listened to some time ago,[8] where he gave example of the authority of the believer with the experience he had with the Lord. According to Kenneth Hagin, he had a visitation from the Lord, where the Lord was telling him certain things and at a point a creature (demon spirit) came in between himself and the Lord and constituted so much nuisance that he couldn't hear the Lord anymore. This went on for a while and Kenneth Hagin was waiting for the Lord to rebuke the demon spirit, but at the same time the Lord was waiting for Kenneth Hagin to rebuke the spirit, as the Lord continued talking. Hagin finally rebuked the demon spirit and the communication between the Lord and himself became clearer. When Hagin asked the Lord why He didn't rebuke the creature, the Lord said, he Kenneth Hagin was the proper person to do that because He has finished His work and all power and authority has been given to him Kenneth Hagin to rebuke every demonic spirit. In the same vein, there are issues that God is looking on us to enforce and unless we do, nothing will be done, because God will not come down to do them. We must realise that everything has ears,[9] and in the spirit realm, there is order. Therefore, when we engage in spiritual communication, we must understand the spirit realm and we must realise our ranking in that realm.

## Conclusion

Despite the numerous definitions and understanding of prayers that we have, the Lord desires for us to progress in our understanding and hence He keeps revealing His mind to us and keeps giving us fresh insights. Jacob prevailed over the angel and in his wrestle, the nation of Israel was birthed.

---

[8] Kenneth E Hagin, 'The Believer's Authority 02 Exercising Our Authority 110188' (between the 10 to 20th minutes of the message. Available at https://www.youtube.com/watch?v=NUvGz0hMezA>

[9] See for example 'O earth, earth, earth, hear the word of the LORD' (**JEREMIAH 22:29; NKJV**). Also, in several places in scripture, Jesus addressed demon spirits that were in people, the demons heard Him and He cast them out. In some cases the demons engaged the Lord in conversations, example is the demons in the mad man of Gadara (**Mark 5:7; NKJV**). Furthermore, **James 2:19** says even the demons hear, they believe the word and they tremble. The Lord Jesus Christ spoke to inanimate things like trees, storms, the dead etc. (See **Mark 11:14; Mark 4:39; John 11:43; NKJV**), which means everything has ears and can hear and obey.

Apostle Paul persisted in Ephesus and the word of God prevailed over the darkness in that City. The same way, we can prevail in our prayers. God is spirit and not only is He spirit, He is Speaking Spirit. He made mankind in His image and likeness, therefore, every human being is primarily a spirit being. Humanity lost it and got disconnected from God when we sinned in the first man – Adam and Eve. For us believers, having received the Lord Jesus Christ into our hearts, our spirit-man has been regenerated, we are now born again and reconciled back to God. This is the primary qualification for engaging in prevailing prayers. There is a call to prayer. The troubles in our world today, the challenges and situations that confront us daily are indications of the urgency to pray more, but we seem to talk more about prayers than actually engage in prayers. I pray that this book will ignite in us the desire to pray more.

CHAPTER TWO

# Prayer is Access

## Introduction

The working definition we adopted for this book is that prayer is spiritual communication that connects us with God, grants us access to the spirit realm to enforce heaven's agenda on earth. As communication must be between at least two people, the first point in the spiritual communication is that prayer is our communication, communion, relationship and intimacy with God. This is why the Lord's Prayer starts with 'Our Father...' **Matthew 6:9** says 'In this manner, therefore, pray: Our Father in heaven, Hallowed be Your name' **(NKJV)** From this perspective therefore, we see prayer as access, communion and intimacy with God. However, the next line in the Lord's Prayer says: 'Your Kingdom come Your will be done on earth as it is in heaven' **(Matthew 6:10; NKJV)**, which means prayer also involves not just access to God but also access to the spirit realm and access to the supernatural.

What gives us legal access to God as believers is the blood and the name of the Lord Jesus Christ. The name of the Lord Jesus Christ has also given us authority in the spirit realm **(Mark 16:17; Luke 10:19; NKJV)**. The question is do other human beings (unbelievers) and spirits have access to God, do they have access to the spirit realm and do they have access to the supernatural? Other human beings can have access to God only through the Lord Jesus Christ, other than that the access they have is to Satan or other gods not the only true Yahweh.[10] Other human beings also have access to the spirit realm.

Satan has illegal access to God because we see in scriptures that due to his rebellion, he had been cast down from heaven and from the presence of God **(Isaiah 14:12; Ezekiel 28:16; Revelation 12:10; NKJV)**. However, when the sons of God gathered to present themselves to God,[11] Bible records that Satan was among them. Satan wasn't meant to be there and that was why the only conversation recorded in that gathering was that between God and Satan, presumably to get him out of God's presence. **(Job 1:6-11; 2:1-6; NKJV)**. This gathering was in the realm of the spirit, while Job who was the subject of the discussion was on the earth realm enjoying his life, living uprightly and making sacrifices for his children in case they went wrong. This implies that negotiations may be ongoing and decisions are being made in the realms of the spirit regarding our lives and therefore we must understand the spirit realm, why and how we can access and function in that realm.

## 2.1 The Spirit Realm

For us to engage in spiritual communication, we must understand the spirit realm. The spirit realm is also referred to as the 'spiritual realm' or the 'heavenly realm' or 'heavenly places' or 'heavenlies'. As expected, and may be common knowledge, every spirit, including Satan and its fallen angels and demonic forces have access to this realm. In fact, they do not just have access to this realm, the most accurate way to put it is that the spirit realm is where they live, function and operate. Interestingly, human beings are spirits and believers whose spirits have been regenerated ought to function

---

[10]  There could be some exceptions here, because in **Acts 10** we see how Cornelius even though unsaved at the time prayed and gave and Bible records that his alms came to God as a memorial. God is sovereign.

[11]  I believe, Satan's access to God is illegal because in the gathering Bible records that 'sons' of God came together, Satan is not a son of God. Also, Satan had been cast out of heaven after his rebellion therefore, even if he comes where we the children of God are gathered, his presence is not legal. But the Lord says a time will come when he and all his demons and fallen angels will be cast into the lake of fire. For now, it is roaming about the earth.

in this realm alongside the physical realm. Man is a spirit, man has a soul and man lives in a physical body. The body is only a suit to enable us function on the earth realm, the hidden man, the spirit man is the real man and should function in the spirit realm.[12]

Why do we have to access God? We have to access God because He is our source, He is our lifeline. God being Spirit, made man in His image and according to His own likeness (**Genesis 1:26-27; NKJV**) and one way we can access Him is through prayer. Therefore, prayer is access to God and access to the spirit realm. Why do we have to access the spirit realm? We need to access the spirit realm for three main reasons, first because we are primarily spirit beings and that is where our Heavenly Father is,[13] secondly everything in the physical (earth realm) has roots in the spirit realm. The third reason is linked to the second one and that is that all the blessings that God has made available to us are in the spirit realm. Therefore, we must be conscious of the spirit realm and our communication must start from that realm. A read of the following scriptures will bring this reality to our consciousness.

> ...and raised *us* up together, and made *us* sit together in the **heavenly _places_** in Christ Jesus, (**Ephesians 2:6; NKJV**)

> Blessed *be* the God and Father of our Lord Jesus Christ, who has blessed us with every spiritual blessings in the **heavenly _places_** in Christ (**Ephesians 1:3; NKJV**)

Any *italicise* word is not in the original text, it is supplied for better understanding, so the scripture was originally meant to read '...who has blessed us with every spiritual blessings in *the heavenlies...*'. The concepts of 'heavenlies' and 'places' imply that there are more than one. This is true because Apostle Paul talked about a man (himself) caught up in the third

---

[12] See Ovo Imoedemhe *Worship: The Essence of Man* (forthcoming), where I did a detailed exposition of the 'Tripartite man'.

[13] We must understand that there are levels in the heavenlies, Apostle Paul talked about 3 heavens, so our Heavenly Father is everywhere but at the same time His thrown is not in the same realm with other beings.

heaven (**2 Corinthians 12:2; NKJV**), which means there could be first and second... so yes, there are spiritual realms not just one realm.

> This also implies that we belong to the spirit realm, as scriptures say: our citizenship is in heaven (**Philippians 3:20**), we have access to heaven now (**Hebrews 10: 19-22**), we are seated together with Christ in heavenly places (**Ephesians 2:6**), we are no longer strangers but fellow citizens with the saints (**Ephesians 2:19**), our treasures are laid up there (**Matthew 6: 19-21**), our desires and affections are there (**Colossians 3:1-2**), our hope is there (**Colossians (1:5**) and our inheritance is there (**1 Peter 1:4**).[14]

The above exposition means that the spirit realm is not a realm to be afraid of. Rather, it should be as natural to us as the earth realm. Man is the only being or specie that is tripartite (spirit, soul and body) and therefore, the only being that can legally function in both the physical and spiritual realms simultaneously.

## 2.2 Facts about the Spirit Realm

There are several facts about the spirit realm which have been dealt with exhaustively by my Spiritual Dad Efe Obuke in his Book entitled *School of the Spirit: Functioning in the Spirit.*[15] Some of them include that the spirit realm runs concurrently or simultaneously with the earth realm. Also, everything that we can see in the earth realm has roots in the spirit realm. In other words the earth is controlled by the spirit realm. The spirit realm is invisible but real and tangible, the earth is physical but the spirit realm is unseen. We are called to function in the spirit realm because we are spirit

---

[14] R.A. Torrey, 'Every Spiritual Blessing: From God, in Christ, By the Spirit' *The Scriptorium Daily* 10 April 2014.
Available at http://scriptoriumdaily.com/every-spiritual-blessing/> (Accessed 12 July 2017).
[15] Efe Obuke, *School of the Spirit: Functioning in the Spirit* (Towdah Publications Benin City Nigeria 2013) pg. 11-15

beings, the spirit realm is where our blessings are located and there is order and ranking in the spirit realm. Most importantly, we have a position of authority in the spirit realm and Satan and all its demons are aware of the believers' authority. I will highlight only a few of these facts here.

## 2.2.1 The Spirit Realm is Tangible

The realm of the spirit is real and tangible, with real activities going on regularly. The conversation in the book of Job between God and Satan is an example of the tangibility of the spirit realm.

## 2.2.2 The Spirit Realm is Invisible but Accessible

It is an invisible but accessible realm. It is invisible because we cannot see or feel it with our natural or physical senses. However, we can access the realm through the help of the Holy Spirit where our spiritual senses are developed and by the gift of the discerning of spirits. As we walk with the Holy Spirit, He enables us to develop our spiritual senses so that as we can see, hear, touch, smell and taste in the physical, we can also begin to see into the realms of the spirit with our spiritual eyes, hear with our spiritual ear, smell and sense things in the spirit realm even though it is invisible to our physical senses. As I mentioned earlier, it could only have been with my spiritual senses that I could sense the Lord smiling over me in my time of discouragement, disappointment and despair.

## 2.2.3 The Realm of the Spirit is more Powerful

The realm of the spirit is more powerful than the earth realm. Everything on the earth realm is subject to the spiritual realm. In other words, the spiritual realm controls what happens on the earth realm. When things are determined in the spirit realm, it takes time before they become manifest in the earth realm. For example, Daniel set himself to fast and pray for 21 days, on the 24th day, the answer to his request came. While delivering the message to Daniel, the angel announced that from the first day Daniel started to fast and pray, his prayers were heard and answers were dispatched.

However, the angel was withheld by the prince of the kingdom of Persia and other princes who withstood him for 21 days until he got reinforcement through Angel Michael who was sent to rescue him from the hands of the princes. **(Daniel 10:10-13; NKJV).**

## 2.2.4 Rules, Order and Ranks are strictly obeyed in the Spirit Realm

There are rules, order and ranking in the spirit realm and everyone in that realm understands and obeys the rules order and ranking. In rank, the 'God Head' ranks first. This includes all of the manifestations of God the Father, God the Son and God the Holy Spirit. Second in the ranking is Man, this includes the unsaved because man is primarily a spirit, made after the image of God. However, the regenerated man i.e. the body of believers in Christ have higher authority. Third in rank are Angels. Admittedly, there are classes of angels such as the cherubim **(Genesis 3:24; NKJV)** and the seraphim **(Isaiah 6:1-4; NKJV)** who are always in God's presence and are constantly keeping watch and bowing before the Most Holy. Nevertheless, in the realms of the spirit, angels do not rank higher than man because it is only man, not angels, that is made in the image and likeness of God.[16] Fourth in rank is Satan, his fallen angels and demonic spirits.

To clarify the position and authority of believers in the spirit realm, from the book of **Ephesians,** we understand that we are risen together and seated, placed, installed and settled together with Christ in heavenly places

---

[16] Several scriptures tell us specifically that we are higher than angels. In **Daniel 10:10-13; NKJV,** angels were sent with answers in response to Daniel's prayers. In response to the prayers of the disciples in the early church, God sent an angel to release Apostle Peter from prison **(Acts 12:7; NKJV);** angels are meant to keep charge/watch over us, lest we dash our feet against a stone **(Psalms 91:11-12; NKJV);** angels are ministry spirits sent to minster to us **(Hebrews 1:14; NKJV).** Apostle Paul writing to the church in Corinth in **1 Corinthians 6:3** said we will judge angels **(NKJV).** The scriptures that seem to confuse some believers about our ranking vis-à-vis angels recorded in **Psalms 8:5** and **Hebrews 7:2** say '...You made him a little lower than the angels...' **(NKJV)** The word translated 'angel' in the verse refers to *Elohim* which means 'God the creator', so the proper rendition of the verse is that we are made a little lower than God the creator.

18

(**Ephesians 2:6; NKJV**) and **Ephesians 1:21** tells us where we belong in this ranking namely, - *Far above all principality, and power, and might, and dominion, and every name that is named, not only in this world, but also in that which is to come* (**NKJV**). This fact is even clearer when Bible describes us as the 'Body' of Christ. The body cannot be somewhere far, neither can it be disconnected, from the head, and so we are situated, located, placed and positioned together with Christ in the heavenlies far above principality, power, might and dominion. Everything else, including Satan and all its demonic forces are under our feet. Glory to God!

## 2.2.5 Communication and Activities in the Spirit Realm

There is ongoing communication in the spirit realm. Although there are various forms of communication such as the non-verbal, which are very important, words are the most potent tools of engagement in the spirit realm. Words spoken by a spirit are taken as the will and legal position of that spirit, and they remain active and potent finding points of entry in the physical realm unless they are withdrawn, cancelled or nullified by words spoken by a superior spirit (**Isaiah 55: 10-11; NKJV**).[17] A clear example was the words spoken by Joshua after the fall of Jericho. In **Joshua 6:26**, Joshua said no man should rebuild Jericho and cursed whoever rises up to build it. It was a curse but they were words.[18] Unfortunately, hundreds of years latter during the reign of Ahab a man called Hiel rose up and rebuilt Jericho and true to Joshua's words, his two sons, first and youngest, died as a result. (**1 Kings 16:34; NKJV**).

Words are spirits themselves, they are containers and carriers. Words are exposed thoughts or ideas. In order to communicate or convey ideas or thoughts, we use the medium of words. Communication therefore, depends on the agreement on the definition of words. The key to effective communication is everyone having the same meaning attributed to the words used. We do not intend to elaborate on communication or words

---

[17] Efe Obuke, (above note 15) pg. 15.

[18] We must realise that blessings and curses are sometimes communicated through words. A blessing is a positive word spoken with the intention and force to make it good. The same applies to a curse in the opposite. A curse is a negative word spoken with the intention and force to make the negativity happen.

but we must understand that words are spirits and they don't die. The word of God the Bible is much more potent. Jesus speaking said '…the words that I speak are spirit, and *they* are life…' (**John 6:63; NKJV**) So when we engage words in prayer, it has to be God's word not words that express how desperate our situations are, of course there are exceptions, such as Hannah who in desperation poured out her heart to God in prayers. Similarly, after praying, we need to constantly align our words and mind-set to God's word because every other word we speak outside of prayers may either negate the prayer or reinforce it. And Bible says we will have what we say not what we pray. The point is not to discourage prayers but to ensure that both in prayers and outside of prayers, we should simultaneously and constantly align our words with the word of God.

## 2.3 Prayer should be orchestrated by God or Be in line with God's divine mandate

From our definition in the preceding chapter, we noted that prevailing prayer is spiritual communication orchestrated by God or in line with God's divine mandate. The second limb of the definition, 'orchestrated by God…' implies that every prayer starts from the heart of God. This is because God made the earth and He has a plan that His will and original intent for creation prevails and the means by which that is to be done is when we enforce God's will on earth through prayer. This implies that God wants us to engage in spiritual communication to bring His Kingdom or His rulership to bear on the earth, as against the forces of darkness.

Our Lord Jesus Christ prayed constantly while on earth and He also taught the disciples how to pray and so He knew that the only way we can prevail over the works and forces of darkness in this world is by prayer. Prayer is our source of spiritual energy. Interestingly, the only request the disciples asked the Lord Jesus Christ while on earth was to teach them how to pray; they didn't ask the Lord to teach them how to fast, or how to raise the dead or how to feed five thousand people. I believe the reason is not far-fetched; they had seen that Jesus did all of those miracles because he spent a lot of time praying. Therefore, when we spend time praying and receiving spiritual energy, we will spend less time with issues that confront us on a daily basis.

God's mandate is already in His word and established in the spirit realm, prayer is the means by which we enforce God's divine agenda on earth. The Bible is God's general mandate or will – the *logos*,[19] but there are times when God wants us to execute certain specific things and at such times we cannot depend on the written word alone, but we must hear specifically from Him – the *rhema,*[20] regarding what He wants us to do and the kind of prayer He wants us to engage per time.

I recall a particular time in my life when all I could do was to pray violently in the spirit for a long time. It was in 2001 while I was pregnant with my second child. Prior to this time, I had only engaged the prayer of thanksgiving and the prayer of faith, but the kind of prayer that the Holy Spirit empowered me to pray in that season of my life was very strange and alien to what I had been used to. Nevertheless, I had to do this because there was a strong burden on me to pray and the Lord had said to me previously that He was going to be leading me through dreams and visions and so in a particular dream, a little girl had given me a knock on my head. The kind of knock that I will never forget, I remember waking up from that dream with severe headache, as though the dream was real. Indeed, it was real because the interpretation of the dream as the Holy Spirit laid it in my heart after I engaged in a three-day fasting and prayer, was that there was a ploy to kill my unborn child, as the knock I had on my head in the dream was directed at my child not me. With this understanding, I began to pray every night from 12 midnight to about 3.00a.m.

This experience is a classic example of how we must hear from God on certain specific issues, so we can be precise and persistent in our prayer. There is no place in the Bible where God would have directed me to in this situation, there is no way I could have taken the prayer seriously if the Lord had not shown me by a night vision and there was no way I could have prayed for so long and so intensely while being pregnant without the help of the Holy Spirit.

---

[19] *Logos* is a Greek word translated to mean, 'word', 'thought', 'principle'. In Greek philosophy, it also referred to a universal, divine reason or the mind of God. Available at https://www.gotquestions.org/what-is-the-Logos.html> (Accessed 17 October 2017). For our purpose *Logos* is simply the 'Written Word'.

[20] *Rhema* is a Greek word which is translated the 'revealed word'.

In addition to the written word of God which commands us to pray, prevailing prayer must be prompted by God or by the orchestration of divine revelation and by the help of the Holy Ghost. Therefore, hearing from God is important because every prevailing prayer should proceed from the heart of the Father. Prayer orchestrated by God or in line with God's divine mandate could be prayer based on the written or revealed word of God, as the Holy Spirit inspires us by divine encounters with specific revelations, instructions, and visitations.

## 2.4 Fervently enforced on earth on a Continuous Basis.

Prevailing prayer is spiritual communication orchestrated by God or in line with God's divine mandate and *fervently enforced on earth* on a continuous basis. The word 'fervent' in the highlighted phrase presupposes that there must be an acceptable posture and attitude to our prayers.

### 2.4.1 Fervent

It is not just prayer but fervent prayer that avails much, that prevails over the works of darkness and makes tremendous power available.[21] Other synonyms of the word fervent are passion, enthusiastic, zealous, eager, earnest, fanatic, avid and keen. They all carry the sense of force, intensity and urgency to get something done. This implies that we must be deliberate and strategic and not casual with prayers. No wonder James enjoins us to engage fervency in our prayer as opposed to casual prayer. We will discuss this in detail later when we talk about proportionality in prayer. However, the point to note here is that we can be fervent in prayer because the man who was given for our example in scripture, Elijah stopped rain and then caused rain to come down after three and half years of drought.[22] He also

---

[21] Confess *your* trespasses to one another, and pray for one another, that you may be healed. The effective, fervent prayer of a righteous man avails much. (**James 5:16; NKJV**).

[22] 'Then Elijah said to Ahab, "Go up, eat and drink; for *there is* the sound of abundance of rain' (**1 Kings 18:41; NKJV**).

called fire from heaven to consume sacrifices that were drenched in water.[23] James likened us to him and said he is of like passion.

In other words, Elijah had the same issues, weaknesses, inadequacies, challenges, limitations, intimidations, fears and seeming failures that we are confronted with in our daily lives in contemporary times. The vivid illustration of Elijah's frailty was reflected in his fear by the threat of Jezebel,[24] which occurred just the next day after he had called down rain and had slain 450 prophets of Baal.[25] Therefore, it appeared that one moment Elijah stood victorious on Mount Carmel and the next he got shrivelled up in fear, intimidation and despair crying to God that he was the only one left of all the prophets and that he was in danger of being killed as well (**1 Kings 19:10; NKJV**). This seems unimaginable because how could Elijah be so afraid of the threat of one woman when he had just annihilated 450 prophets of Baal and 400 prophets of Asherah?

I am sure some of us can readily relate to Elijah's predicament. However, we should not allow our seeming weaknesses, inadequacies, fear and intimidation of the enemy to deter us. Admittedly, like Elijah, our lives are replete with moments of 'highs' and 'lows'. One moment we are on the mountain top in the clouds of glory with some testimonies of spiritual breakthroughs and the very next moment we find ourselves in the valley of depression, despair, disappointment, and these can hinder us from engaging in fervent prayer. But James admonishes us that we should not despair, and allow anything to make us lose our fervency in the place of prayer.

---

[23] And it came to pass, at *the time of* the offering of the *evening* sacrifice, that Elijah the prophet came near and said, "LORD God of Abraham, Isaac, and Israel, let it be known this day that You *are* God in Israel and I *am* Your servant, and *that* I have done all these things at Your word. Hear me, O LORD, hear me, that this people may know that You *are* the LORD God, and *that* You have turned their hearts back *to You* again." Then the fire of the LORD fell and consumed the burnt sacrifice, and the wood and the stones and the dust, and it licked up the water that *was* in the trench. (**1 Kings 18:36-38; NKJV**).
[24] Then Jezebel sent a messenger to Elijah, saying, "So let the gods do *to me,* and more also, if I do not make your life as the life of one of them by tomorrow about this time." (**1 Kings 19:2; NKJV**).
[25] And Elijah said to them, "Seize the prophets of Baal! Do not let one of them escape!" So they seized them; and Elijah brought them down to the Brook Kishon and executed them there. (**1 Kings 18:40; NKJV**).

Jesus in describing Elijah in relation to John the Baptist said he was the greatest amongst those born by women, yet we are all greater than him.[26] So if Elijah could bring down rain and call down fire, we ought to do much more because we are greater than him and we operate in a greater and higher dispensation than he operated in. In fact, in another discussion, Jesus summed it up by saying that we will do greater works than He, Jesus did,[27] and this includes greater works first in prayer and then in doing the miracles that Jesus did.

## 2.4.2 '... Enforced on Earth on a Continuous Basis'

To enforce means we are to ensure that God's will is not only in heaven or in His word or in our heart but also that everything around us is in alignment with the word. Enforce also means there is some amount of **force** to be exerted. The example of law enforcement agents come to mind. Governments equip them not only with training and techniques but with some authority and power to ensure that laws are obeyed in society. They also have the power to punish any recalcitrant behaviour to compel compliance and obedience to the laws of the land. This is the same or even higher power that the Lord has given to us. Therefore, 'fervently enforcing God's will on earth on a continuous basis' implies that God has left us in charge. What an honour indeed that God has entrusted to us the responsibility to decide and determine things, to make negative situations and circumstances align to His divine purpose! A popular cliché amongst believers is 'God is in control', but the truth is that God can only be in control to the extent that we allow Him or make Him in the place of prayer. Therefore, believers; the body of Christ on earth are actually in control. Jesus in his parable of the talents said; 'Occupy till I come' (**Luke 19:13; KJV**), this means we are to take charge and be in control in the place of prayer.

---

[26] "Assuredly, I say to you, among those born of women there has not risen one greater than John the Baptist; but he who is least in the kingdom of heaven is greater than he (**Matthew 11:11; Luke 7:28; NKJV**).

[27] Most assuredly, I say to you, he who believes in Me, the works that I do he will do also; and greater *works* than these he will do, because I go to My Father (**John 14:12; NKJV**).

We must regularly bear in mind this consciousness and without fail bring God's rulership to bear on all the negative situations going on in our lives and around us. This is what '...**Continuous basis**' implies. Jesus gave the parable of the woman and the unjust judge in **Luke 18** and the phrase/words that strikes me there is '...men ought **always** to pray and not to faint'(KJV). This is the expectation of God for us, **to always**, and **on a continuous basis** pray and enforce God's will, superimpose heaven's agenda to bear in every situation.

> What is that situation that has plagued you for so long and you have allowed it, thinking that is how it is meant to be! What is that situation with your child that seems to have settled but you know that it could have been better! What are those conditions with your spouse, siblings or parents that seem to have defiled your prayers! What is that situation that you cannot even say to people because apparently everyone looks at and admire you because everything seems to be in place for you and your family and yet there is an issue that seems to defile God's word and has failed to align to God's divine agenda! I challenge you today to engage in prevailing prayer. In other words, you should keep praying about it and declaring God's word, superimposing God's will on the situation until you stop breathing! Do not give up! Ultimately, every situation will align no matter how prolonged and how dire they may appear. You are a winner, more than conqueror and more than victorious in Christ. Hallelujah!!!

## Conclusion

The different components of our definition of prevailing prayer include (i) spiritual communication (ii) orchestrated by God or in line with God's divine mandate (iii) fervently enforced on earth on a continuous basis have been discussed in this chapter. Primarily, we must realise that prayer is our relationship and communion with God, prayer is access to God, access to the spirit realm and to the supernatural. As believers, we need to realise our ranking in the spirit realm and understand that God has given us authority in that realm. Our consciousness of these facts will help us to engage in prevailing prayer continuously and effectively. The result is that we will be at the centre of God's divine purpose for our lives and everything will align with God's divine mandate. In order to be effective in prevailing prayers, we need to understand the different types of prayer. This is important because there are different kinds of prayers and there is nothing that is destroying the Church in contemporary times other than ignorance. We can only function and be effective in the light that we know per time. Revelation is progressive,[28] and available to us when we ask and are open to the Holy Spirit our teacher and guide. The next chapter will deal with the different kinds of prayers.

---

[28] The concept that 'revelation is progressive' may need unpacking for better understanding and since I may repeat the phrase subsequently, I would proffer some explanation of what I mean here. Revelation is progressive because life itself is progressive, the analogy of how a child is born, starts to feed on milk and grows to toddler, to school age, to teenage and to adulthood and progresses from milk to eating real food, gives us a perfect example of how we grow and progress spiritually. When we got born again in Christ, there were certain truths that we knew but as we studied God's word new revelations come by the Spirit and it looked like we hadn't read the scripture before, the reason is that with every level of growth and maturity, God deals with us and brings new insights per time. Just as we will not give a 12-week-old baby solid food, God deals with us according to the levels we are at. Also, salvation is both an event and a progression. We got saved the moment we received the Lord Jesus Christ into our hearts, but like a physical birth, there is progression in the new birth, i.e. the new life we now have in Christ meaning we are being saved daily as we behold the word of God and as we continue to renew our minds. We shall be saved finally when the Lord returns, the final redemption of our bodies. Therefore, even though our spirit is saved, the progression is that our souls are continuously being saved and our bodies shall be saved. The concept of progression of revelation is reflected in a few scriptures like **John 1:16 '...grace upon grace'; Romans 1:17 '...from faith for faith...'; 2 Corinthians 3:18 '...from glory to glory...'** These scriptures depict the fact that God desires us to progress from one level to another in everything including our revelation and knowledge of Him. Otherwise, He could have taken us 'Home' the moment we got saved. There is work to be done here, there is an assignment for every one of us and we need to be open to receive new revelation by the Holy Spirit to be able to accurately and effortlessly fulfil God's will for our lives. Yesterday's revelation was good for yesterday and today's 'daily bread' we must receive as well as trust God for tomorrow's fresh provision. The same God who said to Abraham to sacrifice Isaac told him not to. If Abraham stuck to yesterday's revelation, he could have killed Isaac. Lord have mercy!!!

# CHAPTER THREE

# Types/Kinds of Prayers

## Introduction

Again, it may appear superfluous to talk about different types of prayers because everyone or most people will say 'prayer is prayer, why do we need to know the different types of prayer. What is important is that we are praying!!!' This is true. However, it is imperative for us to pray intelligently and that can only happen when we have an understanding of the different types of prayer. Perhaps the reason some of us get tired of praying is due to prayers almost becoming routines and mere recitations, maybe we haven't seen the physical manifestation of our prayers because we have not engaged in the right type or maybe we have failed to follow some rules and conditions necessary for answers to some of our prayers? I believe an understanding of the different kinds of prayer is crucial to our engaging in effective lifestyle of prevailing prayers.

From the previous chapter we adopted the definition of prevailing prayer as **spiritual communication orchestrated by God or in line with God's divine mandate...** Although we didn't get into the different forms or kinds of communications, we said that prayer is communication. This implies that there must be different kinds of prayers, just as there are different kinds of communication. There are several kinds of prayers mentioned in scripture. In this chapter I have identified eight. Apostle Paul writing to the Church in Ephesus, instructed that they should pray always with all manner of prayers.

> Pray at all times (on every occasion, in every season) in the Spirit, with all [**manner of**] prayer and entreaty. To that end keep alert and watch with strong purpose *and* perseverance, interceding in behalf of all the saints (God's consecrated people). (**Ephesians 6:18**) (**AMPC**).

In fact, the New International Version uses the phrase; '**All kinds of Prayers**'...

> And pray in the Spirit on all occasions with **all kinds of prayers** and requests. With this in mind, be alert and always keep on praying for all the Lord's people. (**Ephesians 6:18**) (**NIV**).

This implies that there are different kinds of prayer and Apostle Paul admonishes us to engage in all. Having listed the armour of God in previous verses in that Chapter,[29] Paul went on to say that it is not enough to put on these armours, as armours are worn in preparation for battles or warfare. Therefore, the reason we have to put them on is for us to engage in spiritual warfare i.e. prayer and not just prayer but **all kinds of prayers.** From this verse of scripture, it is evident that there are different kinds of prayers and I have identified and discussed eight namely (i) **The Prayer of Salvation/ Redemption, (ii) The Prayer of Consecration, (iii) The Prayer of Faith, (iv) The Prayer of Agreement, (v) The Prayer of Thanksgiving, (vi) The Prayer of Dedication (vii) The Prayer of Intercession/Supplication/ Petition and (viii) The Prayer of Worship/Praise.** However, there are overlaps in some of them, but we will provide some definitions and explanations for better understanding and to identify points of overlap.

---

[29] **Ephesians 6:13-17** listed the armour of God as follows: **belt of truth, breastplate of righteousness, feet shod with the preparation of the gospel of peace, the shield of faith, the helmet of salvation, the sword of the spirit**. Certain preachers have listed **prayer** as the 7th armour, but I think prayer is the warfare that the armours are worn for. Therefore, the reason we are to put on all of the 6 pieces of armours is for us to be thoroughly equipped- like the Roman soldiers in the day, for battle which in our context is prayers- to engage in all kinds of prayers.

## 3.1 The Prayer of Salvation/Redemption

The prayer of salvation or redemption is the prayer that connects every human being on earth to his/her source. God is the creator and maker of human kind. As we said in the preceding chapter, prayer is access and that access is primarily to our source – God Almighty. Therefore, since every human being was created by God, as He said in the beginning, 'Let us make man in our own image and after our likeness',[30] we all came from God. The word 'man' used in **Genesis 1:26** represents the spirit being that encapsulated all of humanity. However, mankind missed it with God when Adam and Eve disobeyed God in the Garden of Eden. The whole of humanity became alienated from their source, we all got disconnected from God because by the sin of one man all sinned.[31] For all have sinned and fallen short of the glory of God **(Romans 3:23)**.

Therefore, beginning from our fore fathers, Noah, Abraham, Isaac and Jacob, through several kings, judges and prophets, God began to put a plan in place to redeem (buy back) mankind from the influence of the devil. Finally, redemption was accomplished in Christ. Essentially, God came down in the form of man, Jesus Christ, to redeem mankind. For God was in Christ reconciling us back to Himself.[32]

Consequently, the first place to begin talking with God i.e. praying to God, is reconciling with God. Without that reconciliation, there can be no access to God in prayer because Bible records that the sacrifice (prayer) of the sinner

---

[30] God said, Let Us [Father, Son, and Holy Spirit] make mankind in Our image, after Our likeness, and let them have complete authority over the fish of the sea, the birds of the air, the [tame] beasts, and over all of the earth, and over everything that creeps upon the earth. **(Genesis 1:26) (AMPC).**

[31] '…For if by the one man's offense death reigned through the one, much more those who receive abundance of grace and of the gift of righteousness will reign in life through the One, Jesus Christ.) Therefore, as through one man's offense *judgment came* to all men, resulting in condemnation, even so through one Man's righteous act *the free gift came* to all men, resulting in justification of life…' **(Romans 5:17-18; NKJV).**

[32] That is, that God was in Christ reconciling the world to Himself, not imputing their trespasses to them, and has committed to us the word of reconciliation **(2 Corinthians 5:19; NKJV)).**

is an abomination to God (**Proverbs 15:8-9; NKJV**). Also, **John 9:31** says that God does not hear sinners (NKJV). With the exception of few instances in which God moves in His sovereignty, the only prayer of an ungodly person that God hears is that of salvation.

Everyone who must qualify to pray to God or engage in prevailing prayer as a lifestyle must go through this prerequisite. It doesn't matter if you were known or called with some prefixes attached to your name such as apostle, prophet, evangelist, pastor or teacher, professor, doctor, engineer, it doesn't matter whether you were a bishop, deacon, born and raised in a Christian home and you attended church services regularly. It doesn't also matter whether you think of yourself as very holy, sanctimonious and righteous, because your parents are/were Christians. We need to acknowledge that we were all sinners by nature and we all had to come to the realisation that by reason of the sin nature, we were spiritually dead, separated and cut off from God.

The great Jewish leader Nichodemus is an example of one who taught the scriptures, yet he was far from being reconciled to God and had to secretly by night go to Jesus to ask the pertinent question of how he could be saved and how he could be born again (**John 3:1-8; NKJV**). The only means by which we can get reconnected is by accepting the sacrifice of the Lord Jesus Christ that He died for our sins so we can become God's children and we can relate and talk with God as our Father again.

Therefore, before you can even engage in prevailing prayer, you need to realise that you are a sinner and you do not qualify, but thank God for Jesus who paid the price for our sins and qualified us, you can now accept Jesus Christ into your heart as your Lord and personal saviour and then become reconciled to God. Apostle Paul said that when we believe in the Lord Jesus Christ that He died for us and that God raised Him from the dead, then we will be saved, for with the heart man believes unto righteousness and with the mouth confession is made unto salvation:

> ...that if you confess with your mouth the Lord Jesus and
> believe in your heart that God has raised Him from the

dead, you will be saved. [10] For with the heart one believes unto righteousness, and with the mouth confession is made unto salvation **(Romans 10:9-10) (NKJV).**

Therefore the prayer of salvation has two-prong elements. First, you have to believe in your heart and second you need to declare or say or confess with your mouth what you believe. Confession is not confessing your sin, it may well include acknowledging that you are/were a sinner and you cannot save yourself but the confession used here is more related to the profession of our faith, the saying or declaration of our faith.

Peter addressing the Council of the Sanhedrin in Jerusalem after the healing of the man at the gate called Beautiful said that salvation is in no other than Jesus

> Nor is there salvation in any other, for there is no other name under heaven given among men by which we must be saved **(Acts 4:12) (NKJV)**

Also, Paul writing to the Church in Philippi said that God has highly exalted the name of Jesus

> Wherefore God also hath highly exalted him, and given him a name which is above every name: [10] That at the name of Jesus every knee should bow, of things in heaven, and things in earth, and things under the earth; [11] And that every tongue should confess that Jesus Christ is Lord, to the glory of God the Father **(Philippians 2:9-11) (KJV)**

Therefore, it is by the name of the Lord Jesus Christ that we are saved, and the prayer of salvation includes our faith in the finished work of redemption on Calvary and our declaration of the same. The Lord Jesus Christ is the express image of the Father **(Hebrews 1:3; Colossians 1:15; NKJV)** and He said no one can come to the Father expect through Him. **(John 14:6; NKJV).**

You may say the prayer of salvation/redemption right now.

**Dear God I come to you as I am. I recognise that I am a sinner and I cannot save myself. I believe that you sent your only begotten son Jesus Christ to die for me and that you raised Him up from the dead. I receive the Lord Jesus Christ into my heart this moment. Dear Jesus, come into my heart, be my Lord and saviour. From now on, Holy Spirit I welcome you into my heart, take up residence in me and please help me to live a life that is pleasing to the Father In Jesus' Name. Amen!**

This is the prayer of salvation. I said it some years ago and if you did now, I welcome you into the family of God. You are born again! Glory to God! A brand new day has begun for you and as Bible says, old things have passed away behold all things have become new (**2 Corinthians 5:17; NKJV**). Receiving the Lord Jesus Christ into our lives is a very important prerequisite to engaging in prayers to God because, it is only through the Lord Jesus Christ that we have access to God. Therefore, Jesus said that whatever we ask the Father in His name will be granted. (**John 14:13-14, 15:7; 16:23; Matthew 18:19, 21:22; Mark 11:24; NKJV**). The prayer of salvation is the 'door' through which we enter into the family of God, we get accepted and then we are able to commune with God as our Father, as well as exercise all of the power and authority that has been given to us in Christ Jesus.

## 3.1.1 Do Believers need to engage the Prayer of Salvation/ Redemption Regularly?

The prayer of salvation is said once and that brings us into the family of God as we are reconciled back to Him through the acceptance of the sacrifice of His only begotten son Jesus Christ. However, some people think that the prayer of salvation should be said regularly or at least it should be repeated now and again. However, I do not think that should be the case if we truly have understanding of the new birth. The new birth involves the recreation of the human spirit and so the nature of sin is taken away and the spirit of Christ is rejuvenated in us.

Once this is done we then need to live the new life in Christ, by reading the Bible, renewing our minds and living according to what the Bible says. It is the new life in Christ that will build our consciousness of what has happened on our inside. This is because in most cases at the new birth, nothing on the outward changes, there could be instant changes in behaviours, appetite and habits in certain people, but we don't grow taller, bigger, shorter or smaller, neither do we experience any outward or physical change when we receive Christ. Nevertheless, the change on the inside is real and it is when we live by the word that the character of Christ begins to reflect outwardly in our thoughts, words, conducts, as well as in the kind of company we keep and the places we go to.

However, when we fall out of relationship with God because of sin or make mistakes and go back into our old lifestyle of unbelief, we need to say the prayer of salvation again to rededicate our lives to God afresh. As demonstrated in the parable of the prodigal son **(Luke 15:11-32; NKJV),** God is ever willing with open arms to receive us when we come to ourselves and we genuinely repent from our sins and mistakes. He does not condemn us.

## 3.1.2 What about the Prayer of Deliverance?

We engage the prayer of salvation regularly only in the sense of when we ask God to save or deliver us from every unpleasant situation. In this sense, the prayer of deliverance from all sorts of evil, danger and afflictions is slightly different from the prayer of salvation/redemption, because in the prayer of salvation, we experience the new birth and we are translated from the kingdom of darkness into the Kingdom of light.

Nevertheless, the prayer made by Jonah in the belly of the whale and the prayer of Apostle Paul in the shipwreck during his voyage to Rome could well be classified as the prayer of salvation i.e. asking God to save us from calamities and imminent dangers. This is more related to the prayer of deliverance. Salvation and deliverance is in Christ and so we can pray to God to save and deliver us from imminent dangers, from oppressions and afflictions of the enemy and from evil forces.

There are several perspectives on the prayer of deliverance and there are ministries that engage in the prayer of deliverance, which I do not have the remit to fault, because the Lord Jesus Christ Himself prayed for people who were sick and cast out evil spirits from those who were demon-possessed.[33] However, I believe revelation is progressive. We need to understand that the people the Lord Jesus Christ prayed for and cast out demon spirits from in the synagogue were 'religious' people, they were not born again believers. Indeed, no one was born again in those days because Jesus hadn't gone to the cross, hadn't shared His blood, the penalty for our sin wasn't yet paid and Jesus was yet to resurrect. Therefore, even though the Lord cast out demon spirits from people during His earthly ministry, He didn't expect His body, His Church to engage in the ministry of casting out devils. Bible says every ordinances and handwriting that was against us and contrary to us were nailed to the cross (**Colossians 2:14; NKJV**). Therefore, living in the new creation realities include that we are conscious that the Holy Spirit dwells on our inside and if the same Spirt that raised Jesus from the dead dwells in us how can an evil spirit still be in us? Our body, Bible says, is the temple of the Holy Ghost**... (Romans 8:11; 1 Corinthians 6:19; NKJV).**

Also, I believe the greatest deliverance we have comes from God's word. Bible says, *'... and you shall know the truth and the truth shall make you free.'* (**John 8:32; NKJV**). If peradventure we engage the prayer of deliverance for anyone and we ask them to undertake a session of 7, 14 or 21 days fasting and prayer as the case may be, it is advisable to follow-up with an understanding of God's word to maintain the deliverance. We need to tell such people to continue in the study and meditation of the word of God otherwise, such days and efforts spent in prayer of deliverance will be efforts in futility. The demons may come back with seven more wicked ones to repossess the empty space (**Matthew 12:42-45; NKJV).** Therefore, my recommendation is for us to saturate ourselves with the word of God so that we can constantly live and experience the new creation realities and there will be no room for the devil or its demons. Moreover, Jesus, in His death, burial and resurrection,

---

[33] For example, in **Mark 1:21-34 NKJV** and **Luke 4:31-41 NJKV,** Jesus taught and cast out demon spirits (unclean spirits) in the synagogues and then, He went and healed Peter's mother-in-law. Jesus healed so many others who were sick and were brought to Him and He cast out demon spirits from those who were possessed.

spoilt principalities and powers and made an open show of them triumphing over them... Indeed, every handwriting against and was contrary to us has been blotted out by the precious blood of the Lord Jesus Christ. (**Colossians 2:14-15; NKJV**). All we need to do is enforce these victories and make them our realities in the place of prevailing prayers.

## 3.2. The Prayer of Consecration

Consecration is also sometimes called sanctification or dedication, which involves the setting apart of certain things and people for God's use. However, here we will liken and restrict the prayer of consecration to the prayer of total submission and surrender to God's will. It is the kind of prayer that we engage in when we say **'let your will be done'**. It is the prayer we engage in when we have options and the power of choice to determine what options to pick. In other words, the prayer of consecration demonstrates that we have a will and the power to choose, but we'll rather submit to the will of the Father. This is the prayer that Jesus engaged in the garden of Gethsemane. There are times in our lives where we have options and we can simply choose the simple or what appears to us to be the best one. Nevertheless, there is this uneasiness in our hearts that seems to suggest that the 'simple' or 'best' option may not be God's will for our lives. We know that God gave us a will and therefore, God will not force anyone to do His will, all we need to do therefore is to constantly align our will to God's divine will.

## 3.2.1 Biblical Example – The Lord Jesus Christ in the Garden of Gethsemane

For the Lord Jesus Christ, He knew God's will was for Him to die for the sin of mankind. He knew it and talked about it several times during His earthly ministry. Yet when the time came for Him to die, the pain of going through that death, bearing the sin of the whole world when He didn't do any wrong and being separated from the Father, came upon Him. As a matter of fact, He could have chosen a 'simple' or what might have appeared to be the 'best' option of not submitting Himself to death. This was why He had to say that prayer thrice, Bible records that he went again and again saying the same words (**Matthew 26:36-44; NKJV**).

> **He went a little farther and fell on His face, and prayed, saying, "O My Father, if it is possible, let this cup pass from Me; nevertheless, not as I will, but as You *will* (Matthew 26:39; NKJV).**

The phrase '**nevertheless, not as I will**' implies that Jesus had a will or an option, which is 'let this cup pass from me' meaning He didn't want to submit to death, which entailed separation from the Father. The prayer of consecration was the decision to submit His will to the will of the Father. Thus, when we are faced with unpleasant situations and it appears that we must got through them, even though there could be some other seemingly simple and best options, we must be willing to check with the Lord and submit our will to His will. The prayer of consecration is an ongoing prayer for the believer, especially where critical decisions are to be made. We must learn to say '...*Nevertheless, not as I will, but as You will*'.

There are several other examples in scriptures but another one that readily comes to mind is Peter. Having toiled all night long and caught nothing and despite his expertise and experience in fishing, Peter had to submit to the will of God and said '...*nevertheless, at Your word I will let down the net*'. (**Luke 5:5; NKJV**). He had completed his job for the day and all he got was disappointment and in that state of despair all he wanted to do was go back home and probably have some rest and hopefully come back the next day, which is an expected reasonable option. However, against all that his brain and body may have told him, he submitted to the instruction of the Master. This example may not relate directly to prayer in the sense that we conceive and have compartmentalised prayer but there is a lot to learn from it and I think it is applicable to the prayer of consecration, especially as it teaches us to submit to God's will in every area of our lives regardless of how we feel or what we know by our training or experiences.

## 3.2.2 Personal Example and Testimony

After we got married, my husband and I finally settled in Lagos Nigeria, which I found very exciting. I loved it there not only because it was the capital at that time, but also because it is the commercial hub of the country, with diverse institutions, organisations, multinational companies, NGOs and major government offices having their headquarters there. Also, all consulate offices and the only functional international airport at the time were located in Lagos. I love travelling so the idea of travelling from another part of the country to Lagos to obtain visas and to connect the international airport before travelling out of the country was taken care of with our being in Lagos. In addition, I thoroughly relished my job. As the Group Company Secretary/Legal Adviser to an oil servicing company at that time, my job provided me loads of travelling opportunities.

However, after about seven years of being in Lagos, my husband got a job in another City, Benin City and it was not a problem initially, because we were happy with the arrangement that he relocated alone and left the children and I in Lagos, as long as he came every weekend or every fortnight to spend some time with us. As you would imagine, even before the suggestion of whether we were to relocate to join my husband in Benin City came up, I suspected that would be the case, so I began to pray. Essentially, I prayed and asked God if that job my husband got was His will and if not, for God to shut the door. Obviously, I did not want to relocate to Benin City, I didn't like it there. I took my prayer to another level with fasting and declarations all just to get the Lord to say what I wanted to hear. But the Lord spoke so clearly to me one day and it was a question: *'Why are you praying so hard; if the job your husband got is with an institution in the UK or America or even Ghana or South Africa will you pray this hard?'*

This was like a 'blow below the belt', because it revealed to me how selfish I had been; praying not necessarily because I wanted God's will to be done but mine, because I didn't want to relocate. Well, at that point, and going forward, I began to say the prayer of consecration like our Lord Jesus said at the Garden of Gethsemane: *Dear Lord you know me, I don't want to go to that City, I really don't want it, nevertheless, not my will but let your will be done.* The conclusion was that we relocated to Benin City and all that I am today started when we did, I began my lecturing career and all the opportunities to travel outside the country opened up with participating in international conferences. The beautiful thing was that in the early days of my travels, the University liaison officers helped with procurement of visas for academic staff especially where such travels were for academic purposes, so I didn't go through the chores of travelling to obtain visas. Most of the travels were also partly funded.

The lesson is that when we submit to God's will, we have more to gain. He knows us from the cradle to the grave, even before we were conceived, our days were already written in His book **(Psalms 139:16; NKJV)** and the Lord said 'Lo I have come in the volume of the books to do thy will oh God!' **(Psalms 40:7; Hebrews 10:7; KJV)**. Although the point of yielding comes with pain and tears because we don't usually see the full picture, surrendering to God's will just makes life easy. I encourage us to always engage the prayer of consecration especially when we don't feel like taking certain steps but we know that that is the way God wants us to go.

## 3.3. The Prayer of Faith

Faith is needed in every prayer, because Bible says, he that comes to God must believe that He is and that He is a rewarder of them that diligently seek him **(Hebrews 11:6; NKJV)**. Therefore, it is faith that makes us approach God in prayer. However, there is the type of prayer that is called the prayer of faith. It is the prayer that we pray once and ideally, it needs no repetition. However, we must be certain that what we pray or ask God for is available i.e. it is provided in scripture.

Therefore, before we engage the prayer of faith, we must spend time to **search the scriptures** to see what the scripture says about the issue or ask God to tell us if the issue is specific and not dealt with in scriptures. Once you have a word either from scripture or from the Lord on the issue then you are ready to engage the prayer of faith. The hallmark of this kind of prayer as the name portrays, is that it is the prayer of **faith** and as noted earlier, it should be prayed once. There is no need to repeat it otherwise you will be negating the prayer, or walking in unbelief, in doubt or doublemindedness and of course we know that a double minded person is not only unstable in all his ways, he also cannot receive anything from God (**James 1:6-8; NKJV**).

After the prayer of faith, between when we prayed and when we see the physical manifestation of what we prayed for, we then engage the prayer of thanksgiving. This is so because when we engage the prayer of faith, we do not sometimes see the answers manifest instantly. Most believers do not understand and they think God has not answered and then they begin to pray again repeatedly. However, the most appropriate thing to do when waiting for the physical manifestation after engaging the prayer of faith is to switch to the prayer of thanksgiving. James asked:

> Is anyone among you sick? Let him call for the elders of the church, and let them pray over him, anointing him with oil in the name of the Lord. [15] And **the prayer of faith** will save the sick, and the Lord will raise him up. And if he has committed sins, he will be forgiven (**James 5:14-15; NKJV**).

The phrase '…and the *prayer of faith* shall save the sick' presupposes that for the sick this is the kind of prayer to engage. In context, James did not expect that any one should be sick amongst God's people, this is evident when he said '*is anyone* sick among you?' In other words, James was saying, I don't expect that any should be sick but peradventure there is any sick person, let the elders pray…

This expectation that there should be no sick persons amongst God's people is the truth as founded in scriptures because God's wish and desire is for us to prosper and be in health even as our soul prospers (**3 John 2**). Bible says '…He [Jesus] Himself took on our infirmities and bore our sicknesses' (**Matthew 8:17, Isaiah 53:4; NKJV**). Indeed, 'He was wounded for our transgressions, He was bruised for our iniquities, the chastisement of our peace was upon Him and by his stripes we are healed' (**Isaiah 53:5; NKJV**); 'who Himself bore our sins in His own body…by whose stripes you were healed' (**1 Peter 2:24; NKJV**); 'it is not right to take the children's bread and toss it to the dogs' (**Matthew 15:26; NKJV**) (Healing is the children's bread). These scriptures establish absolute truth about the divine health and healing that God intends for us and which He has made available in His word, purchased, signed, sealed and delivered by the sacrifice of the Lord Jesus Christ in His death, burial and resurrection. Glory to God!

Therefore, the prayer of faith regarding healing and provision should be engaged once and accompanied with an expectation of an immediate and instantaneous answer. James said '*...and the prayer of faith shall save the sick, and the Lord shall raise him up...*' The prerequisite is to come with knowledge. We must know what God has made available for us in Christ, the things that accompany salvation. Salvation is a total and complete package and with it came healing, deliverance, liberty, peace, protection, provision, preservation, total well-being, joy etc. but the enemy will always keep believers in the dark making us feel we are still in bondage. No wonder Hosea said '**My people are destroyed for lack of knowledge...**' (**Hosea 4:6**), God's people who are meant to be in charge of God's creation are perishing for lack of knowledge; what a tragedy! This is why we need the knowledge of all that we have in Christ, we need faith to access them, without doubting or wavering.

The prayer of faith is a prayer based on all that Christ has done for us and made available to us. Therefore, we must know the things that God has made available to us through Christ. We can engage the prayer of faith when it relates to personal needs, such as food, clothing, shelter, healing, protection, financial breakthroughs etc. I have heard a few preachers say there should be a time when we don't have to pray for food, clothing and shelter because the Lord says we should not *worry* about them (**Matthew 6:25-31; NKJV**). Indeed, depending on our level of faith walk with God, that may be correct. We should mature in our walk with God and get to the point when we don't ask for daily provision because God knows and He will supply anyway. We can then focus our prayers on other 'more pressing' issues.

However, I believe we should pray for everything including these basic needs because Bible did not say not to pray for them but that we should not *worry* about them, we should not be anxious about them. In fact, I believe that failure to pray may inevitably lead to worrying about these things. He said *'Be anxious for nothing, but in everything by prayer and supplication with thanksgiving let your requests be made known to God'* (**Philippians 4:6; NKJV**). In addition, in the Lord's teaching on how we should pray, he said pray in this manner *'...give us this day our daily bread...'* (**Matthew 6:11; NKJV**). Although this may not relate only to literal food, but it suggests that the Lord wants us to ask for daily provision, He also said to 'ask, seek and knock' (**Matthew 7:7; NKJV**). Therefore, it is in order to pray for our basic needs but the appropriate prayer is the prayer of faith after which we engage the prayer of thanksgiving.

Admittedly, in the western world, some of these things are non-issues because housing, food, clothing etc. are somewhat basically taken care of, but this is where the prayer of faith overlaps with the prayer of thanksgiving. We may not pray for these things in the sense of asking God for them but we need to thank God for them. Therefore the prayer of thanksgiving overlaps with the prayer of faith here. Also, both prayer of faith and thanksgiving overlap in the sense that since we already know that God has provided these things for us as stated in scriptures, we simply thank Him for supply, i.e. for making it possible for us to enjoy them as a physical fact. We shouldn't even take for granted the air we breathe, we need to thank God for seemingly inconsequential things like sleeping and waking up, the ability to smile, talk, walk, thank God for family, friends, and even for foes. Thank God for the air, water and all the basic things we take for granted...

## 3.4 The Prayer of Agreement

The prayer of agreement is almost the same as the prayer of faith. The difference is that the prayer of agreement involves another person, as it is an opportunity to agree with two or more believers regarding any issue. **Ecclesiastes 4: 9-12**, says that two are better than one because they have a good reward for their labour and a threefold cord is not easily broken (NKJV). Also, the Lord says that whatsoever two shall agree upon it shall be done for them.

> Again I say to you that if two of you agree on earth concerning anything that they ask, it will be done for them by My Father in heaven **(Matthew 18:19; NKJV).**

Therefore, the prayer of agreement is apt when we need someone else to help our faith and to take advantage of the promise in this scripture. It is the kind of prayer that couples and family members should engage in, as well as friends, prayer partners and believers generally. On the other hand, the prayer of faith can involve two or more people, as well as it could just be an individual private prayer.

We will discuss agreement and faith as essential ingredients in all kinds of prayers in subsequent chapters, but here we must note that the same requirements for the prayer of faith apply to the prayer of agreement. Therefore, with the prayer of agreement, first, there must be a specific condition, an issue, a challenge or a request. Second, we must **search scriptures** to see where that issue has been provided for, or made available. Third, we must **comply with relevant conditions** attached to receiving the promise in scripture and finally, we need to **get someone on the same level of faith with us or someone on a higher level of faith.** This last point is critical because two cannot walk together except they agree.

Searching scripture is something we must do. We don't want to pray blindly and especially regarding specific issues, we need to search and find where similar things have been done and provided for in scriptures. God is bound by His word so it is His word that we must pray to Him or we must anchor our prayers on. Failure to search scriptures may inevitably result in frustration because praying our problems and challenges may not yield appropriate outcomes.

Also, we need to comply with conditions attached to any promise in scripture. For example, forgiveness is a general prerequisite that God has instructed us to engage in, we must forgive others just as God forgives us. Therefore, most prayers will not prevail if we harbour unforgiveness, bitterness, resentment, malice, and grudge in our hearts against anyone. In fact most times, we may not need to engage any form of prayer, just doing or obeying the instruction alone brings our miracle.

The last element of the prayer of agreement, which entails finding someone on the same or higher level of faith, is very critical because we do not want to engage the prayer of agreement just for the sake of doing it, we want such prayers to prevail. Therefore, the person you agree with or who you call to agree with you in prayer concerning any issue must be on the same level of faith, not just a believer, but someone who knows the word on which you are standing and believes on the same level or someone whose level of faith is higher.

I once asked a young Christian lady to agree with me concerning an issue. It was a health condition (heavy menstrual flow) that was recurring at a particular season of my life. I was convinced having read the scriptures that I have been healed by the stripes of Jesus over two thousand years ago, I had prayed and declared the word, but I hadn't received the physical manifestation of my healing. So I thought I might tell this Christian lady to agree with me and in accordance with the scripture that God will grant what two people agree on, my healing will manifest. I was shocked when the lady said maybe it was God's will... Anyone who knows me would have guessed my immediate reaction, but in order not to make her feel hurt, I allowed her to finish her exposition on 'maybe it is God's will' and then we prayed and of course the content of her prayer was laced with phrases of 'God let your will be done...' Of course, there are things we are clear on, particularly things that are clearly provided in scriptures like healing, divine health, protection, provision etc. and for such things we don't pray this kind of prayer of 'let your will be done'. This is because we already know God's will, that He wants us healed and delivered from every form of sicknesses, diseases and afflictions. As you would imagine, the condition continued after our prayer of agreement and even worsened, as it progressed from recurring to continuing, non-stop kind of bleeding and I became anaemic and couldn't do most things that I usually did with ease. Ultimately, it was at a camp meeting that the word of knowledge came specifically on my health condition, I was prayed for and the bleeding ceased.

**Amos 3:3** says two cannot walk together unless they are agreed (NKJV). It is better you engage the prayer of faith than agree with someone who is not at your level of faith especially regarding the particular issue. The Christian lady I asked to pray with me is a believer and I respect her faith walk with God. However, being a Christian or a believer is not the prerequisite here, we all are at different levels of faith walk and growth in God. Therefore, to maximise the benefits of the prayer of agreement, we need a believer who is at the same level of faith walk like we are or a believer who is at a higher level.

## 3.5. The Prayer of Thanksgiving

Here, I would like to say that there is the **general** and **specific** prayer of thanksgiving. General prayer of thanksgiving is the prayer that every believer engages in on a regular basis. It is basically thanking God and not asking Him for anything. As noted above, we need to thank God for everything, including the fact that we are alive. Life is a privilege not a right so we need to be truly thankful for the gift of life and for the gift of a brand new day and for all the benefits that He daily loads us with (**Psalms 68:19; NKJV**). Let us maintain a heart of gratitude at all times for the things we see and the many things we do not and cannot see with our physical eyes. This is what I call **general** prayer of thanksgiving; thanking God for what He has done, for what He has given to us and for what He chose to withhold from us for our own good. Generally, believers are expected to and we do thank God regularly. Apostle Paul says 'in everything give thanks; for this is the will of God in Christ Jesus for you' (**1 Thessalonians 5:18; NKJV**).

The major difference between the prayer of faith and the prayer of thanksgiving relates to the **specific** prayer of thanksgiving. As noted earlier, with the prayer of faith, we ask God for certain things. We know that God has made all things available (**Ephesians 1:3; 2 Peter 1:3; NKJV**), but we ask Him for supply and delivery. *Provision is what is available and supply is what is delivered to our doorstep or to us physically per time.* So even though we know that God has made all things available, they are only within our reach but not in our hands and so the prayer of faith places a demand by specifically asking for those things to be delivered to us as a physical fact. The relationship therefore between the prayer of faith and specific prayer of thanksgiving is that we engage the prayer of faith by asking for specific things to be delivered to us. Thereafter, we engage the **specific** prayer of thanksgiving in the interim while we are waiting for the supply or physical manifestation, as well as when we receive the things as a physical fact. This is specific prayer of thanksgiving. Thanking God in anticipation of the physical manifestations and thanking Him when we have received our miracles as a physical fact. With time, this other arm of thanking God after we have received the specific things we asked or prayed for, becomes our 'deposits' of general thanksgiving. When we look back in retrospect, we can thank God generally for all His miracles in our lives.

## 3.5.1 Biblical Example – The Syrophoenician Woman

The example of the Syrophoenician woman comes to mind. This story may not exactly mirror prayer as some of us conceive prayer, but permit me to use the analogy here. This woman had heard that Jesus of Nazareth was around and she had heard that He has healings in His hands, based on this information that the Great Physician the Lord Jesus Christ was around, she knew that healing was available to her daughter but not within her reach and so she went and asked the Lord to heal her daughter - prayer of faith- Jesus' response to her request was a NO: *'I am only sent to the lost sheep of Israel'*, the Lord said to her.

In other words, even though I have healing to disseminate, you don't qualify because you do not belong to the family of God! The next thing she did whiles in anticipation was bow in worship, she began to engage the **specific** prayer of thanksgiving and began to thank the Lord Jesus because since she already asked -prayer of faith-, she was sure to receive her request physically and tangibly if she engaged in **specific** prayer of thanksgiving. Of course she did receive her miracle and she continued to thank God specifically for the same afterwards.

As a Canaanite woman she couldn't engage any kind of prayer, not even the general prayer of thanksgiving because she is alien to God, she didn't belong to the family of God and she didn't qualify, but by the sovereign power and mercy of God, certain protocols and rules were bye-passed for her sake when she engaged the prayer of faith and **specific** prayer of thanksgiving. (**Matthew 15:21-28; NKJV**).

## 3.5.2 Biblical Example – The Ten Lepers

The story of the ten lepers that were healed is another clear example. Only one out of the ten came back to say thank you and for doing that he did not only get healed of the disease, he was made whole. In other words, when he engaged **specific** prayer of thanksgiving for the healing he received from the Lord, he was not only healed and cleansed, he was made whole, so much so that there was no trace, scars or signs of the disease in his skin. (**Luke 17:11-19; NKJV**). When we engage **specific** prayer of thanksgiving, not forgetting what God has done for us, but recalling all of His goodness and thanking Him specifically for them, God is sure to do much more for us.

## 3.5.3 Personal Example and Testimony

Academic excellence is something I always placed a high demand on during my undergraduate days because I belong to an excellent God and so I believe I must excel in every area of my life including in my academics. Moreover, the word says to me that God has made me the head and not the tail, above only and never beneath; greater is He that is in me than he that is in the world; I have more understanding than my teachers; I have favour in the sight of all men... (**Deuteronomy 28:13. 1 John 4:4; Psalms 119:99-100; Psalms 5:12; NKJV**). However, there was a particular examination I wrote that I just couldn't boldly declare these truths. I had marked my script in my mind and I had failed. In fact, I had concluded that the examiners will be justified to give me a fail mark because that was what I deserved based on what I had written.

Nevertheless, a scripture came to my mind that says, the king's heart is in the hand of the Lord, like rivers of waters, He turns it wherever He wishes (**Proverbs 21:1; NKJV**), and on the basis of this scripture, I prayed to God to have mercy on me and to touch the heart of whoever is going to mark my script to give me a pass mark. I prayed this prayer once -prayer of faith - but after that, several thoughts came to my mind why I cannot pass, but each time the thoughts and fears came, I recalled another scripture that says; *casting all your cares upon him for He cares for you* (**1 Peter 5:7; NKJV**) and so I got into specific prayer of thanksgiving:

> *(Father God I thank you because according to your word, you will turn the hearts of kings in my favour, whoever is marking my script his or her heart is in your hand to turn them in my favour. Thank you Lord because not according to what I deserve but your mercy will prevail on my behalf. Thank you Lord because your mercy will prevail over judgement. Thank you Lord because concerning this examination I will have a pass mark, because your word says you compass me with favour as with a shield. No man is permitted to fail me, thank you Lord because I cast this care, worry and anxiety upon you because you are my Father and you love and care for me. Thank you Lord!)*

I repeated this prayer of thanksgiving consistently for about a month, anytime I got anxious and I continued until the result came and guess what? I passed! Glory to God! I then continued in the **specific** prayer of thanksgiving, declaring that if it had not been for the Lord on my side, the story would have been different, and I thanked Him specifically again and again for giving me that specific miracle.

In retrospect, although this happened over two decades ago, it has become part of my general thanksgiving, especially as I counsel and encourage people to excel in life and specifically in their academic pursuits. I can relate with people who though are diligent in their studies but for one reason or the other have not done very well in an exam. If you are in that situation or your friend, sibling, child, colleague, parent, could you just encourage them that if they could make a switch from worrying to engaging the prayer of faith and the specific prayer of thanksgiving as I did above that God will give them a testimony? 'How do I stop worrying?' I can almost hear you ask? Admittedly, this is the most difficult part, how to quit worrying. I tell you it is hard, but one thing that can put you over is the word of God. He will give us peace if our minds are *stayed* on Him and on His word and if we trust Him (**Isaiah**

47

**26:3; NKJV)**. God is no respecter of persons, if He did it for one He will do it for all. God is bound by His word. He is infallible, impeccable and His word is immutable. Hallelujah!

## 3.6. The Prayer of Dedication

The prayer of dedication is a regular prayer of surrender, devotion and commitment to God. It is a prayer in which we pledge our allegiance to God. Again, there seems to be an overlap between the prayer of dedication and the prayer of consecration. However, the subtle difference is that with dedication, we are not asking for God's will to be done specifically. Rather we are dedicating our lives to God, we are pledging our loyalty, total surrender and submission to Him. The prayer of consecration on the other hand relates to a specific issue in which we already kind of know the will of God but we are unwilling to go that route and there also seems to be some options, which if we are allowed to 'pick and choose', we would rather choose other options than follow God's will. The prayer of consecration, therefore, relates to where there are conflicts between what we want and what God wants, conflict between our will and God's will for our lives, we then painfully and tearfully pray the prayer of consecration of 'nevertheless not my will but God's will be done'.

On the other hand, we dedicate our lives to God regularly, we dedicate our children to God when they are born, and throughout their lifetime, we dedicate our houses, cars, ship, aircrafts and any major acquisition or material possession to God. By so doing, we make a declaration whether publicly or privately that all we are and have belong to God, because no man receives anything except it is given to them by God (**John 3:27; NKJV**). Simultaneously and implicitly, we undertake to give them all up if the Lord so directs. (**Matthew 19:16-24; NKJV**). We should be willing to freely give to those who are in need, widows and orphans, brethren in the household of faith, for the work of the ministry or to charity. When we engage the prayer of dedication, it would be easy to part with our physical possessions, because the prayer of dedication gives us the consciousness that they don't belong to us, but to God and when God asks us to give to a particular person or project, we would not resist.

The prayer of dedication will also help us to live holy and righteous lives daily, because we consider our lives not to be ours but God's. We came from God, we belong to Him and therefore we will live for Him all our days.

> *Dear Lord, help us to dedicate our lives to You daily. Help us to live for You and if need be die for You, because this life is not our own, to You we belong and so we pledge to love You and live for You all our days. Help me, help us Holy Spirit. IJN Amen.*

## 3.7. The Prayer of Intercession, Supplication/Petition

I have decided to put the prayer of intercession, supplication, and petition together because I think they all interrelate with subtle differences. The prayer of intercession is the prayer we pray for other people, places or things other than for ourselves. The word intercession means mediation, negotiation and intervention with the aim to prevent, it means to step into the shoes of the wrongdoer. In other words, you take on the wrong or sin of the person, as if you were the offender and therefore the punishment and penalty that the person should have received should come upon you.

Significantly, 'intercession' comes from the word 'intercede' which has its origin in two Latin words '*inter*' which means 'between', and '*ced*' which means 'go'. So literally it means 'go between'.[34] The prayer of intercession is usually referred to as 'standing in the gap'. The concept of 'gap' signifies a place of weakness, vulnerability and danger. It is a defenceless location of exposure and limitation, the place where people face real threats.[35] Standing in the gap therefore means 'to fill in the gaps'.[36] We could see the term 'standing in the gap' in **Ezekiel 22:30** that says, *'So I sought for a man among them who would make a wall, and stand before Me in the gap on*

---

[34] 'Standing in the Gap'? What does that Mean?' Available at http://www.myredeemerlives.com/intercession.html> (Accessed 28 June 2017)

[35] First United Methodist Church Shreveport, 'Standing in the Gap'. Available at http://firstshreveport.org/2014/09/19/standing-in-the-gap/> (Accessed 28 June 2017)

[36] 'Standing in the Gap'? (above note 34).

*behalf of the land, that I should not destroy it, but I found no one'* (**NKJV**). In Bible times, cities had walls around them to help protect the people from external attacks. However, with time some broken parts of the wall created physical gaps in the wall. Although Ezekiel, used the concept of 'wall', which the people could relate to, he spoke about the injustices and oppressions that were prevalent at the time for which no one could stand in the gap because they were all complicit in the atrocities. Therefore, this speaks prophetically about the Lord Jesus Christ who eventually came to stand in the gap for humanity.

Therefore, 'standing in the gap' means standing as a mediator between a people who have done wrong and God. This is correct and accurately mirrored in the Lord Jesus Christ. Both prophets Ezekiel and Isaiah prophetically declared about how God sought for a man and found none and how He (God) would have to come down in the person of Jesus Christ to save humanity. Isaiah declared, 'He saw that *there was* no man, And wondered that *there was* no intercessor; Therefore His own arm brought salvation for Him; And His own righteousness, it sustained Him' (**Isaiah 59:16; NKJV**). Therefore, in its strictest sense, the phrase 'standing in the gap' and the word 'intercession' are mirrored in the lives of only two people in scriptures; Moses and the Lord Jesus Christ. Moses who was a type of Christ interceded for the children of Israel preferring for the people who sinned to live and for his name to be blotted out of the book of life. The only person who can stand in the gap and who has done it is the Lord Jesus Christ, because He mediated between humanity and God in His death, burial and resurrection. He took upon Himself the sin of humanity and substituted His righteousness for our sin nature and took on the penalty of sin which is death and which we rightly deserved. He continues to advocate, mediate and intercede for us (**Hebrews 7:25; 1 John 2:1; NKJV**).

Since the Lord Jesus Christ stood in the gap for all of humanity, and has committed into our hands the ministry of reconciliation, we need now to engage the prayer of intercession in the same way as Jesus did. Not necessarily in physical death, but in laying down our lives for others in the place of intercession. Indeed, we can apply the principles and follow in the footsteps of the Lord Jesus Christ. This means that when we engage the prayer of intercession, we shouldn't pray from the 'outside'.[37] Rather, we should actually see ourselves as standing in the place of the person, people, city or situations that we pray for. Indeed, we ought to stand in the place of the people we pray for because that is what intercession is all about. Two classic prayers of intercessions in the Bible that I'd like to mention here are the prayer of intercession by Abraham for Sodom and Gomorrah and that of Moses for the Israelites.

## 3.7.1 Biblical Example - Abraham

God said he wouldn't do anything without telling his servant Abraham **(Genesis 18:17; NKJV)** and so before He destroyed Sodom and Gomorrah, God told Abraham and Abraham began to engage the prayer of intercession until he gave up **(Genesis 18:23-33; NKJV)**. Abraham did intercede for Sodom and Gomorrah, but he stopped after he interceded to a point, because he couldn't believe that in a whole city there wouldn't be at least 10 righteous people. However, if Abraham had gone up to one i.e. the point of asking if there was one righteous person, I believe God may have spared Sodom and Gomorrah because his nephew Lot and his family were there and I think arguably, they were righteous people for which God may have spared Sodom and Gomorrah? Here, with all due respect, it appears that Father Abraham remained in his comfort zone and 'threw' prayers from the 'outside' in the hope that God will change His mind? This is how some of our intercessory prayers appear in contemporary times. Our prayer of intercession kind of lack fervency, appears lethargic and too casual as though nothing is at stake. This appears to be the case, especially when the people or issues we pray for don't relate to us personally and directly and therefore, we don't step in to fill the gap and take on the pain of the person or people we are praying for.

---

[37] Praying from the outside is being dispassionate and not identifying with the people and situations we intercede for. As we would see in the difference between the prayer of intercession by Abraham and Moses, there is a way we can engage in the prayer of intercession that reflects that our lives are at stake that brings us into the very situation of other people we pray for. Conversely, there is also a way we pray with no sense of identification, with no passion, no zest, and no conviction, that looks like we pray from the outside.

Here is a little digression but it buttresses the point. Once upon a time, a king was sick to the point of death and God sent a prophet to tell him to put his house in order that he will surely die. The prophet had not finished delivering his message before this king turned to the wall and began to petition God with tears, praying and asking for more years to live. He wept bitterly in prayer to God to the extent that God had to change His mind, told the prophet to turn back to the king and tell him that He (God) would give him another 15 years to live. This king was healed of the affliction and lived another 15 years according to the word of God (**2 Kings 20; Isaiah 38; NKJV**). Thank God for answers to prayers. Thank God for His mighty deliverances. However, unfortunately, the 15 years addition proved to be unproductive, because this same king exposed the treasury and wealth of Israel to Babylonian envoys who came to spy Israel but disguised as emissaries to visit the king because they learnt of his ailment. Not only did he expose the wealth of Israel to these people, he also did not consult the prophet as to what he should do regarding the visit. Long story short, find below excerpts of the conversation between the prophet and the king.

> Isaiah the prophet went to King Hezekiah, and said to him, "What did these men say, and from where did they come to you?" So Hezekiah said, "They came from a far country, from Babylon." Isaiah said, "What have they seen in your house?" Hezekiah answered, "They have seen all that *is* in my house; there is nothing among my treasures that I have not shown them." Then Isaiah said to Hezekiah, "Hear the word of the LORD: 'Behold, the days are coming when all that *is* in your house, and what your fathers have accumulated until this day, shall be carried to Babylon; nothing shall be left,' says the LORD. 'And they shall take away some of your sons who will descend from you, whom you will beget; and they shall be eunuchs in the palace of the king of Babylon.' So Hezekiah said to Isaiah, "The word of the LORD which you have spoken *is* good!" For he said, "Will there not be peace and truth at least in my days?" (**2 Kings 20:14-19; NKJV**).

It is mind-boggling that at the news of his imminent death King Hezekiah prayed, wept, reminded God of his good works and didn't allow God rest or peace until God changed His mind. Yet, when the same prophet told him about the consequences of his actions and how his children would be impacted negatively as a result, his response was casual and careless as though nothing was at stake. By virtue of his exposure of the treasury to the Babylonians, Isaiah told King Hezekiah that they would come, not only to carry the wealth but that everyone will be taken captives to Babylon, including his own sons. His response was '...*The word of the LORD which you have spoken is good...Will there not be peace and truth at least in my days?'* (2 Kings 20:19). In other words, as long as there was guaranteed peace in his lifetime and during his reign as king, everything else was good. It didn't matter to him that his own children would be taken captives. How self-centred! Not a word of prayer proceeded from King Hezekiah's mouth to avert this imminent danger. If God heard, averted his death and gave him 15 more years to live, I believe God could have had mercy and averted the captivity had he prayed. Arguably, Daniel, Hananiah, Mishael and Azariah (Shadrach, Meshach and Abednego) were some of his children that were eventually taken captives and became eunuchs in Babylon.

May the Lord help us not to be careless, casual and self-centred. When His word comes to us, may we take it seriously and engage the prayer of intercession to save not only our lives but those of our children and generations yet unborn. Our lives may be going on well, we may have made and probably still making ground breaking achievements in our careers, ministries, families and in all spheres of human endeavours, but may I ask us to pause and think about our children and the next generation and what legacy we leave behind? If all we plan to leave behind are material wealth, such as large amount of money, cars, houses, shares, companies, gold and silver, then we may be missing it, because we saw that with King Hezekiah the treasuries together with his sons were taken into captivity. Therefore, if the Lord tarries, in addition to material wealth, we should leave untouchable legacies of 'spiritual deposits' by engaging the prayer of intercession for our children. King Hezekiah was self-centred and he failed to intercede for his nation and children. Therefore, one key requirement of the prayer of intercession is *selflessness*. Although Abraham interceded for Sodom and Gomorrah, his intercession did not reflect a stepping in, to fill the gap because it lacked other basic requirements of true intercession such as *identification* with the people and situations we pray for and *persistence*.

## 3.7.2 Biblical Example - Moses

The second prayer of intercession I'd like to refer to is that by Moses. At a point God really got tired of the Israelites and was ready to wipe them out because they truly provoked Him by their continued unbelief, complaints and murmuring. On this occasion, they had made for themselves an image to worship instead of God. However, Moses a true intercessor, stepped into their shoes and took on the wrong and sin of the nation of Israel by presumably saying; 'you know what God; better wipe my name out of the book of life instead of destroying these people because your name is at stake here. Other nations will say you couldn't take them to the Promised Land hence you destroyed them, so let me go for them instead' (**Exodus 32:31-32; NKJV**). This is a classic prayer of intercession. No wonder Moses is a type of Christ because he mirrored exactly what our Lord Jesus Christ did to redeem us all. No sin was found in the Lord Jesus Christ, yet He took on the sin of humanity and stood in our place of death, died for us so that we may be reconciled back to God. Glory to God!

## 3.7.3 Features of Prayer of Intercession

The core of the prayer of intercession is that we pray for other people not for ourselves and we pray for situations that do not relate to us directly. We pray for family members and friends, presidents, prime ministers, and those in positions of authority generally. The prayer of intercession also includes praying for God's peace and righteousness over the atmosphere and the land in our city and country of residence and other cities and nations of the world. Therefore, a key requirement for this kind of prayer is *selflessness*. Regrettably, King Hezekiah displayed selfishness instead of selflessness, and we must learn the lessons from the consequences of his actions and inactions.

Other requirements or characteristics to bear in mind are *identification,* *persistence* and *discernment.* We must **identify with** the people or situation we pray for. In other words, it is not enough to pray for people or situations, we should descend into the arena and step into the situation and practically carry the burdens like the examples of Moses and our Lord Jesus Christ provided above. In some cases, the situations may have come about as a result of sin, and in those instances, we must assume that we are the ones that sinned and repent on behalf of the people. This is vital because sometimes we engage the prayer of intercession for people who cannot pray, because they do not have a relationship with God and therefore they lack the *locus standi* (legal standing) to access God in prayer.

Sometimes, it may well be that the people had a legal standing but they sinned and now they cannot stand before God to plead their case because of guilt. Therefore, like the Lord Jesus Christ is for us, we need to be advocates for these people. At other times, they may not even be aware of the precarious situation they may be in or the imminent danger looming. Unlike King Hezekiah, we should be selfless, we should engage the prayer of intercession, and decree into the future to avert things that our children may be oblivious about thereby saving and securing their lives. Sometimes walls are broken because of sin, and people are exposed to attacks by the enemy. However, as prophesied by Ezekiel, where the people didn't realise that their walls were broken, the same way, the people we pray for, may not be aware that they have become vulnerable and exposed to attacks. This point is vital because it will help us to, for example, pray for people around us; family, friends, neighbours, classmates and colleagues who are in danger of hell should they die suddenly or should the Lord Jesus Christ return. We need to intercede for the salvation of their souls because they may be oblivious of their state. Bible says that God does not wish that any man should perish but that all should come to the knowledge of the Lord Jesus Christ and be saved. (**1 Timothy 2:1-4; 2 Peter 3:9; NKJV**).

The third distinctive feature of the prayer of intercession is '**persistence or continuity**' that is we must pray through until we see the physical manifestation of what we are praying for. Therefore, repetition is allowed in this kind of prayer because unlike the prayer of faith, which ideally we should pray once, the prayer of intercession is continued repeatedly and persistently. This is permitted in scripture because Bible encourages us to remind God of His word and He said we should not keep silent until we see the physical manifestation.

> For Zion's sake I will not hold My peace, And for Jerusalem's sake I will not rest, *Until* her righteousness goes forth as brightness, And her salvation as a lamp *that* burns. I have set watchmen on your walls, O Jerusalem; They shall never hold their peace day or night. You who make mention of the Lord, do not keep silent, And give Him no rest *till* He establishes And *till* He makes Jerusalem a praise in the earth' (**Isaiah 62:1; 6-7; NKJV**).

While repetition is allowed, we should also constantly be attentive to the Holy Spirit to know when to engage the prayer of thanksgiving. In fact the prayer of thanksgiving accompanies and completes all prayers. Similarly, there are times when God puts certain burdens on us and we have to pray until such burdens are lifted. In fact, the burdens make us restless until they are lifted, which is an indication that the matter has been dealt with. Thereafter, we engage the prayer of thanksgiving until and after we see the physical manifestation.

Simeon and Anna were two examples of people who demonstrated **persistence and continuity** in intercessory prayers (**Luke 2:26-38; NKJV**). Bible records that the Holy Spirit revealed to Simeon presumably in the place of prayer that he would not die **until** he had seen the Lord Jesus Christ. Also, Anna continued in the temple and served God with fastings and prayers night and day **until** the Lord Jesus Christ was brought to the temple by Mary and Joseph. The operative word in the prayer of intercession is 'Until'.

When I think of the persistence required in the prayer of intercession, I couldn't help but tell a young girl in my local church to write out this testimony for me to insert in this book, of course with the express permission of her mother Bunmi Ibrahim. At the time of writing, Ayi Ibrahim is 10 years old. Here is Ayi's testimony of her persistence in the prayer of intercession.

> **I had a friend called Jacob. He was riding his bike one day and he fell off. I felt sorry for him so I prayed for him to get better so he could come back to school on Monday. On Monday, Jacob didn't come back to school. I was disappointed but I still had faith in God. So I prayed again. Unfortunately, the next day, he did not come back to school. I was still determined so I prayed once more. The next day, Jacob was at school feeling all better! I was very grateful so I thanked God.**

It is amazing how Ayi persisted in the place of prayer of intercession for her friend and schoolmate. She was disappointed initially when she didn't get the desired outcome, but she was determined I like her '*...I was still determined so I prayed once more*'. Therefore, her persistence in prayer finally brought about the physical manifestation of her intercession. See how beautifully Ayi engaged the specific prayer of thanksgiving for that specific miracle of answers to her prayer; '*I was very grateful and so I thanked God*'! This is truly awesome! May Ayi Ibrahim and all our children continue in this path of persistence in the prayer of intercession in their generation.

Due to the fact that we pray for other people and situations that we don't know about with our physical senses, we need **discernment** in order to be effective. Praying with discernment means that we need our spiritual senses sharpened. Just as we possess the physical senses of sight, smell, taste, hear and feel, we do have all of these as spiritual senses as well. Therefore, we need to be alert and spiritually sensitive when we pray. One way to achieve this is by praying in the Holy Ghost. **Praying with discernment by praying in the Spirit** is a distinctive feature of intercessory prayer that cannot be overemphasised because Bible says we know not what to pray for as we ought but the Spirit Himself helps our infirmities with groaning that cannot be uttered. Our weaknesses and shortcomings are reflected in our limitations. We are limited in what we see, hear and know physically, and our language is limited as well, therefore we must rely and depend absolutely on the Holy

Spirit to help us in all kinds of prayer, especially in intercessory prayers. The Holy Spirit knows the mind of God and knows what and how we should pray.

Some years ago, a young lady was always coming around my friend Cynthia and for some reasons the relationship wasn't such that Cynthia could terminate and she couldn't stop the lady from coming to her. However, whenever, the lady came around Cynthia, she observed that there was an unpleasant odour that the lady exudes, and that she smelt like a corpse. 'How do you know how a corpse smells and how do you know this young lady smells like one?' I was curious as I asked Cynthia! 'I don't know' said Cynthia, 'all I can say and the only way I can describe the stench is that the young lady smelt like a corpse and I don't know what to do about it'! This was very strange because Cynthia didn't know and she couldn't describe why she felt the smell was that of a corpse and I was as clueless as she was. Since I didn't understand much at the time, I advised Cynthia to seek counsel with her pastor which she did. 'You are the only one who perceive that smell' was the response from Cynthia's Pastor '… if the young lady comes in here now I am sure I will not perceive the smell…' 'She may not even be aware that she carries such fragrance…these are spiritual matters.' Cynthia's Pastor concluded and prayed with her.

After that session of counselling and prayer, Cynthia went home and continued to pray and the Holy Spirit began to reveal certain truths to her about the young lady. Apparently although unknown to the young lady, there was an evil spirit that followed her, that wherever the lady went something sinister happened, especially if she remained in a place for a long time. It is either that somebody in that environment would die or something close to death would happen. So the Lord began to teach Cynthia to pray against death and rebuke the spirit of death. Cynthia continued this prayer for as long as the young lady came around her and whenever she perceived that unpleasant smell. Cynthia continued praying for the length of time her relationship with the young lady lasted and for that period, God enabled Cynthia to pray to avert any evil that could have come to her or a member of her family because of her association with the young lady. This was the gift of discernment of spirit in operation through the spiritual sense of smell. The need for discernment in the place of prayer cannot be overemphasised.

One way to be discerning in prayer is to ask the Lord to help us. Too many times we have too many prayer points. It is not what we bring to God in prayer, not our many prayer points but what the Lord prompts or inspires us to pray about that matters. I am not discounting having a list of prayer points. We could have prayer points but at the same time we must be open, sensitive and be willing to promptly obey the Holy Spirit when He inspires a prayer that is not on our list. Let's allow Him to disrupt our list because if all the time we pray, we already have prayer points that we must stick to, then we will remain limited and cannot pray with discernment and enforce heaven's agenda on earth.

There are several instances in which the Lord has helped me to pray with discernment and it happens when I say to the Lord 'I don't know what or how to pray, Lord teach me, reveal to me what you want done and what you want me to pray about'. Sometimes, He tells me to pray for cities and situations I had no idea existed, sometimes He tells me to pray for somebody and most times He does it by showing me pictures. I believe these are the most effective times of prayers I have had and I am immensely grateful to the Lord because it is as He wills, it is entirely His prerogative to reveal per time.

Long ago, while coordinating a prayer session on a Friday evening, the prayer time had ended and we had come together to hold hands in a cycle and to share the benediction when suddenly the Lord showed me a picture of a little boy who was about 5 years old or less at that time. On this little boy's forehead was the number '17' and the word 'insanity'. Immediately, I saw this divine picture, I requested everyone in the prayer meeting to pray in the spirit for a while. While we prayed in the spirit, the Lord brought an understanding to me that we should rebuke the spirit of insanity from that boy, because apparently the devil had planned to plague him when he becomes 17 years old.

If we had put the issue aside, said the benediction because time was far spent, we could have recorded that we went for prayer meeting that evening but in heaven's agenda perhaps this little boy's issue was the only prayer that the Lord needed us to tackle? Glory to our God who sees and knows our days and years long before we were conceived and who by His mercies reveals to us per season what is most important to pray about. The Lord wants to reveal to us where or when the devil is planning perversions in our lives, the lives of our loved ones, in His Church, in our cities and nations of the world and prevailing prayer with discernment is the awesome opportunity to partner with God to avert such perversions.

Also, a few years ago, while at home preparing for a prayer meeting in church, a picture of a child picked up by a teacher in his school was shown to me. Shortly afterwards the teacher put the child down and I noticed that the child's legs had been terribly twisted. I was so shocked and wondered why the child's legs were so bent and I asked what had happened. The Lord said to me to begin to pray for our children against any perversion, derailment and distortion of their destinies. For while we send them to school with the innocuous belief that they are being taught and trained in the regular approved curriculum, certain philosophies and doctrines may be inculcated in them, thereby derailing their destinies. We did handle this in our prayer meeting that evening at my local church AGP and a few times afterwards. It was shortly after this that all of the changes in the education sector in the UK, which purport to teach relationship education, transgender fluidity, same sex marriage in schools began to shore up. Thank God for discernment! We know that since God inspired us to pray we already took care of it in the spirit realm. Although we continue to pray for God's will to be done in every sector, especially the education sector both in the UK and all the nations of the world, discernment will help us to pray proactively rather than reactively.

When next you want to pray could you just ask the Lord what He wants you to pray about? You will be amazed at what He will tell you! Sometimes, He may not say or show you anything and if that is the case be happy to just worship Him and be sensitive and spiritually alert. The only way we can pray with discernment is when we pray in the spirit and when we come asking the Lord i.e. when we truly wait on Him like a chef or a waiter waits on us when we go to our favourite restaurant to have a meal.

In addition to the distinctive characteristics of intercessory prayers, which include selflessness, identification, persistence and discernment, Bible describes the intercessor as a watchman and a watchdog.[38] This means that we must be able to see into the realm of the spirit the direction that our prayers should take per time. As 'watchdogs', we should also be able to 'bite' and not remain mute. Referring to Jacob, Isaiah prophesied that although hitherto, Jacob/Israel had been perceived as a worm that God has made him a new sharp threshing instrument having teeth.[39] We are God's 'Israel' in this dispensation. Therefore, God says He has made us new sharp threshing instrument with teeth to thresh the 'mountains' and 'hills' symbolic of challenging situations and make them small, null, void and of no effect. Whilst the tongue and teeth are vital organs in the mouth, they carry out distinct functions. The concept of the 'teeth' refers to enforcing God's mandate on earth, which as we noted earlier involves some amount of *force.* **Matthew 11: 12** says that since the day of John the Baptist the Kingdom of heaven suffers violence and only the violent takes it by force (NKJV). Praying with discernment helps us to be effective watchmen and watchdogs that can see and bite.

At other times the prayer of intercession could also be made for believers, especially when God reveals certain things about their situations to us. This is not the time to go gossiping about what God has revealed, because God reveals to redeem and to deliver and if we are privileged to receive such revelation it means that God trusts us enough that we will intercede to avert any imminent dangers concerning our brethren. The devil is known to attack in our areas and time of vulnerability and therefore, the prayer of intercession is the opportunity we have to stand in the gap for our brethren in those times and areas so the enemy does not have a foothold in our lives. **Galatians 6:1-5** enjoins us to pray for one another and therefore bear one another's burden (NKJV).

---

[38] For Scriptural references for Watchmen and Watchdog see **Isaiah 56:10-11; 62:6; Ezekiel 3:17; 33:7 NKJV**. Also, Habakkuk said, 'I will stand upon my **watch**, and set me upon the tower, and will **watch to see** what he will say unto me...' **Habakkuk 2:1 KJV** (emphasis added).

[39] See **Isaiah 41:14-15** 'Fear not, you worm Jacob, You men of Israel! I will help you," says the LORD And your Redeemer, the Holy One of Israel. [15] "Behold, I will make you into a new threshing sledge with sharp teeth; You shall thresh the mountains and beat *them* small, And make the hills like chaff' NKJV.

## 3.7.4 The Prayer of Intercession and Supplication: Any Difference?

It is in this regard i.e. praying for brethren that I think intercession differs slightly from the prayer of supplication or petition. Although these are usually used interchangeably, and I think it is not entirely wrong to use them interchangeably, but I also think that there is a subtle difference. I think that while it is correct to engage the prayer of intercession for unbelievers, those in positions of authority, governments, cities and nations etc., the prayer of supplication or petition is apt for when we pray for ourselves, for fellow believers in Christ, and especially for believers who are going through protracted situations or those going from one challenging situation to another and have become 'battle-weary'.[40]

I believe the prayer of supplication is apt when we pray for fellow believers because supplication means entreaty, appeal, plea, request and petition. Therefore, as believers who have legal standing with God, we can actually petition or supplicate for and by ourselves. Although we 'intercede' for other believers when they are in situations in which they are unable to pray, such as for example if they fall into sin, or they need support because of the enormity of the challenge they are going through, nevertheless, 'supplication' and 'petition' seemed more apt when we pray for believers because they also may be praying for their situations and the challenges of others as well. However, because at the particular season, they may feel discouraged, disappointed, depressed, downcast, in despair and seemingly defeated, they may not be able to pray as they ought, being overwhelmed by the particular situation or

---

[40] At a worker's retreat held in Leicester UK sometime in November 2015, I had the opportunity to speak on the topic '**Workers: Refreshed or Burning Out?**' I identified three types of burn out or three things that could lead to burning out, one of which was battle weariness. Battle weariness occurs when believers are constantly engaged in spiritual warfare. This could range from being constantly engaged in prayers that involves confronting the powers of darkness, to being surrounded by multiple troubles, which lead to exertion of both physical and spiritual energy. Although these may relate to physical rather than spiritual warfare, examples in scriptures are **Elijah in 1 Kings 17-19**, **David** as reflected in **Psalms 3:1; 25:19** and **King Saul in 1 Samuel 13:8-9**. Although arguably, King Saul's battle weariness was as a result of his disobedience.

circumstance. It may well be that such brethren have become battle-weary due to the several challenges they are faced with. In this context, I think that when we pray for ourselves, for fellow believers in the body of Christ, for our pastors and church leaders, the accurate kind of prayer is the prayer of supplication or petition.

Therefore, when Apostle Paul wrote to Timothy he used the words; 'supplications', 'intercessions' and 'giving of thanks' presumably because the people contemplated to be prayed for may fall into one of the categories. Supplications for those in the position of authorities who are believers, intercessions for those who are in authority but are not believers and giving of thanks for all.

> Therefore I exhort first of all that **supplications, prayers, intercessions,** *and* **giving of thanks** be made for all men, [2] for kings and all who are in authority, that we may lead a quiet and peaceable life in all godliness and reverence. [3] For this *is* good and acceptable in the sight of God our Savior, [4] who desires all men to be saved and to come to the knowledge of the truth. (**1 Timothy 2:1-4**) (**NKJV**)

During the dedication of the temple, King Solomon prayed:

> …(For they *are* Your people and Your inheritance, whom You brought out of Egypt, out of the iron furnace), [52] that Your eyes may be open to the **supplication** of Your servant and the **supplication** of Your people Israel, to listen to them whenever they call to You. (**1 Kings 8:51-52**) (**NKJV**)

Also, in the letter to the Church in Ephesus, Apostle Paul noted;

> …praying always with all prayer and **supplication** in the Spirit, being watchful to this end with all perseverance and **supplication** for all the saints (**Ephesians 6:18**) (**NKJV**)

Paul used the word *supplication* twice in this verse and it is in relation to praying for the saints, namely, believers or the body of Christ. Therefore, I think that the prayer of intercession is for unbelievers, people and situations that are not clear-cut and we are not very sure of, while the prayer of supplication/petition is for ourselves, fellow believers and the body of Christ generally.

However, regardless of the foregoing distinction, I have categorised intercession, supplication/petition together here because they are usually used interchangeably and I sincerely do not think it is wrong as long as we are praying and the Holy Spirit is enabling us to pray aright. Moreover, scripture doesn't particularly make any distinction between these different kinds of prayers. Nevertheless, I think revelation is progressive and as the Lord reveals to us per time, we will be able to understand and pray more intelligently, so I enjoin us to pray with understanding so that even though we may use them interchangeably, we should seek discernment when we pray. The distinctive characteristics of **selflessness, identification, persistence** and **praying with discernment by praying in the Holy Spirit** discussed in relation to the prayer of intercession, all apply to the prayer of supplication/ petition as well.

## 3.8. The Prayer of Worship

The prayer of worship is the highest form of prayer. It is praise. This is where prayer and praise merge. There is actually a mix and a blend where prayer and praise synthesise to bring to the Lord a sweet-smelling savour, which would be discussed later. The prayer of worship is mirrored several times in the Bible. For example, a leper met Jesus and in the midst of a great multitude, this man offered a prayer of worship;

> And behold, a leper came and **worshiped Him**, saying, "Lord, if You are willing, You can make me clean (**Matthew 8:2**) (**NKJV**)

This act of worship did not only attract the healing power of God, but the healing was accompanied with a touch. Jesus touched him and he was healed. This implies that when we engage the prayer of worship we can receive a touch from the Lord and we can be sure of healing and wholeness to our being-spirit, soul and body.

Also, in **Acts 13**, Bible records that certain prophets and teachers got together to pray and fast.

> Now there were in the church that was at Antioch certain prophets and teachers; as Barnabas, and Simeon that was called Niger, and Lucius of Cyrene, and Manaen, which had been brought up with Herod the tetrarch, and Saul. As they **ministered** to the Lord, and fasted, the Holy Ghost said, Separate me Barnabas and Saul for the work whereunto I have called them. And when they had fasted and prayed, and laid their hands on them, they sent them away. (**Acts 13:1-3**) (**NKJV**).

Here, we see that these people came together to fast, pray and worship. The word '**minister**' used here is actually **worship** and the New International Version used the word specifically; it says 'While they were **worshiping the Lord** and fasting...' (**Acts 13:2**) (**NIV**). So they did not only fast, they prayed and they did not only fast and prayed, they also worshipped and it was while they were engaged in all three that the Holy Ghost gave specific instruction that began all of Paul's missionary journeys. This means that we can be sure that when we need a specific direction or a word from the Lord, He is sure to speak to us by the Holy Spirit when we engage the prayer of worship.

Furthermore, we could see from the example of the Syrophoenician woman earlier mentioned that she came asking i.e. praying for healing for her daughter but she didn't get any positive response. However, immediately she switched to the **prayer of worship**, we saw that even though she didn't qualify for what she asked for, she got it instantly because faith was activated by her worship. The prayer of worship provokes all manner of miracles. People say when all fail, engage the prayer of worship but I would say that we should engage all forms of prayer. Let us have a blend of all kinds of prayer and regardless of the focus of our prayers, let us always depend on the help of Holy Spirit.

## Conclusion

The reason for this exposition of the different types of prayers is to bring understanding and clarity. Admittedly we cannot compartmentalise them in practice and in reality, as Apostle Paul admonishes, let us engage all kinds of prayers. Nevertheless, it is good to have the understanding of the different types of prayers. For example in 'Believers' Meetings[41] the only type of prayer that is appropriate is the prayer of worship because it is a time to minister to the Lord and tarry in His presence. It is not a time to ask and so all other types of prayers may be inappropriate. However, we cannot box the Holy Spirit so if the Lord directs that certain other kinds of prayers be engaged, then we must follow the leading of the Holy Spirit. It may well be that peradventure there are unbelievers in a believers' meeting, then a little exhortation and the prayer of salvation need to be said to lead such persons to Christ first and for the baptism of the Holy spirit. It may well be that the Lord would have us do certain things in certain meetings. Therefore, we must remain sensitive and yielded to the Holy Spirit at all times in the place of prayer.

---

[41] The concept of 'Believers' Meeting' is reflected in **1 Corinthians 14:26** that says, 'How is it then, brethren whenever you come together, each of you has a psalm, has a teaching, has a tongue, has a revelation, has an interpretation. Let all things be done for edification' (NKJV). Several believers' meetings were recorded in Roberts Liardon, *God's General: Why they Succeeded and why some Failed* (Tulsa, Whitaker House 1996) where people came together to minister to the Lord i.e. to worship and tarry in God's presence with no agenda or specific order of how the meeting would proceed.

# CHAPTER FOUR

# Categorisation/ Classilcation of Prayers

## Introduction

Prayer can be categorised broadly into two, namely private and public prayers. Private prayer include personal and individualised prayers between us and our Heavenly Father; God, but even then the Holy Spirit dwells on our inside so it is not really accurate to say it is just one person and God. The person of the Holy Spirit indwelling us makes it a tripartite partnership. Within private prayer is also prayer with family, friends, and prayer partners. By public prayer, we mean corporate prayer that involves church members, whole communities, families etc. This broad classification of prayers means that at every point, prevailing prayer will always require the essential ingredients of agreement and faith.

## 4.1 Agreement in Prayer.

Although we mentioned that agreement and faith are types of prayers in the previous chapter, underlying every prayer are the two essential elements of agreement and faith. This is because if we agree that prayer is access to God then we must believe or have faith that God is real even though invisible to our physical eyes and that we have a relationship with Him. We must also agree with His word, because one of the primary ways He communicates with us is through His word. God and His word are one. Hence in the following sections we will discuss the forms of prayers and how faith and agreement are indispensable requirements in prayers.

At no time is prayer a monologue. Prayer is communication as we said and, in any communication, there must be more than one person. Therefore, our prayers are usually between us, the Holy Spirit who resides within us and our Father the unseen God through our Lord Jesus Christ. Sometimes, prayers could be between us, the Holy Spirit and spiritual beings in the unseen realm. This presupposes that there must be some agreement in any prayer.

Agreement means having the same opinion, two or more people approving and accepting something. It means accord, concurrence, consensus and harmony. Agreement also means consistency, compatibility and conformity. There are several other meanings of the word, but these may well be sufficient for the purpose of analysis in our context. Amos wrote; 'can two walk together except they be agreed?' (**Amos3:3; KJV**). The answer is NO. Therefore, for us to come to the place of communion with our Heavenly Father in prayer, we must be in harmony with Him, there must be a synergy in the spirit, especially in our words, thoughts and actions aligning with God's word. Indeed, agreement is the underlying and unseen foundation for all prevailing prayers.

## 4.2 Faith in Prayers

Prayer addresses God. As believers, our prayers are primarily addressed to God our Heavenly Father. Admittedly, there are times when our prayers are directed at the devil and demonic spirits, especially when we take authority over the spirit of oppressions and afflictions and we take back what rightfully belongs to us in Christ Jesus. In such instances, we take authority and address the demonic spirits behind the afflictions. However, most or all of our prayers start with addressing our Heavenly Father hence the Lord in teaching us how to pray said to start with 'Our Father, in Heaven. Hallowed be your name…'.

If in our prayers, we address God primarily and we know that God is unseen, the invisible, the only wise God and He is Spirit, then we must come to

Him with faith believing that He is and truly is Almighty God. Faith is the foundation of our walk with God. Without faith no man can please God and therefore, if faith is lacking there can be no prevailing prayer. One way to have faith and to build it is by the word. Bible says faith comes by hearing the word again and again. When we read, study, listen to, confess and meditate the word of God regularly, faith will be built in us and we can be sure to engage in prevailing prayers continuously.

Faith is so intricately linked to the word. Concerning the Centurion whose servant was sick, Jesus marvelled at his faith because the Centurion said to the Lord to **only speak the word** that his servant will be healed (**Matthew 8:5-10; NKJV**). In addition to being a man of authority he understood the power of words and particularly when backed with or spoken by someone in authority.

## 4.2.1 Biblical Examples of Faith in Prayer

In several places in scriptures, the Lord didn't have to say anything than '...your faith has made you whole' or 'I have not seen such great faith...' This presupposes that faith is crucial in our walk with God and especially in our prayers. To the woman with the issue of blood who had suffered haemorrhage for several years, the Lord said to her 'your *faith* has made you well' (**Matthew 9:22; Mark 5:34; NKJV**). To the only leper who returned with prayer of thanksgiving, Jesus said 'your *faith* has made you whole' (**Luke 17:19; NKJV**). To Blind Bartimaeus, He said 'Go your way; your *faith* has made you well' (**Mark 10:46-52; NKJV**). To the paralytic man whose four friends brought down through the roof of the building, Bible said 'When Jesus *saw their faith*, He said to the paralytic, Son, your sins are forgiven you' (**Mark 2:1-5; NKJV**). The fact that Jesus didn't just heal these people but relied on their faith to connect with his healing power means that in all situations there is always the human part. In prevailing prayers, our part is to come with faith like these people did.

## 4.2.2 What is faith? Faith is Our Confidence in God

*Faith is our <u>confidence</u> in God*. Our <u>**absolute trust**</u> that He is! Our God is Almighty God and we need to trust that He can do what we want Him to do for us. This is so important that James said that we must not waver, doubt or be doubleminded, as all of these will prevent us from prevailing in our prayers. Paul wrote in **Ephesians 3:20** that '… [God] is able to do exceeding abundantly above all that we ask or think…' (NKJV). God is not a man to lie neither the son of man to repent. What He promised, He is able also to perform. He watches over His word to perform it… (**Numbers 23:19; Romans 4:21; Jeremiah 1:12; NKJV**).

Where is our confidence? Sometimes we pray but our confidence is on someone or somewhere or something else, we need to have absolute confidence and trust in God and the place to build that confidence is in the word. We need to build our faith, our absolute confidence and trust in God's word.

## 4.2.3 What is faith? Faith is Acting on God's Word

*Faith is <u>acting</u> on the word of God*. Faith is not passive, it is *active; involves a doing.* In the instances in scriptures described above, all of the recipients of miracles did something, they acted i.e. they took deliberate steps. The woman with the issue of blood pushed her way through the crowd regardless of the fact that she may have been smelling, looking and feeling frail, pale and faint due to weakness arising from the excessive loss of blood. The four men who brought their paralytic friend could have been justified to return home and say to their friend; we will try another day since the crowd was too much today and there was no way to go through the door, which is the legal entrance to reach Jesus. Blind Bartimaeus could have kept quiet when they told him to, or he could have even asked for money when Jesus asked what he wanted but his faith made him to shout louder so much so that Jesus stopped and called for him. What is our faith doing? It is not enough to read, study and meditate the word, it is not even enough to believe the word, because demons also believe and they tremble (**James 2:19; NKJV**). The difference is in our action. Faith acts…

## 4.2.4 What is faith? Faith is Corresponding Action

*Faith is corresponding action…* We have just said that faith is active not passive, but we need to understand that faith is not just acting. Rather, faith is corresponding action i.e. actions that corresponds to, are in accordance and proportionate to what we know, hear, receive and believe in His word. The actions or steps I should take in my walk with God may not be the same with the actions I expect my teenage son to take, but at his level, I expect him and God expects him to walk in faith i.e. take corresponding actions to the proportion of his faith and understanding of God's word. This is not an absolute example as age has got nothing to do with it because a teenager may have a deeper walk with God than a man or woman who is 50 years old.

I can imagine that on the street of Jericho on that fateful day that Bartimaeus received his sight that there could have been a few other blind folks on the street begging, but it was the man who acted based on the information he received that got his miracle. What are we doing with what we hear, know and believe? Faith is corresponding action. Our action must be concomitant, correlate and consistent with the word of God that we hear daily.

## 4.2.5 The Tangibility of faith

Faith is tangible. To the four men who brought their paralytic friend through the roof, Bible said; 'When Jesus _saw_ their faith…' (**Mark 2: 5; Luke 5:20; NKJV**). In other words, faith is tangible and can be seen. To the Centurion Jesus marvelled!!! Wow; what great faith to make the Lord Himself to wonder and gap in admiration!

> When Jesus heard these things, He marveled at him, and turned around and said to the crowd that followed Him, "I say to you, _**I have not found such great faith**_, not even in Israel!" [10] And those who were sent, returning to the house, found the servant well who had been sick (**Luke 7:9-10**) (**NKJV**).

We need to demonstrate our faith both in our actions and our words. The centurion did with his words, the four friends of the paralytic did by their actions, blind Bartimaeus did with his words and actions and the woman with the issue of blood did with her words and actions. Faith can be seen when we speak the word and take corresponding steps in line with the word. When we engage in prevailing prayers, these things must be demonstrated in our lives both during prayer time and in our regular daily living.

With these two ingredients; agreement and faith, in mind, we will explore the classifications of prayers. The main importance is to increase our understanding and to know at any point in time whether we are engaging in prevailing prayers or not. Where these elements of faith and agreement are present, then we can be sure that our prayers will prevail over any situation and when they are lacking, it is better we put the prayer on hold and fix things first so our prayers will not be futile or pointless. When we pray alone or with somebody or a group of people what must we watch out for to ensure that our prayers are not pointless? We need to have understanding, be alert, and watch so we can move from engaging in pointless to prevailing prayers.

## 4.3 Private Prayers

This is the prayer we engage in personally and individually. This does not mean that the prayer must be said or made only in private places, but it means that we don't need another person, we pray alone all by ourselves and wherever we are, just like Jonah prayed in the belly of the fish. In this sense prayer is relationship; we can talk to God because we are in a relationship with Him, just like we wake up in the morning and we talk to our parents, siblings and friends and during the day, we say hi to check up on them and to update them of where we are and what we are doing… it is the same thing that happens in our personal private prayers. The point is we should wake up early in the morning to pray and speak to our Heavenly Father, which is very important, but also, we should never go the whole day and not have a moment to commune with our God.

Therefore, private prayer should ideally start in our bedroom, and at the early hours of the morning, but it could be at any other more comfortable and quiet place. It then continues in the day; while in the bathroom, on the street, in the bus, on the train, on the aircraft, at the park, during our break time at work or school, anywhere is fine, as long as we do not constitute a nuisance to people around us. This is very important because we are going to be talking about Daniel later how he maintained a lifestyle of prayer and he had a specific place where he prayed. Does this point of praying anywhere contradict that fact? No not at all, the point is that much as a specific place of prayer is ideal and should be maintained by believers, we cannot circumscribe our prayers to only when we are in that place, otherwise, there will be a serious break in communication. A lifestyle of prevailing prayer means that regardless of where we are physically and regardless of our personal circumstances, we are in constant communion with our Heavenly Father. It means that God can depend on us to listen to Him whenever He speaks to us, that we will yield to Him when He instructs and we will enforce His will in every situation.

In addition to private prayer being between us individually and God, private prayer may involve family members, friends, and prayer partners. In this sense, we pray with other people. Whether we pray alone or we pray with other people, agreement is an essential ingredient in prayer. On the individual basis, we must agree with God and His word before we can have any meaningful conversation or communication with Him. When family or other people are involved, then we must not only agree with God and His word, we must also agree with one another. This is very essential because unless and until we are on the same page with the people who pray with us, it is better we pray alone. And when we pray alone, unless and until we agree with God and His word, it is better we don't pray because such prayers will be futile and pointless. We should rather engage in prevailing prayers and for that, agreement is essential. This does not discount the fact that people are at different levels of faith walk with God. Rather, it means that regardless of the diverse levels, everyone agrees with God's word and we are all yearning for more of God and growing in Him.

### 4.3.1 Biblical Example: Paul and Barnabas

This is not strictly in relation to prayer but Paul at a point had to separate from Barnabas and both went their separate ways because they were not in agreement with respect to the work of ministry that God had commissioned them to do. **(Acts 15: 36-41; NKJV).** While Barnabas wanted John Mark to go with them, Paul disagreed because John Mark had deserted them earlier. Bible records that Barnabas went with John Mark while Paul went with Silas. Significantly, they continued the work and still accomplished it and even came together in the end **(1 Corinthians 9:6; 2 Tim 4:11; Colossians 4:10; NKJV).** The point here is, there must be agreement in everything we do and especially in prevailing prayer. Anything done outside of it amounts to futility. It is better we disagree temporarily and trust God to resolve all issues than to continue with resentment, bitterness and malice because where there is strife there is every evil work and our prayers cannot prevail in such circumstances.

### 4.3.2 Personal Example

I once met a lady who had a health condition. She had boils in some parts of her body. I asked to pray with her, she hesitated and then she said '…well, if you want to but…' with that reluctance I suspected there was something so I asked; 'why; is there anything you would like to share…?', because she is a believer, I thought every child of God should automatically, willingly and happily want to be prayed for especially regarding a health situation. 'I think prayers will not take them away because it feels normal as it runs in my family, especially at a particular age', she said. I shared with her from scriptures how at the new birth she is a new creature, how she is now engrafted in Christ and even though certain things have been prevalent in her family she can break the chain and break out of them… but she couldn't agree with me and she couldn't agree with the word of God. At that point, there was no need to pray because no kind of prayer will prevail in that circumstance. Without agreement there can be no prevailing prayer.

Another example was with a lady; one of my 'Mums' in the Lord, I call her Mummy. She was visiting with her daughter in the UK, and I went to see her, as the city where I lived was only about 45 minutes' drive to where her daughter was staying and where she was visiting. We had a lovely time catching up, laughing and sharing with each other. At the end of the visit as I was preparing to return, we decided to pray. We had finished praying and I was about to leave when she said there was a pain on her back that has been there for a long time and that as she climbed the stairs to get something for her grandchildren, she said the Holy Spirit asked her to tell me to pray for her. I didn't know anything, but since she told me what the Holy Spirit impressed in her heart, we decided to pray again this time specifically on the back condition. As soon as we started or just before we held our hands to pray, the Holy Spirit dropped the word 'bitterness' in my heart. The Lord impressed in me that she is harbouring unforgiveness and as long as that is not dealt with she cannot be healed even if I prayed for her. 'We need to talk' I said to her with a somewhat serious tone in my voice. '"Bitterness" is what the Lord just impressed in my heart and there is no point praying when the prayers will not prevail over the situation. For us to pray you have to forgive whoever has wronged you'. She immediately broke down and started crying and of course in the end she forgave the person and then we prayed, and she got healed instantly.

Agreement is so powerful that without it our prayers cannot prevail. If this Mummy didn't admit that she was indeed walking in unforgiveness and if she didn't agree according to the word of God to forgive, we could have prayed but the prayer couldn't have prevailed over the situation and she couldn't have gotten healed of the back condition. She could have continued with it and who knows if that may have taken her life prematurely? But glory to God, with agreement on the background, we didn't have to pray for too long. God heard and answered us! Hallelujah!!!

## 4.4 Public Prayers

Public prayer is the same as corporate prayers. It involves groups of people coming together to pray like in a church setting. Therefore, it could be a local assembly involved in prayers together as a congregation, it could be a community of believers in the Lord Jesus Christ coming together to pray and it could be two or three or more families coming together to pray. Public prayer also implies that the prayers could be said in public places, such as in a church building, in the park and on the street. My local Church Amazing Grace Parish (AGP) participates in Street Fairs biannually on Queens Road Leicester. It is the Clarendon Park Summer and Winter Fairs, which usually provide unique opportunities for everyone in the community to showcase who they are and what they do, as people come to display their products and the services they render. As a local Church, AGP seizes the moment to share the love of Christ, sing and pray for peace for the community, as well as pray for people individually as they request.

AGP also holds Church in the Park during the summer where on a designated Sunday instead of having the regular church service in the usual church building, AGP goes to the Victoria Park and holds its Sunday service there. It is usually a great opportunity to pray over, shift and recalibrate the atmosphere, to enforce God's will for peace, stability and prosperity in the city and country as a whole. All of the prayers said at those times; within the church building, at the Street Fairs and at the Park can rightly be classified as public prayers. If I may digress a little, this idea of coming out to interact with and impact the community by holding worship services outside a building is phenomenal, because the Church is not the physical building. The Church is the *Ecclesia* (the called out ones), people who have received the Lord Jesus Christ and who have received the assignment to reconcile the world back to God. Believers are therefore, the light of the world and the salt of the earth individually and collectively, not the light and salt of a building. Congregating in a building is good and biblical, but in addition, finding ways to impact the communities positively is equally important and biblical.

Public in the sense used here entails not just the fact that the place of prayer is a public place but also involves the participation of many people. The more people you have praying together, the more the necessity for agreement and faith. This is important because concerning the children of Israel it was the sin of one man Achan that made them to be defeated at the battle against Ai, which was a smaller opponent/city compared to Jericho (**Joshua 7**). The congregation of the children of Israel numbered close to two million people and in the sight of God, His people must be in complete obedience to His instruction and they must be holy. Nevertheless, the disagreement and disobedience of one man brought calamity to the entire nation of Israel. Similarly, the more the number of people that gather either physically or virtually (online conference) to pray, the more the necessity to ensure that everyone is in agreement and walking in obedience to God's word because if one person fails then the entire team is polluted and there can be no prevailing but pointless prayers in such instances.

Several times in scripture we see the Lord Jesus Christ calling people out of the crowd. Sometimes outside the town to the outskirts of cities before he prayed for them. I believe one of the reasons was to take them out of the crowd, out of the atmosphere of unbelief and disagreement because even with the anointing, Jesus couldn't do mighty works in his home town due to unbelief. If the Lord Jesus Christ needed an atmosphere of faith and agreement to pray for people, I think we need it much more…

## Conclusion

There are many ingredients to prevailing prayers, some of them include being born again, living a holy and sanctified sin-free life, walking in love, having a forgiving heart, walking in complete obedience, etc. These are very fundamental, but in this chapter, we have broadly classified these requirements into two namely agreement and faith. This is because all other elements can be subsumed under them. The different types of prayers discussed in the previous chapter need these two elements to prevail. With the prayer of salvation/redemption anyone coming to Christ must first agree with and believe in the gospel of our Lord Jesus Christ and then they must have faith in God and be able to relate with Him as their Father. Also, the other types of prayers, namely, the prayer of consecration, dedication, prayer of faith, prayer of thanksgiving, intercession/supplication and worship all have at their rudiments these key ingredients of agreement and faith.

# CHAPTER FIVE

# The Place of Prayer:
# The Upper Room

This part of the book will include an exposition of **Daniel 6:10**. Recall in the beginning, I mentioned that this book was prompted by the Prayer Weekend we had in my local Church in February 2017 in which I was privileged to be one of the speakers. The theme for the prayer weekend was '**The Lifestyle of Prayer**' coined from **Daniel 6:10.** It was in the course of my prayer and preparation for my session that the Lord dropped 'Prevailing' in my heart and hence I came up with 'Prevailing Prayer Lifestyle'. In this part of the book, in addition to an exposition of the verse, we will use Daniel as a Case-Study looking at how he prevailed in prayers.

> Now when Daniel knew that the writing was signed, he went home. And in his **upper room**, with his windows open toward Jerusalem, he knelt down on his knees three times that day, and prayed and gave thanks before his God, as was his custom since early days. (**Daniel 6:10**) (**NKJV**).

Interestingly Bible Scholars agree that Daniel was in his 80s at this time and was serving under the third King in Babylon.[42] Despite his busy schedule and old age, Daniel continued with his life-long practice of praying and he had a specific place of prayer – the Upper Room. This chapter will give a

---

[42] See for example, Steve Shirley, 'Q: 374. How old was Daniel when he was thrown into the Lion's Den?' Available at http://jesusalive.cc/ques374.htm>; John F. Walvoord, 'Daniel in the Lions' Den' https://bible.org/seriespage/6-daniel-lions-den>

brief exposition of the different component of the verse as follows: **(i) Daniel went into his house (Upper Room) - Place of Prayer; (ii) Daniel kneeled down upon his knees three times - Posture; (iii) Daniel Prayed and gave thanks before his God - Purposeful, Precision & Priority and (iv) As was his custom since early days – Persistence and Proportionality in Prayer**

## 5.1 Daniel went into the Upper Room – the place of prayer

Daniel went home and in his **Upper Room** which is the **Place of Prayer,** he prayed and gave thanks to his God. Certainly, there are activities and events that characterised the upper room in scriptures. It is interesting to note that both positive and negative things happened in the upper room.

## 5.1.1 Positive Incidences in the Upper Room – The Place of Prayers

In **1 Kings 17:19 NKJV,** Elijah raised the son of the widow of Zarephath to life at the *Upper Room.* Similarly, in **1 Kings 4:10-11 NKJV,** Elisha raised the child of the Shunamite woman from the dead at the *Upper Room* because the woman had prepared that *Room* for him to rest whenever he came on his evangelistic missions. Also, in **Acts 1:13 NKJV,** the Apostles went to the *Upper Room* where they appointed Matthias to replace Judas Iscariot, it was also at the *Upper Room* that the Holy Ghost came upon them on the Day of Pentecost and since then the Holy Ghost has not returned; He remains in us, continues with us, helping us to continue and complete the work of ministry that the Lord Jesus left for us to accomplish.

In addition, in **Acts 9:37-39 NKJV,** the great philanthropist Dorcas Tabitha had died but the disciples laid her at the *Upper Room* and sent for Peter who came from Joppa and raised her from the dead. Furthermore, in **Acts 10:9 NKJV,** Peter fell into a trance at the *Upper Room* at which God showed him that nothing is unclean and therefore, God was interested in both the Jews and Gentile nations alike and instructed him to get ready to respond positively and promptly to a call from **Cornelius** who became the first Gentile to receive the gospel.

Therefore, the **Upper Room** was not only known as **The Place of Prayer**, but it was also a place where great miracles took place, where the dead were raised to life, as well as the place where divine encounters, generational and life changing transformations occurred. The question is; is the Church, the Body of Christ in this generation keeping the Upper Room? The Upper Room is symbolic of the place of prayer and like Daniel, we need to **prioritise the place of prayer** both individually and collectively in order to have positive **Upper Room** experiences; divine encounters and transformations in our lives, God's interventions in His Church, in our cities and in the nations of the world.

## 5.1.2 Negative Occurrences in the Upper room – When we fail to heed the call to Pray

Despite the above positive incidences that happened in the upper room, two notable negative and unsavoury situations were also recorded in scriptures. The first was in **2 Kings 1:2 NKJV**, where **King Ahaziah** fell down from the **Upper Room** because he was sleeping. The second incident was recorded in **Acts 20:8 NKJV**, when Apostle Paul preached into the night and a young man **Eutychus** slept and fell from the **Upper Room** and died, but Paul raised him up. This clearly tells us that the **Upper Room** is meant for prayer and not for sleeping.

## 5.1.3 Our Choice

Do we sleep at midnight hour in our homes in the **Upper Room** when the Lord wakes us up to pray? Do we make excuses when it is time to pray? Sleeping could be symbolic of excuses that we give for not heeding the call to pray and these excuses might appear legitimate. However, we must realise that there are grave consequences if or when we sleep in the **Upper Room** instead of praying, because somebody for whom prayer is urgently needed at that time might die. May the Lord have mercy on us; that death will not be upon us or upon our loved ones or anybody because their blood may just be on our heads. But we do have a choice to make.

I recall back in Law School, how I did very strange things to overcome sleep so I could read and pass my Bar Exams. My friend Chi-Chi had a good laugh because one of the strange things I did was to practically stand on top of my reading table with my text book in my hands and I said to myself that if I sleep while standing on this table, I will not only fall down, I will also sustain injury, serious enough to keep me awake to read for my exams (laughs). I can't remember taking such drastic measures when it comes to prayer. Lord have mercy on me!!!

In the case of **King Ahaziah**, his error was double and hence there was no remedy for him. It was bad enough that he slept in the **Upper Room** when he was meant to be praying, but he also made a wrong choice to have consulted a strange god. Therefore, while in his case, he eventually died because he consulted a strange god about his sickness, which occurred as a result of the fall, God's mercies and resurrection power raised **Eutychus** from the dead. There is resurrection power available to us but we cannot afford to let things go bad. We have a choice to make, which is to deal decisively with sleep and all seemingly 'legitimate' excuses that takes us from the place of prayer. We may not have a specific location in our homes where we pray, but God expects us to keep the hour of prayer whatever place and time that may be.

## 5.2 His windows were opened – Purposeful in Prayers

> Now when Daniel knew that the writing was signed, he went home. And in his upper room, with **his windows open toward Jerusalem**, he knelt down on his knees three times that day, and prayed and gave thanks before his God, as was his custom since early days. **(Daniel 6:10) (NKJV).**

Daniel had his **windows opened**. This seems contrary to Jesus' instruction to us in **Matthew 6:6 to go into our closet and shut our doors when we pray**. However, this is distinguishable from **Matthew 6:6** because in context, our Lord Jesus Christ was teaching us to avoid every form of hypocrisy when we pray, we shouldn't engage in prayers just because we want to be seen or heard by people.

In contrast, Daniel's opening of the window signified two things. First, it signified **open demonstration of his uncompromising stance, resolve, diligence in his devotion and dedication to his God.** He demonstrated that he was neither ashamed of worshipping Jehovah, the God of his fathers, nor afraid of the law that had just been passed prohibiting his worship and the imminent consequences. Second, although far away from his home country, Daniel had affection for the Holy City, Jerusalem.

Daniel turned his face towards Jerusalem when he prayed. Traditionally, prayer made in the Temple was guaranteed to prevail because God's presence and glory, symbolised by the Ark of the Covenant, abode there. Thus, when the temple was dedicated, it was anticipated that this would be the practice that when the people prayed there God would answer and deliver them from whatever trouble they might be in. Similarly, if they were taken captive to a strange/far country or land or wherever they might be, they should pray facing Jerusalem and possibly where the temple is located.

Therefore, Jews in exile prayed facing Jerusalem, while those in Jerusalem prayed facing the Temple. This became a regular practice amongst Jews who lived in their home country to pray in the Temple or if far away to pray with their faces turned towards the Temple in Jerusalem. God had promised that every prayer made in the Temple would prevail as God represented by the Ark of the Covenant was in the Temple and would hear and answer His people when they cry to Him in prayers. Thus, in the prayer of Solomon, at the dedication of the Temple, he said;

> When Your people go out to battle against their enemy, wherever You send them, and when they pray to the LORD toward the city which You have chosen and the temple which I have built for Your name, then hear in heaven their prayer and their supplication, and maintain their cause. (**1 Kings 8: 44-45**) (**NKJV**).

Furthermore, in **verses 46-53** Solomon said

> When they sin against You (for there is no one who does not sin), and You become angry with them and deliver them to

the enemy, and they take them captive to the land of the enemy, far or near; [47] yet when they come to themselves in the land where they were carried captive, and repent, and make supplication to You in the land of those who took them captive, saying, 'We have sinned and done wrong, we have committed wickedness'; [48] and when they return to You with all their heart and with all their soul in the land of their enemies who led them away captive, and pray to You toward their land which You gave to their fathers, the city which You have chosen and the temple which I have built for Your name: [49] then hear in heaven Your dwelling place their prayer and their supplication, and maintain their cause, [50] and forgive Your people who have sinned against You, and all their transgressions which they have transgressed against You; and grant them compassion before those who took them captive, that they may have compassion on them [51] (for they are Your people and Your inheritance, whom You brought out of Egypt, out of the iron furnace), [52] that Your eyes may be open to the supplication of Your servant and the supplication of Your people Israel, to listen to them whenever they call to You. [53] For You separated them from among all the peoples of the earth to be Your inheritance, as You spoke by Your servant Moses, when You brought our fathers out of Egypt, O Lord God." **(1 Kings 8: 46-53) (NKJV).**

Typically, when the temple was dedicated, these were the prayers and expectations and the tradition had been passed down from one generation to another so much so that even in exile in faraway Babylon, Daniel did not forget this culture of praying, he did not only pray, but he also prayed in the prescribed manner. The act of being purposeful in prayer is one that is gradually being eroded in Christendom and we need to bring it back, reinforce it and continue steadfastly in praying so that the next generation can carry on with it wherever they find themselves whether in exile in faraway countries or at home.

Purposefulness in prayer relates to open demonstration of our faith and relationship with our God without pretence. In contemporary times, it appears we seem to be silent and we seem to always desire to be quiet in the name of political correctness? We don't want to offend, we don't want to break the laws of the land? The point here is not to encourage us to constitute nuisance in our schools and work places with our prayers, but we need to realise that there is freedom of thought, belief and religion,[43] by which we are free by law to participate in whatever religious group, belief and express ourselves freely in prayer. So being purposeful in our prayers doesn't mean we are in breach of the laws. Rather, it is understanding that within the confines of the law, we are allowed to exercise our right to profess our faith and express our worship and prayer to God. Daniel provides us a good example that even though a law has been passed prohibiting his worship of God, he did not pretend. Rather, he continued purposefully and deliberately in his prayer and worship to God. If this generation cannot be purposeful in our prayers to God, I wonder what will become of the next generation if the Lord tarries. Like Daniel, we need to arise and be purposeful in prayer regardless of the laws that may be targeted at us.

## 5.3 Daniel kneeled down upon his knees three times - Posture and Proportionality

The act of **Kneeling** was considered the most appropriate **posture** in prayer, as it is most expressive of **humility**, **reverence** and **submission** to God. Although Daniel was a **great man**, he did not consider himself too dignified to be on his knees before his Maker three times a day. Although he was an 'old man' (being above 80 years old), and it had been his practice from his youth up, he was not weary of this kind of well-doing; and though he was a **business man, of great and important position**, and his services,

---

[43] See Human Rights Act 1998. Article 9 - Freedom of thought, belief and religion, which protects the rights of people to have their own thoughts, beliefs and follow religions of their choice; it also includes the right to change their religion or belief at any time. Religion and belief is one of the protected characteristics within the Equality Act and it is unlawful to discriminate against workers because of their religion or belief or lack thereof. See also Articles 9 & 14 of the European Convention on Human Rights (ECHR).

duties and responsibility were of high demand by the general Babylonian society, he didn't think these should be sufficient excuses for him to stop or reduce or readjust this daily act of thrice kneeling before God in prayer. How inexcusable then are we who have but little to do, even if we are busy, I do not think our busy schedules unparalleled Daniel's. By kneeling in prayers thrice daily, Daniel demonstrated the right posture and proportionality in prayer that we must emulate.

## 5.3.1 Posture in Prayer

Daniel demonstrates to us that regardless of our high position and importance in society, regardless of how demanding our responsibilities have become, our humility and submission to God should be reflected in our posture when we pray. Posture is everything, you cannot be casual and say God sees the inward – the heart and not the outward, because it is what is in our heart that shows on the outward and Bible says God is a God of knowledge and by Him actions are weighed (**1 Samuel 2:3; NKJV**). Therefore, God looks at the heart as well as our outward appearance which is our posture. Let our heart synchronise with our posture, as we maintain the right posture in prayer. I do recognise that due to certain health conditions, or some other reasons, some people may not be able to kneel down physically, and these can be permissible exceptions. Apart from these, the general rule is that our posture in prayer, which is to kneel down reflects humility and submission and it is as important as the content of our prayers. We need to approach God with reverence both in our hearts and physically.

## 5.3.2 Proportionality in Prayer

> ... [Daniel] knelt down on his knees **three times** that day... (**Daniel 6:10**)

'**Three times**' signified **Morning, noon, and evening.** These were the hours of prayer observed by devout men of former times. This was continued by the apostles, who observed the **third**, the **sixth**, and the **ninth hours** (**Acts 3:1; 10:30; NKJV**) as times of prayer. In contemporary times, these would represent **9.00am, 12.00noon and 3.00pm**. So many things are recorded about these different times of prayers in scripture but we will limit our discussions to the **ninth hour** which is **3.00pm.**

It was at the **ninth hour** that Jesus died on the cross. Bible records in **Matthew 27:45-51** that at the **ninth hour** Jesus cried out '*Eli, Eli Lama sabachthani?*' that is '**My God My God why have You forsaken me?**'(NKJV) and Bible records that Jesus cried out with a loud voice and yielded up his spirit and instantaneously, the veil of the temple was torn in two from top to bottom... In other words, it was at the **ninth hour** that the price for the reconciliation of humanity to God was paid, as mankind through the death of our Lord Jesus Christ, His burial and His Resurrection on the third day, regained the hitherto lost access to God. In **Acts 3:1 NKJV**, Peter and John prayed for the man at the gate called Beautiful at the **ninth hour** on their way to pray and the man was healed. Similarly, in **Acts 10:3&30 NKJV**, Cornelius was praying at the **ninth hour** when an angel appeared to him and asked him to send for Peter. It was this experience that led to his conversion, because simultaneously on the sixth hour of prayer, Peter fell into a trance in the upper room and was shown a vision in which God told him not to discriminate.

Proportionality in prayer will be discussed in detailed in the last chapter, but here, proportionality is in relation to the number of times that Daniel prayed. Praying thrice daily is presumably a tradition Daniel learnt from his home country and has become his lifestyle and because he already had that on-going relationship, he didn't have to add or remove from it. He didn't get angry, it wasn't recorded that he cried, grumbled or murmured! His response was proportionate in that he prayed just as he has always done. He did not respond in fear, neither was his prayer intensified by reason of the law targeted at him. On the contrary, what we see in contemporary times is that our prayers are reactionary and because we react to things when they happen, sometimes our actions are motivated by fear and not faith and therefore, we respond disproportionately. 'Your kingdom come Your will be done on earth...' is a mandate that God has given us to enforce His will on earth. This means we do not have to wait until unpleasant situations occur before we take this mandate seriously. The Church should be proactive in prayer, making the news and not allowing the news to dictate the proportion or intensity of our prayers. Also, Apostle Paul admonishes in **1 Thessalonians 5:17** that we should pray without ceasing (NKJV). Therefore, while in Daniel's dispensation praying thrice daily and at specific times, was the tradition, in this dispensation we could adopt those times, but in addition, we need to be in constant communion. This will help us to be alert and sensitive to the Holy Spirit so that we can be able to constantly enforce heaven's agenda in our lives and situations all over the world.

## 5.4 He prayed and gave thanks before his God - Precision and Priority

> '...and [Daniel] prayed and gave thanks before his God...' (Daniel 6:10)

From our previous discussions on the different types of prayer, we can safely conclude that Daniel engaged two kinds of prayer, namely the *prayer of supplication* and the *prayer of thanksgiving* in his daily devotion, by which he is an example for our emulation. This is important because we need to know that approaching God with our fears, tears and feeling of defeat and intimidation does not help our prayers, neither will any of these make our prayers to prevail. It is precise prayer orchestrated by God's word and promises in scriptures that prevails over every unpleasant situation and circumstances in our lives.

## 5.4.1 Daniel Prioritised Prayer

The prayer of supplication is one of the prayers we pray for ourselves and other believers alike. The premise is that we already know God, we belong to Him, we have a Father/Son/Children relationship with Him so we can approach Him with boldness and confidence. Also, because we belong to God and we have a relationship with Him, we already know that whatever comes our way, we are going to make it. Therefore, Daniel prayed precisely the kind of prayer that is required here because of relationship. We are not told the content but I suppose it may have been something like this:

**'Dear God behold their laws, behold their threats, behold my conspirators, nothing is hidden from You and I know that in this situation, You remain God, You will save and deliver me from their hands and You will ensure they do not prosper in all that they have imagined to do and they will not be able to carry out their evil enterprise...'**

I imagine this could have been the kind of prayer Daniel prayed. This demonstrates trust and confidence, which comes from knowing God and knowing God comes from having a relationship with Him in the place of prayer and study of His word. It is important that we engage the right kind of prayer per time.

Also, it is interesting that Daniel did not allow the laws that was made to upset him. He may have been provoked, but he was propelled to pray. In other words, Daniel prioritised prayers in the midst of imminent danger. He didn't pretend, rather, he prayed. Instead of being provoked to anger, he was propelled to prioritise prayers. Unfortunately, it appears the contrary is the case with believers in contemporary times because the first thing we do sometimes when faced with challenges is not prayer. Most times we complain, we cry and we kind of do every other thing but pray. However, we must learn from Daniel, and even though we may cry and we may be provoked to anger, we should nevertheless be propelled to *prioritise* prayers.

## 5.4.2 Daniel Gave Thanks.

In addition to what we noted above as what may have been the content of Daniel' s prayer, since he also 'thanked God', presumably, he may have concluded his prayers with these lines *'...Thank You God for You are the Almighty God. The Great God who hears and answers me always... Thank you God because You will save and deliver me from the hands of my conspirators and from this obnoxious law...*

The prayer of thanksgiving ought to be a vital part of every of our prayers, regardless of what situation we find ourselves. Bible commands us to give thanks in every situation because that is the will of God concerning us, not that it is His will for us to be in negative situations, but He wants us to thank Him because He is able to turn every negative situation around. Therefore, when we pray to God to ask Him for the mercies we want, we ought to thank him for those we have received, as well as thank Him in anticipation of the answers to what we prayed for, knowing that He is able to do exceeding abundantly above all that we can ask or think…

Daniel did not engage more prayer than necessary. He did as he was used to doing, i.e. prayed and gave thanks. This also depicts proportionality in prayer. In our day, some of us will enlist prayer partners and prayer warriors to engage all kinds of prayer and most of them born out of fear. Whilst calling for support in prayer and praying all kinds of prayers are not wrong, we must ensure that fear is not the underlying motivation, because as we said earlier, the crucial core elements of faith and agreement must accompany our prayers. Therefore, our prayer should not be propelled by fear but by faith built in the place of intimacy with God that has been cultivated overtime.

## 5.4.3 …Before His God

It is interesting that Daniel did not pray **to but <u>before</u> his God.** This may not sound different but we must realise that there is a huge difference here because *'to'* means there is some gap or distance, while *'before'* reveals closeness, presence and being with. It depicts intimacy. Recall what we said earlier that prayer is communication and access to God. Yes, we can talk to relations, family and friends in distant places on phone, chat, through skype etc., but we know that there is a big difference in talking face to face. Here, we could see that Daniel's relationship with God transcended a remote and distant relationship. Daniel had an intimate relationship with God and therefore, He prayed and gave thanks *before* his God. **(Daniel 2:9 6:22; NKJV).**

Moses was one example in the Old Testament who talked with God face to face and we saw the difference in the glory that he radiated **(Numbers 14:8; Matthew 11:26; 18:14; Luke 12:6; NKJV).** Moses' relationship with God was classically distinct from the relationship of the Israelites with God in that Moses knew God's ways while the Israelites knew God's acts. This means that for us to prevail in the place of prayers, we need to have that intimacy with God. We must transcend the seasons of praying *to God* and get into praying *before God*. Activating His presence is what makes the difference. This means when we develop a closer walk and intimacy with God, we are conscious of His presence always and especially in prayers. Just the same way we talk with our earthly parents in a conversational, relational way, is the exact same way we can have conversations with God and He wouldn't appear far away from us. Intimacy is fuelled by a holy and righteous living, being obedient and having a hunger for more of God always.

## 5.5 As was his custom since early days - Lifestyle of Persistence in Prayer

The last element to consider in the **Daniel 6:10** is the last phrase, namely, *'...as was his custom from early days.'* Daniel had persistently practiced the act of prioritising the place of prayer and from this scripture, this is something he may have imbibed probably from his parents, because from his early days may be something he cultivated from home and yet while in a foreign land he did not forget this act. No wonder the Bible enjoins us to train up our children the way they should go and when they grow up they will not depart from it (**Proverbs 22:6; NKJV**). The big question is what are we teaching our children? How are we training our children up? Teaching and training our children go beyond what we say or instruct them to do or to refrain from doing. It also includes our culture, values and lifestyle. We can be confident that when we have the culture of prioritising the place of persistent, purposeful, precise and proportionate prayers with the right posture and we deliberately teach our children, they will continue in it wherever they find themselves.

It is noteworthy that Daniel did not stop his prayers because of the law and because of the fear of death since the penalty was to be thrown into the lions' den. It is important to note also that Daniel did not break the law deliberately since he did no more than he had been doing previously, he only persisted and persevered in his former long-continued course. For us, the instruction is to make our stance known, have a close intimate walk with God and pray without ceasing. Also, we should not be afraid or be anxious about anything but in everything, by prayer and supplication with thanksgiving let us make our request known to God (**Philippians 4:6; NKJV**), and He is faithful to save and deliver us.

## Conclusion

Daniel had a lifestyle that the Body of Christ needs to emulate in order to respond appropriately to envies, jealousies, unhealthy competition and rivalries that leads to obnoxious laws, policies and decisions being made against the Church in recent times in our cities, and in the nations of the world. These obnoxious laws are evident in our schools, organisations, institutions and corporations, as well as businesses and work places. However, when we prioritise the place of prayers, when we are persistent, precise, purposeful, and proportionate in prayers, then we are sure to prevail over the opposition. Like Daniel, even though we may be provoked to anger, especially since these laws are obviously targeted at us, we must be propelled to pray instead. We must **prioritise** the **place** of prayer wherever that may be (Upper Room), because failure to prioritise prayer may result in some unpleasant negative experiences. We have to be **persistent** in prayers. We also need to take the right **posture** in prayer, as posture reflects our humility, submission and reverence for God and finally, our prayers need to be **purposeful, precise and proportionate.** These 7 'P' words will be discussed in more detail in the concluding chapter of this book.

# CHAPTER SIX

# Daniel's Lifestyle Mirrored - Daniel and the Early Church

Significantly, Daniel is a type of the Church and so in this chapter we shall explore how his lifestyle foreshadowed the early Church. Soon after the Lord Jesus Christ resurrected and ascended to heaven, the Apostles received the promise of the Holy Ghost on the Day of Pentecost and with the Holy Ghost in them they began to live and walk like Christ. One of the prevalent characteristic of the early Church was the presence and the working of the Holy Spirit in and amongst them. Nevertheless, despite being filled with the Holy Spirit, the early Church was persecuted and beaten on account of their faith.

First, Daniel prayed in the Upper Room, the early Church also prayed in the Upper Room and it was from there they appointed Mathias to replace Judas Iscariot and got baptised with the Holy Spirit. Second, Daniel was hated and persecuted, just as the early Church was hated and persecuted. Third, due to jealousy and envy, Daniel was the target of obnoxious law, just as the early Church was also the target of obnoxious laws. Daniel had a company of the other three Hebrew children Shedrack, Meshach and Abednego and he went to meet his company (**Daniel 2:7; NKJV**). Similarly when Peter, James and John were arrested and beaten and warned not to preach about Jesus, they also went to meet their company the other disciples (**Acts 4:23; NKJV**). Lastly, Daniel was put in prison (lions' den) and had angelic assistance (**Daniel 6:22; NKJV**) the same way the early Church were imprisoned but had angels come to their rescue (**Acts 4; 5:17-20; 12:7-10; NKJV**).

These similarities indicate that Daniel prefigured the early Church and by extension the Church in this generation and for all ages.

## 6.1 Prioritised the Place of Prayer

Just as Daniel prioritise the place of prayer and spent his time in the Upper Room praying, the early Church went into the Upper Room to wait and pray. The Lord had instructed them to tarry in Jerusalem until they were endued with power from on high (**Luke 24:49; NKJV**). It was at the Upper Room that Matthias was appointed to replace Judas Iscariot and while they were there in one accord, praying and waiting, the Holy Ghost came on them on the Day of Pentecost. Without this important visitation and outpour of the Holy Spirit, the early church would not have functioned effectively. They became active witnesses for Christ, even though hitherto they were cowardly, intimidated and devastated by the departure of the Lord Jesus Christ, the Holy Spirit gave them boldness to be witnesses for Christ.

Similarly, the body of Christ in contemporary times should exemplify the lifestyle of prioritising the place of prayer. If Daniel did it in a foreign land and in the face of imminent life threatening danger, and if the early Church engaged in praying and tarrying in the Upper Room in obedience to the Lord's instruction, then we should also prioritise the place of prayer. It is in the place of prayer that tremendous power is made available. The Lord Jesus spent lots of times alone in the early hours of the day praying. Sometimes, Jesus departed to lonely places to pray, and because He spent a long time praying early hours of the morning, during the day, He exerted less energy. In some cases, He only gave thanks – Lazarus raised from the dead **John 11:41; NKJV**, the feeding of the Five Thousand **John 6:11; NKJV**; and at other times, He just said '...so that they might believe that YOU sent me' **John 11:42; NKJV.**

## 6.2 Hated and Persecuted

Daniel was hated by his colleagues because of jealousy and envy. Among three supposedly equal governors, Daniel was preferred and appointed to head not just the two other governors but also the whole of the 120 Princes who were appointed to rule over the 120 provinces.

> It pleased Darius to set over the kingdom an hundred and twenty princes, which should be over the whole kingdom;[2] And over these three presidents; of whom Daniel was first: that the princes might give accounts unto them, and the king should have no damage. [3] Then this Daniel was preferred above the presidents and princes, because an excellent spirit was in him; and the king thought to set him over the whole realm. [4] Then the presidents and princes sought to find occasion against Daniel concerning the kingdom; but they could find none occasion nor fault; forasmuch as he was faithful, neither was there any error or fault found in him. **(Daniel 6:1-4) (NKJV).**

The reason for Daniel's preference was because an excellent spirit was found in him. In other words, the excellent spirit of God distinguished Daniel and brought him promotion and lifting, but the lifting provoked jealousy. In the same vein, the early Church didn't function until they had a deluge of the Spirit on them. This is crucial to the body of Christ in contemporary times that seems to function without the Holy Spirit. It is the Holy Spirit in us that can cause us to be distinguished and excellent in all we do, therefore, we need to spend time in the place of prayer to receive an overflow of the outpour of the Holy Spirt in order to function effectively. Prioritising the place of prayer will certainly activate more of the presence and expression of the Holy Spirit in our lives. Not too long after the distinction brought promotion, hatred and persecution came knocking on Daniel's door. This also happened with the early Church, as the Apostles performed signs and wonders by the power of the Holy Ghost, specifically with the healing of the man at the gate called Beautiful, they soon began to gain popularity and prominence. Nevertheless, this was accompanied with hatred and persecution from members of the Sanhedrin.

## 6.3 Target for Obnoxious Laws and Policies

Interestingly, Daniel's haters searched for ways to fault him, but found none. With regards to the discharge of his responsibilities to the public, he was diligent, presumably, he was never late or absent from work, he never violated the laws of the land and he spoke to his subordinates and everyone politely. With regards to his duties to the Kings of Babylon under whom he served, Daniel was diligent and impeccable. The only place they sought to fault him was in relation to his devotion and dedication to God (**Daniel 6:5; NKJV**). This was epitomised in the early Church as well, because when Peter and John were interrogated for healing the man at the gate called Beautiful, the only error or fault they found with them was in relation to the miracle that had just occurred.

> And when they had set them in the midst, they asked, "By what power or by what name have you done this?" [8] Then Peter, filled with the Holy Spirit, said to them, "Rulers of the people and elders of Israel: [9] If we this day are judged for a good deed *done* to a helpless man, by what means he has been made well [10] let it be known to you all, and to all the people of Israel, that by the name of Jesus Christ of Nazareth, whom you crucified, whom God raised from the dead, by Him this man stands here before you whole (**Acts 4:7-10) (NKJV).**

It appears this is also exemplified in contemporary times where the body of Christ is being interrogated because of her devotion and dedication to the one true God? However, these have been written for our learning so we do not think that some strange things have befallen us. As Jesus admonished, if the world hated Him the Lord Jesus Christ, then we would be hated as well.

> If the world hates you, you know that it hated Me before *it hated* you. [19] If you were of the world, the world would love its own. Yet because you are not of the world, but I chose you out of the world, therefore the world hates you. [20] Remember the word that I said to you, 'A servant is not

greater than his master.' If they persecuted Me, they will also persecute you. If they kept My word, they will keep yours also. [21] But all these things they will do to you for My name's sake, because they do not know Him who sent Me. **(John 15:18-21) (NKJV).**

Since Daniel was flawless, a law had to be promulgated. A royal statute was legislated declaring; anyone who prayed to any other God or made request or petition to any God other than the king within these days should be thrown into the den of lions **(Daniel 6:7; NKJV).** It was only a few lines to be in force for 30 days. The law was targeted at him to make him compromise his faith, to stop him from continuing in his lifestyle of prevailing prayer and to make him deny his God.

Similarly, the early Church did not only receive a verbal warning but they were beaten and sternly prohibited from talking about the Lord Jesus Christ. Like Daniel, the warning and beating only propelled them to pray more. They went to their company after they were released and they prayed much more fervently to the extent that the place shook and they got filled with the Holy Spirit again **(Acts 4:23-31; NKJV).** We need to follow in the footsteps of the early Church, that when we are threatened by laws, whether written or verbal, it is not the time to confront our haters or explain why the laws are wrong. Rather it is the time to prioritise the place of prayer. Like the Apostles were empowered again by another infilling of the Holy Spirit, we can be sure to receive power when we prioritise prayer in the midst of persecution. And take notice that they did not pray to be delivered, they prayed for boldness to continue to proclaim the resurrected Christ. What is the content of our prayers when we face persecution?

## 6.3.1 Instances of Obnoxious laws in the Bible – Pharaoh

Promulgating obnoxious laws against God's people dates back to many generations. In Exodus, a Pharaoh who didn't know Joseph arose and felt intimated by the multiplication of God's people in the land. The only way he sought to check or eliminate them was to legislate laws and policies on hard and harsh labour, which imposed on the people stiffer and tougher measures in carrying out their daily tasks. When that did not work, a second legislation was passed, namely, to kill all male children of the Hebrews. The Pharaoh went as far as appointing law enforcement agents among the midwives called Shiphrah and Puah to ensure that the law was enforced to the letter. However, God put His fear in the hearts of the midwives and they couldn't carry out Pharaoh's evil enterprise. Therefore, although the law to annihilate God's people was in full force in Egypt, the enforcement was haphazard and sometimes impossible because of God's intervention, which made the birth of the deliverer of the time -Moses- a reality.

## 6.3.2 Instances of Obnoxious laws in the Bible - Haman

Similarly, in the palace at Shusha, Haman was determined to annihilate the entire Jewish nation because Mordecai a Jew, refused to kowtow to him. It was one of the ways a group is targeted by genocidal laws, because for the presumed 'error' of one man, Haman made king Ahasuerus to promulgate the law to destroy the entire Jewish people. However, by prayer and fasting, God overturned the laws by allowing Queen Esther and Mordcai to legislate a superior law, which ensured that not only was Haman and his sons executed but also all non-Jews and the enemies of God's people so much so that everyone turned to become Jews to save their lives (**Esther 8:15; NKJV**). Indeed, as prophesied by Isaiah, the time is coming and now is that time when people shall run to the Lord and His Church for salvation (**Isaiah 2:1-3; 4:1; NKJV**). We are in the best seasons of time! All we need is courage, boldness and spiritual energy which comes from the Holy Spirit when we engage in fasting and prayer.

## 6.3.3 Instances of Obnoxious laws in the Bible – King Herod

One would have expected that with the birth of the Lord Jesus Christ, the promulgation of obnoxious laws would have ceased. Nevertheless, fast-forward to the New Testament and despite the fact that the birth of Jesus had been predicted and prophesied for many years, King Herod was intimidated by the announcement of the birth of the King of the Jews. Determined to secure his kingship and kill the newly born Messiah, King Herod legislated a law to destroy every child that was 2 years and below. Glory to God for the way of escape orchestrated by the divine angelic visitation by night vision to Joseph that instructed him to escape with Mary and Jesus to Egypt.

Also, the laws against the early Church were widespread, as Saul before his conversion, took letters of authorisation to carry out the campaign of persecution and enforcement of obnoxious laws against the followers of Christ throughout the region of Jerusalem, and as far as Damascus (**Acts 9:1-2; NKJV**). Interestingly, it was on his way to Damascus to persecute Christians that the Lord Jesus Christ appeared to him and that encounter led to Saul's conversion, who became Paul and wrote more than half of the New Testament.

Therefore, I declare that regardless of the laws and policies seemingly targeted at Christians:

> *...the Church must be strong in this day because it is written woe unto him that decree unrighteous decree and that write grievous laws. The Lord executes righteousness and judgement to all that are oppressed; God's people shall be far from oppression and terror for we shall not fear. Behold they shall surely gather but not by me saith the Lord, and because their gathering is not of the Lord, they shall fall for your sake. No weapon formed or fashion against God's people shall be able to prosper and every tongue that rises against you in judgement is condemned already. The Lord will disappoint the devices of the crafty and prevent their hands from performing their evil enterprise. He shall frustrate the token of lairs and make the diviners mad...*[44]

When we are propelled to prioritise the place of prayer and we continue to declare God's word then we can be sure that as Gamaliel counselled the Sanhedrin concerning the Apostles, the laws will not see the light of day (**Acts 5:34-39; NKJV**). We shall laugh as scripture said he that sits in the

---

[44] Excerpts from the following scriptures; **Isaiah 10:1; Psalm 103:6; Isaiah 54:15; Isaiah 54:17; Job 5:12; Isaiah 44:25 (NKJV)**.

heavens shall laugh because the Lord shall have them in derision **Psalms 2:4; NKJV.** The Lord will yet fill our mouths with laughter and our lips with singing and shouting. He will cause us to laugh in the face of destruction and famine and we will not be afraid of the beasts of the earth (**Job 8:21; 5:22; NKJV**).

## 6.4 Daniel's Lifestyle of Dedication/Devotion, Diligence and Determination

Daniel was dedicated to God and all through the Book we find how his devotion set him apart. This was prophetic of the early Church and symbolic of what the Church in contemporary times should be. The same dedication and devotion was reflected in the early Church, because even though they had been with the Lord previously during His three years of earthly ministry, the Lord instructed them to wait in Jerusalem until they were endued with power. This separation and dedication is important because without it the early Church couldn't have functioned maximally. The result of obedience, devotion and dedication was the outpour of the Holy Spirit on the Day of Pentecost and subsequently, the Apostles continued in their dedication and devotion to prayer, fasting and breaking of bread from house to house. They also responded promptly by appointing deacons and men of faith, full of the Holy Spirit to serve when discrimination began to creep in between the Grecian/Hellenistic Jews and the Hebraic Jews. This enabled the early church to stay focused, dedicated and devoted to prayer and the word (**Acts 6:1-7; NKJV**).

## 6.4.1 Dedication/Devotion

From the onset, the lifestyle of dedication to God was reflected in Daniel and the three Hebrew children. Therefore, it didn't matter when they found themselves in a foreign land, a solid foundation was already laid and crafted within them. Daniel demonstrated his dedication and devotion to God by deciding not to participate in the eating and drinking that went on in the Babylonian palace.

But Daniel purposed in his heart that he would not defile himself with the portion of the king's delicacies, nor with the wine which he drank; therefore he requested of the chief of the eunuchs that he might not defile himself. (**Daniel 1:8**) (**NKJV**).

## 6.4.1.1 Make your Stance known from the Onset.

Right from the day Daniel and the three Hebrew children were brought to Babylon, we were made to understand that they did not compromise their faith in God. Despite being in a foreign land and supposedly being away from their parents, pastors, family and friends and despite being in a place where they seemingly had no right and could only live at the mercy of the Babylonians, they dedicated themselves to God and made that fact glaringly known to their host - the Babylonians.

Daniel dedicated himself to God and by so doing he distinguished himself from the regular Babylonian youth when he decided that he will not eat of the king's meat or drink his wine. This is a huge challenge in our day where there seems to be no difference between the Church and the world. Compromises and being politically correct seems to be the order of the day. However, like Daniel, when we find ourselves, in a new job, new school, with new business associates, with a new organisation or institution, we need to make our stance clear and known. We need to say who we belong to and what we will do and not do because of our belief. There are so many ways in which we have denied our God. Most times we say we need to be careful, we need to be wise, we need to ensure not to offend ... but the Bible says if we are ashamed to confess the Lord before men, He also will not confess us before the Father. When we make our stance known from the onset it sets us apart from others and God backs us up. We may still get into trouble but in the end God will back us and deliver us like He did for Daniel and the three Hebrew children. Let our dedication and devotion to God be known to all regardless.

## 6.4.1.2 *Do not be Afraid of Trouble.*

The story of Daniel and the three Hebrew children Shedrach, Meshach and Abednego in Babylon is one that many of us can relate to in our day. However, one thing that stands out in their story is not just their devotion but the fact that it appeared almost always that God did not hear or answer their prayer and God did not honour their faith. When King Nebuchadnezzar made the golden image and proclaimed its worship in the whole of Babylon, it was interesting that Shedrach, Meshach and Abednego did not bow to worship the golden image. At this point we expect that God would immediately come down and honour them for their dedication and devotion to Him. However, this was not the case. The report got to the king and he summoned them to ask if it was true that they refused to obey his order. Interestingly again, right before the king, the boys said:

> ..."O Nebuchadnezzar, we have no need to answer you in this matter. [17] If that *is the case,* our God whom we serve is able to deliver us from the burning fiery furnace, and He will deliver *us* from your hand, O king. But if not, let it be known to you, O king, that we do not serve your gods, nor will we worship the gold image which you have set up **(Daniel 3:16-18) (NKJV)**.

Again, at this point we would have expected that God will show up for them, but the king had to order that the fire be heated up seven times more.

> Then Nebuchadnezzar was full of fury, and the expression on his face changed toward Shadrach, Meshach, and Abed-Nego. He spoke and commanded that they heat the furnace seven times more than it was usually heated. [20] And he commanded certain mighty men of valor who *were* in his army to bind Shadrach, Meshach, and Abed-Nego, *and* cast *them* into the burning fiery furnace **(Daniel 3:19-20) (NKJV)**.

I have been in situations where I have had to ask God; where are You? Yet those situations were not as dire as this one faced by the three Hebrew children. Bible records that the men who threw them into the fiery furnace were burnt and yet right in the middle of the fire the fourth man the Lord Jesus Christ appeared with them. This is truly amazing, the amazement is in the when and how God answered, in a most 'terrible' way I must say!

Could it be that right in the very calamitous situations, in the dreadful danger, in the mess and shame you have found yourself God is with you? Like He descended into the fire with the three Hebrew children, I believe strongly that the Lord is indeed with you, otherwise, you wouldn't be reading these lines right now. The mark of God's presence in your life is not only in when things are going well, not only in the promotions in work places, God's presence is also manifested when we are in trouble, terrible enough to destroy us yet we remain standing. Thus, while certain dreadful situations cause the death and destruction of unbelievers because they do not know or have God, our God keeps and preserves us through them all. Joseph was sold, he was in Potiphar's house as a slave and then thrown into prison and yet at every point Bible records that God was with him. The presence of God is not the absence of trouble. Rather the presence of trouble signifies that God is actually with us especially when such trouble was due to our stance for truth and righteousness. We must not fear trouble, we have the Great Deliverer on our side.

## 6.5 Diligence

In addition to being dedicated, Daniel has a lifestyle of diligence. Diligence connotes hard work, having and showing care and conscientiousness in one's work or duties. Someone who is diligent works hard in a careful and thorough way.[45] The writer of Proverbs says a diligent man will always stand before Kings (**Proverbs 22:29; NKJV**). It was diligence that made Daniel to work successfully with four different Kings spanning decades.

---

[45] Definition of Diligent. Available at https://www.collinsdictionary.com/dictionary/english/diligent>

> And I, Daniel, fainted and was sick for days; afterward I arose and went about the king's business. I was astonished by the vision, but no one understood it. **Daniel 8:27**

Despite being in high position, God constantly visited Daniel with revelations and on this particular occasion, Bible records that he was sick for days. Yet he arose and went about the King's business. He didn't excuse himself from work because of being sick. This is a huge challenge to some of us who at the slightest opportunity we excuse ourselves from work and stay at home. However, to be diligent we need to arise like Daniel and be about our duties and daily businesses.

As noted earlier, Daniel served under four (4) different kings in Babylon. In Chapter 6 of the book, **Darius** was the reigning king. From Chapters 1-4 of Daniel, **Nebuchadnezzar** was the king, in Chapter 5, **Belshazzar** Nebuchadnezzar's son was king and in Chapter 10 **Cyrus** was the king. Daniel served under these four different kings and regimes and yet he was not only found to be above board, he was also dedicated to his God, as well as diligent in his duties. Significantly, Daniel was not diligent in church and home and then neglected his work. His diligence was routed in his disciplined lifestyle, which he imbibed from early days.

## 6.6 Determination/Doggedness

Daniel's determination both to pursue excellence in all he did and to pursue after His God was demonstrated throughout the book. In Chapter 1, his determination was demonstrated in his decision not to eat and drink what others were eating and drinking. In Chapter 2, King Nebuchadnezzar had a dream and because nobody could interpret the dream he had ordered the killing of all the magicians and astrologers. However, when Daniel heard, he was determined to find the solution to the problem and determined to save not only his life but the lives of others. When certain decrees have been made and it appears everyone must follow in the direction, do we try to make an exception when we become aware of the laws? Are we determined to find a solution that will save not only our lives but also the lives of others and our children? Daniel refused to be a regular, ordinary person. He was determined to find solutions and by so doing he saved his life and others'.

## 6.7 The Benefits of Daniel's Lifestyle

Certain benefits readily come to mind in the character study of Daniel. Indeed, there is always a reward for diligence, faithfulness and steadfastness. For Daniel, there was **provision** for him. Although Daniel and the other three Hebrew children refused to eat the normal king's delicacy they had supernatural provision that made them to look ten times better than others. Second, Daniel had **prowess.** This is demonstrated all through the book as God granted Daniel an excellent spirit culminating in supernatural abilities, skills, competence, and intelligence that made him to do things which ordinarily he couldn't have done. All through the book, it was recorded that an excellent spirit was upon Daniel. A third benefit was **promotion.** With every temptation that was meant for his downfall and even death, Daniel was not only protected and preserved, he was also promoted again and again.

> Then King Nebuchadnezzar fell on his face, prostrate before Daniel, and commanded that they should present an offering and incense to him. [47] The king answered Daniel, and said, "Truly your God *is* the God of gods, the Lord of kings, and a revealer of secrets, since you could reveal this secret." [48] Then the king **promoted** Daniel and gave him many great gifts; and he made him ruler over the whole province of Babylon, and chief administrator over all the wise *men* of Babylon. [49] Also Daniel petitioned the king, and he set Shadrach, Meshach, and Abed-Nego over the affairs of the province of Babylon; but Daniel *sat* in the gate of the king. (**Daniel 2:46-49**) (**NKJV**).

Also King Darius honoured Daniel and made a national decree for everyone to worship the God of Daniel

> And the king gave the command, and they brought those men who had accused Daniel, and they cast *them* into the

den of lions—them, their children, and their wives; and the lions overpowered them, and broke all their bones in pieces before they ever came to the bottom of the den. (**Daniel 6:25**) (**NKJV**).

Then King Darius wrote:

To all peoples, nations, and languages that dwell in all the earth: Peace be multiplied to you. I make a decree that in every dominion of my kingdom *men must* tremble and fear before the God of Daniel. For He *is* the living God, And steadfast forever; His kingdom *is the one* which shall not be destroyed, And His dominion *shall endure* to the end. [27] He delivers and rescues, And He works signs and wonders In heaven and on earth, Who has delivered Daniel from the power of the lions. [28] So this Daniel prospered in the reign of Darius and in the reign of Cyrus the Persian. (**Daniel 6:24-28**) (**NKJV**).

Finally, Daniel enjoyed ***preservation***, Daniel's life was preserved because he was persistent in his lifestyle of prevailing prayer. Therefore, the lions could not devour or harm him because the Angel of the Lord (**The Lion of the Tribe of Judah Revelation 5:5; NKJV**) appeared and shut their mouths.

## 6.8 Relationship, Revelation, Relevance

Other benefits relate to his sustained ***relationship*** with God which in turn led to ***revelation*** of deep and secret things, culminating in his continued ***relevance*** in Babylon, despite being a foreigner. Daniel was relevant regardless of the changes in the regimes in Babylon. Daniel remained ***relevant*** because he knew his God, no wonder he said they that know their God shall be strong and do exploit (**Daniel 11:32b; NKJV**). The knowing was a result of his ***relationship*** with God despite the ungodly environment he functioned in. This relationship was fuelled and strengthened by his persistent lifestyle of prayer. Therefore, God ***revealed*** deep and secret things to him. Daniel became a solution to the nation of Babylon, not his own country but a country where he would be rightly classified as immigrant.

Likewise, for the Church to remain *relevant*, we must prioritise our relationship with God and get deeper in Him. It is the place of close intimacy and deep relationship that God will begin to reveal to us solutions to the political, economic and social problems in our world. **Deuteronomy 29:29** says that the secret things belong to the Lord our God but the things that are revealed belong to us and our children (NKJV). Therefore, God is committed to revealing things relating to our work places, institutions, governments, schools and situations regarding our cities and nations around the world to us if we maintain intimacy with Him.

## Conclusion

The book of Daniel mirrors the early Church and the Church in contemporary times. Therefore, Daniel being a type of the Church reflects us individually and corporately, because we can readily relate to his context especially with jealousy, hatred and obnoxious laws being promulgated just to 'corner' him; to make him deny his God. Yet he stood strong and overcame because he prioritised and persisted in the place of prayer. Similarly, when as individuals and as a Church we prioritise and are persistent in the place of prayer, we will certainly prevail over the darkness in our schools, institutions, governments, in our cities and in all the nations of the world both in our day and in the next generation. Also, intimate relationship with God will culminate in revelation, which will in turn make the Church to continue to be relevant.

# CHAPTER SEVEN

# The Biblical Fast and Prevailing Prayer

Like prayer, everyone engages in one form of fast or the other. Therefore, we qualify our kind of fast here by using the words 'Biblical Fast'. The biblical fast is the fast that the Lord instructed all who are His followers to embark on. Fasting is mandatory for every child of God because in **Matthew 6:17,** He said '**when** you fast...' (NKJV). The word *when* suggests that fasting is compulsory not optional. The Lord Himself fasted for 40 days and He said to us that certain issues cannot be dealt with by prayers alone except our prayer is accompanied with fasting. When we fast, our spiritual senses are sharper and we become more sensitive and yielded to the Lord. Interestingly, Daniel engaged fast in his prayers as well and in his day, he had engaged in a 21 day fast, and on the 24th day, 3 days after he had concluded his fast, the physical manifestation or answers to his prayers came.

## 7.1 What is the biblical fast?

The biblical fast is abstinence from food and natural pleasures for a spiritual purpose. It is a wilful and personal commitment to renounce the natural in order to invoke the spiritual. Fasting involves the dedication of a certain period of time to devout oneself to spiritual priorities of prayer, intimacy with God by studying and meditating the word. It also involves adjusting our schedules, such as reducing the use of our phones, internet and television, also, reducing our engagements in meetings and on social media platforms to dedicate and consecrate ourselves to God.[46]

From the above definitions, the biblical fast carries dual equally important implications. The first is the physical abstinence from food. This is very important because physical abstinence from food separated Daniel, Shedrach, Meshach and Abednego for excellence and distinction in Babylon. Furthermore, Daniel abstained from food for 21 days and the result was that right from the first day of his fast, God dispatched answers to him. Therefore, we cannot discount the importance of physical abstinence from food. However, in addition to abstinence from food, we also need to abstain from the internet, cell phones and television. Abstaining from food only without a corresponding abstinence from social media, the internet and phones defeats the purpose of the biblical fast. Sometimes abstinence from television, social media and phones is referred to as 'soul fast'.

The second limb of the biblical fast is the spiritual aspect, which entails spending time with the Lord in prayer and studying the word. This is what completes the biblical fast and makes it different from every other kind of fast. The reason we deny ourselves of food and other pleasures that satisfy our body and soul is because we desire to get closer to God, so as to build our spirit man – the inward man. Therefore, without a vital prayer time and vibrant fellowship with the word, the biblical fast is incomplete.

## 7.2 Types and Lengths of Fast

The biblical fast can be categorised broadly into three. The normal, partial and absolute fast. The normal fast is when we skip some meals and fluid for the day. For example, when we do not take our breakfast but we take lunch and dinner or we skip both breakfast and lunch and take only dinner, this can constitute the normal fast. I encourage people, especially children to start with this kind of fast because we need to understand our bodies and be real with ourselves when we fast. Fasting is not a competition. Engaging in normal fast, can help us to be more focused with prayer and studying the

---

[46] Myles Munroe, 'How to Pray and Fast Effectively' Available at https://www.youtube.com/watch?v=l3kKSsUwUOI>

word and thereby achieve more intimacy with God while we fast. Therefore, instead of taking your regular breakfast at 7.00am or 8.00am, you could decide to stay till 12 noon and gradually build up to 3.00pm or 6.00pm. The main focus is to spend the time in fellowshipping with the Lord in prayer, worship, studying and meditating His word.

The partial fast is when we decide to abstain from certain food. This is the kind of fast that Daniel engaged in alone and also when he together with Shedrach, Meschach and Abednego refused to eat the king's delicacies but requested for vegetables only. This is because, they did eat, but their meal was not the regular meal that other youths or other people ate at that time. The partial fast honours God, especially as we devote the time to Him. In response to their partial fast God caused Daniel and his friends to be more refreshed, robust, stronger and ten times better than those who ate the regular king's meal. **(Daniel 1:1-20; NKJV).** This kind of fast is recommended for those who for one reason or the other cannot abstain from food completely.

The absolute fast is when we abstain from food, water, sex (for married folks),[47] social media and everything else for a period of time in order to spend time with God in prayer and studying of His word. Significantly some people engaged in this kind of fast in scriptures. For example, Moses, Elijah and the Lord Jesus Christ, fasted 40 days and 40 nights without food and water.

Admittedly, these categorisation is not clearly stated in scriptures but I think if there are other kinds of fast, they may be subsumed under any of these three broad categories. Some people have discounted the partial fast as not amounting to biblical fast because it does not reveal a complete abstinence from food. However, I think it is a biblical fast because fast is not just the abstinence from food but the prayer, communion and intimacy with God during the time that matters. Also, the biblical fast can be engaged in individually or corporately.

---

[47] Paula White, 'The Power of Fasting' https://www.youtube.com/watch?v=QJWCOG-Zb9g&t=855s>

## 7.2.1 Individual Fast

Daniel's fast was an individual/personal one. In **Daniel 9:1-2 NKJV,** Bible records that Daniel found where it was recorded that the years of Israel's captivity in Babylon was 70 years (**Jeremiah 29:10; NKJV**) and since this time was almost approaching he began to fast so they can be delivered from the captivity. This is very important because as we study scriptures, we will be provoked to fast as we find where it is expressly written that we are not meant to be in certain situations for so long or we are not meant to be in them at all. However, without finding where it is written, ignorance will keep us wallowing in situations we shouldn't have any business with, because we've already been delivered from them. Therefore, what prompted Daniel's fast was knowledge and that knowledge came because he searched and found where it was written. Have we searched to find where it is written? Concerning every situation we are faced with, there is need to search the scriptures and ask the Holy Spirit to know the mind of God in relation to it. Prevailing prayers must be informed and prompted by a deep and accurate knowledge of the word and mind of God on the particular issue.

## 7.2.2 Corporate Fast

Also, there is the corporate fast. In **2 Chronicles 20:3 NKJV,** King Jehoshaphat proclaimed a fast, in **Joel 2:12 NKJV,** Joel proclaimed a fast that included everyone with no exception, also in **Jonah,** the entire City of Nineveh embarked on a corporate fast. There are more instances but these are a few examples of the corporate fast that we will be referring to in the discussion below.

## 7.2.3 Length of Fast: How Long should we Fast for?

Sometimes a few questions may be asked as to what is the most appropriate length of fast? The length or duration of fast varies. However, in Scriptures, Moses, Elijah and our Lord Jesus Christ fasted at different times for 40 days. Scripturally, this is the longest period of fast. However, people and congregations do engage in longer fast. While this is not bad, the danger is that more often than not, a few people get weary, while others do not engage in the spiritual aspect after a while, thereby making the fast to become only the physical abstinence from food. It is important to note that abstinence from food is only the first half of the biblical fast, the second limb, which is equally and even more important is the spiritual that entails our intimacy with God. It must also be mentioned that while the 40 day fast engaged in by Moses, Elijah and the Lord Jesus Christ at different times were absolute fasts, some of our fasts even though longer sometimes, are not absolute but partial or normal.

While Daniel engaged in a 21 day personal fast, the people of Nineveh embarked on a day or three day fast. Everyone including their king, the highly elitist members of society to the lowest and mundane, even including the cattle and animals in Nineveh were involved in the nation-wide fast (**Jonah 3:5-10; NKJV**). The result was that God changed His mind regarding the destruction of the great City He already asked Jonah to announce. The exact length of this fast was not recorded, although it might have been a 3 day fast because of the reference to Nineveh being a 3-day journey.

> So Jonah arose and went to Nineveh, according to the word of the LORD. Now Nineveh was an exceedingly great city, a three-day journey *in extent.* ⁴ And Jonah began to enter the city on the first day's walk. Then he cried out and said, "Yet forty days, and Nineveh shall be overthrown!" (**Jonah 3:3-4) (NKJV).**

Regardless of the length, it was so effective that God changed His mind. We know God as ageless, changeless or unhanging, but here is an instance amongst others where He changed His mind. Therefore, what is most important is not the length of fast but the effectiveness that matters. What makes for an effective fast?

## 7.3 What is the requirement of an Effective fast?

Fasting is not just missing a meal or mere abstinence from food. Fasting is not dieting. For married couple, fasting is not staying away from sex. However, as admonished by Apostle Paul in his letter to the Church in

Corinth, based on mutual agreement, it is good for couples to stay away from sex while they engage in a fast, but for lengthy fast of 21 days or 40 days or more, it is wise not to stay away from sex for too long because not every married person can handle such long abstinence from sex. Nevertheless, married couples can always depend on God's sustaining grace on occasions where long abstinence from sex is required whether for fasting, health or other purposes. The bottom line is that there must be mutual agreement between the couple regarding abstinence from sex during the period of fast.

## 7.3.1 An Effective Fast must be prompted by the Word

From the story of Nineveh, the fast was prompted by a message. There was a divine instruction to the people through Jonah informing them of the impending danger and destruction of the City. This message provoked remorse and repentance and the people proclaimed a fast. It is interesting that even before the King got the information and proclaimed the nation-wide fast, the people already started fasting, they didn't wait for the King. It was while they already started fasting that the King made the proclamation:

> Let neither man nor beast, herd nor flock, taste anything; do not let them eat, or drink water. [8] But let man and beast be covered with sackcloth, and cry mightily to God; yes, let every one turn from his evil way and from the violence that is in his hands. [9] Who can tell *if* God will turn and relent, and turn away from His fierce anger, so that we may not perish? (**Jonah 3:7-9**) (**NKJV**).

Also, Daniel's fast was prompted by the word. Bible records that Daniel understood by the books. The 'books' here refers to the **Torah,** the **Prophets** and maybe the **Psalms**, because in those days the Bible hadn't been written in a well organised referenced compendium like we have it today. Therefore, I believe Daniel must have done some research and study before he found where a specific prophecy and promise concerning his situation and that of the nation of Israel was recorded.

> ...In the first year of his reign I, Daniel, understood by
> the books the number of the years *specified* by the word of
> the LORD through Jeremiah the prophet, that He would
> accomplish seventy years in the desolations of Jerusalem
> (**Daniel 9:2**) (**NKJV**).

These two instances of personal and corporate fast demonstrate that
effective biblical fast should be prompted by the word of God. The word
could either be the *logos* (the written word i.e. scriptures) or the *rhema* (the
revealed or spoken word).

## 7.3.2 An Effective biblical Fast must be accompanied by True Repentance

The people of Nineveh did not just engage in a fast by merely abstaining
from food to fulfil all righteousness. Rather they did it genuinely confessing
their wrongs publicly. Therefore, what God saw was the true remorse,
repentance and change of heart. God saw that they turned from their evil
ways. Similarly, although Daniel did not physically participate in the sin of
the people, he did not only repent on behalf of the people, he *identified with*
their sin and prayed as though he sinned.

> We have sinned and committed iniquity, we have done
> wickedly and rebelled, even by departing from Your
> precepts and Your judgments. [6] Neither have we heeded
> Your servants the prophets, who spoke in Your name to our
> kings and our princes, to our fathers and all the people of
> the land. [7] O Lord, righteousness *belongs* to You, but to us
> shame of face, as *it is* this day—to the men of Judah, to the
> inhabitants of Jerusalem and all Israel, those near and those
> far off in all the countries to which You have driven them,
> because of the unfaithfulness which they have committed
> against You. (**Daniel 9:5-7**) (**NKJV**).

Identifying with the sin and situation of the people is a very critical and
distinguishing feature of the prayer of intercession, as we discussed in

Chapter 3. Nehemiah did the same, and in the case of Moses, he went as far as asking to take the place of the Israelites and go to hell just so that God could change His mind and forgive them, which was prophetically symbolic of the substitutionary and redemptive work that the Lord Jesus Christ did for us all. Therefore, true remorse and repentance are crucial to effective biblical fast.

### 7.3.3 Do we have to put on Sack clothes for our fast to be effective?

The hallmark of both Daniel and Nineveh's fasts and indeed fasting as recorded in the Old Testament was that they wore sack clothes and put on ashes. In Jonah, the people of Nineveh believed the message and proclaimed a fast and put on sack clothes

> So the people of Nineveh believed God, proclaimed a fast, and **put on sackcloth**, from the greatest to the least of them (**Jonah 3:5**) (**NKJV**).

Also Daniel said:

> Then I set my face toward the Lord God to make request by prayer and supplications, with fasting, **sackcloth, and ashes** (**Daniel 9:3**) (**NKJV**).

These instances demonstrate that in ancient times, there were certain physical ways to show remorse and repentance, which was acceptable to God because with the people of Nineveh, Bible records that God saw their works and that they have repented and turned from their evil ways (**Jonah 3:10; NKJV**).

This practice became a dominant custom with the people so much so that God had to speak to them through Prophet Isaiah in **Isaiah 58**. It will be good to have a read of the entire chapter because the people began to pride in the custom and ceremony of putting on sack clothes and ashes while they fasted and neglected the most important things of the heart, such as forgiving one another, doing good, being fair and enthroning justice. Essentially, **Isaiah 58** reeled out why their fast could not be seen by God and detailed certain requirements of how a true biblical fast should be done.

Consequently, in the New Testament, the Lord Jesus Christ commands that during the fast we must look good (**Matthew 6:16; NKJV**). Thus, in our dispensation physical look does not determine an effective fast and we do not have to wear sack clothes or put on ashes for our fast to be effective.

## 7.4 The Effects or Impact of a True Biblical Fast

### 7.4.1 Realisation, Remorse and Repentance

The first impact of a true fast occurs in us not with God. With the examples of Daniel and the people of Nineveh, we could see that there was first a realisation when the revelation came to them. Therefore, the fast should bring a **realisation** in us and that **realisation should provoke remorse and repentance,** a change of heart, a turning away from what was wrong to what is right and what is required of us.

### 7.4.2 Humility

Second, there must be **total humility**. In both instances, both the King of Nineveh and the entire population from the highest to the lowest humbled themselves before God. Similarly, although Daniel was second in command to King Darius in Babylon at the time, his high position did not prevent him from humbling himself to fast. Daniel's personal fast is important because he didn't have anyone come to preach or declare the word to him, he didn't wait for anyone to proclaim a fast for him to participate in. He read the Book, he saw where it was documented and despite his high position, his busy schedule and despite being in a foreign land, he declared a personal fast to seek God's face. Much as corporate fast is good, Daniel's example should challenge us to humble ourselves to engage in individual/personal fast.

### 7.4.3 Refining and Purifying

A third impact of a true fast is that **it purifies us**. When we engage in the biblical fast, we are refined and purified, we become holy and acceptable vessels and once that happens we become separated for God's use. A good example that comes to mind is Queen Esther's fast. Presumably, Esther was already prepared and groomed for the palace by her Uncle; Mordecai. However, despite being the Queen, by a decree (obnoxious law) devised by Haman and signed by the King, Esther's life and the lives of the entire Jews were marked for destruction. Beauty and position could not exempt her. Therefore, she proclaimed a 3 day fast after which she was sanctified for God's use to save the entire nation. She was not only refined, purified and prepared to change the course of the whole Jewish people by averting their total annihilation, but she also made decrees that superseded those of the ruling king.

### 7.4.4 Greater Sensitivity

The voice of God becomes clearer when we engage in the biblical fast. God speaks all the time but because of the cares, challenges and troubles of life, we don't hear Him clearly sometimes. However, when we engage in the fast, the voice of the Holy Spirit becomes clearer and the prophetic becomes more visible. Indeed, fasting increases our spiritual capacity, it helps our spiritual senses to be more alert and we become more discerning and sensitive to the leading of the Holy Spirit. This is a necessary consequence of fellowship and intimacy, as the fast brings us closer to God in prayer and study of His word. Therefore, we must hook up to God through praying, studying and meditating the word during the biblical fast and since He speaks back to us in prayer, His voice becomes clearer and distinct, helping us with accuracy and precision both in hearing and in promptly obeying Him. In **Acts 13:1-2 NKJV**, some prophets and teachers in the Church at Antioch gathered together to pray and fast. The result was that they heard the Holy Spirit speak clearly to them regarding the next phase of ministry that Paul and Barnabas were to come into.

## 7.4.5 Divine Favour and Reversal

The biblical fast attracts the favour of God. For the people of Nineveh, God's wrath was appeased by their genuine remorse and repentance and they attracted God's mercy and favour. Instead of destruction, God showed them favour, reversed death and they lived. Also Esther found favour before the king after she engaged in the 3 day fast. Therefore, what ordinarily would have resulted in her death, God reversed (**Esther 4:11-15; 5:1-7; NKJV**). Fasting attracts God's favour in our lives and helps us to become bold and untouchable.

## 7.4.6 Inevitable Change

In conclusion, we know God as unchanging, but from what we have seen in scriptures, especially with the people of Nineveh, the biblical fast can make God change His mind and if God can change, what or who else cannot change. In the Book of Joel, the biblical fast was marked with a total change from poverty to prosperity and restoration. When the biblical fast is accompanied with prevailing prayers, change is inevitable. Indeed, we should expect tremendous positive changes in our lives, in our cities and indeed in all the nations of the world.

## 7.5 Spiritual Benefits of the Biblical Fast

There are overlaps in some benefits and the impact of the fast that we discussed above. Therefore, this may seem repetitive. However, like Apostle Paul said, repetition does not harm.[48] Some benefits of the biblical fast are outlined in **Isaiah 58.**

> Then your light shall dawn in the darkness, And your darkness shall *be* as the noonday. [11] The LORD will guide you continually, And satisfy your soul in drought, And strengthen your bones; You shall be like a watered garden,

---

[48] '...To write the same things to you, to me indeed is not tedious, but for you it is safe' (**Philippians 3:1; NKJV**)

And like a spring of water, whose waters do not fail. [12] Those from among you Shall build the old waste places; You shall raise up the foundations of many generations; And you shall be called the Repairer of the Breach, The Restorer of Streets to Dwell In (**Isaiah 58:10-12**) (**NKJV**).

## 7.5.1 Intimacy with God

In addition to the benefits outlined in **Isaiah 58,** the first spiritual benefit of the fast that comes to mind is intimacy with God. Fasting brings us closer to God, as it increases our hunger for God and helps us to hear God more clearly and accurately. This is the same as the impact of greater spiritual sensitivity discussed above. The biblical fast helps our spirit to gain ascendency over our flesh and helps us to put our bodies under. The fast also helps us to see things in the right perspective.

## 7.5.2 Breaks ungodly habits

The fast brings true freedom and helps to break ungodly habits and every appetite for fleshly desires. I believe this must have happened to Daniel and the three Hebrew youths when they decided they would not participate in the eating and drinking in the King's palace in Babylon.

## 7.5.3 Right Positioning for Speedy Manifestations of our Prayers

Fasting makes us to be rightly positioned for God's favour and protection. Fasting makes the answer to our prayers to manifest more speedily. Examples are Daniel, Esther and Nineveh fasts.

## 7.5.4 Sensitivity to the Needs of People Around us

The biblical fast makes our light to shine and helps us to develop the fruit of the spirit. It also helps us to be more sensitive to the needs of people and to find ways to support them. This was a conversation I had some years ago. 'Hi Sist Ovo, I will be helping you with school run this period; I will be taking Ono to school and back' said our youth pastor; Kehinde Odude (Kay). I was shocked because, we, my children and I, had just concluded a discussion on how we need some support with the school run especially because it was winter and my Ono gets really tired walking to school and back. 'Really? What about work, are you off work or on holidays?' was my question to Kay! 'Yes really, no am not off work and not on holidays, but the Lord laid it in my heart and I felt I might do it as part of my good works during this period of fasting' replied Kay. I was overjoyed and called my children to announce the news of how awesome our God is. This has been a regular occurrence with us, and my children can testify to it that when we discuss anything and it is a need, almost immediately somebody brings the answer or supplies the need even when we haven't prayed or asked anyone about it. It is almost as if the people were privy to our discussions and my thoughts. This particular instance stood out to me because combined with family and church programmes, Kay is usually very busy at work and for him to undertake to help with school run despite his busy schedule at the time was just amazing to me. But his response was even more phenomenal '...*the Lord laid it in my heart and I felt I might do it as part of my good works during this period of fasting'*. This is a classic example of how the biblical fast helps us to develop the fruit of the spirit and helps us to be more sensitive to the needs of people.

## 7.6 Physical or Natural benefits of the Fast

Paul writing to Timothy in **1 Timothy 4:8** said that '**bodily exercise profits a little...**'(**NKJV**). Although used in a different context, I believe the reverse is also true that spiritual exercise can profit much more. I believe that the biblical fast is a spiritual exercise that can result in both spiritual and physical gains.

## 7.6.1 Health and Longevity

**Isaiah 58:8** talks about our health springing forth speedily. Indeed this is both a spiritual and physical benefit. The biblical fast ensures physical wellness to our bodies, which can lead to long life.

119

Then your light shall break forth like the morning, Your healing shall spring forth speedily, And your righteousness shall go before you; The glory of the LORD shall be your rear guard (**Isaiah 58:8**) (**NKJV**).

## 7.6.2 Detoxification of the body

Other physical benefits include, cleansing and purifying of the body by detoxifying i.e. getting rid of toxic that are not good for the body. This overlaps with refining and purifying effects discussed above. However, while refining and purifying are internal positive impacts leading to sanctification and separation for the Master's use, detoxification has results or outcomes that reflect both internally and externally.

## 7.6.3 Loss of unnecessary Weight and fats

Fasting could lead to loss of weight, can prevent obesity and can prevent the possibility of developing terminal diseases. The biblical fast can make us feel lighter and less irritable, we become more patient and tolerant when we fast.

## 7.6.4 Mental Alertness

Fasting also has mental benefits, it brings mental alertness and clarity as it increases our retention capacity. We are able to retain mentally because there is less distraction when we fast.

## Conclusion

There is no way we can engage in prevailing prayers without engaging in the biblical fast. In fact, the Lord commanded and expects us to fast. In **Matthew 17:21**, when the Lord had just alighted from the mount of Transfiguration, He met his disciples with the man who brought his son for healing but the disciples could not heal the son. After Jesus healed the son, He told the disciples the secret that '*...this kind does not go out expect by prayer and fasting*' (**NKJV**). Interestingly, on this occasion, the Lord Jesus Christ did not tell the man to take his son away and bring him back after He (Jesus) would have fasted so He could heal the boy. Rather, He rebuked the demon spirit immediately and the boy was healed instantly. Jesus' explanation that this kind of situation cannot be dealt with except with fasting and prayers implies that we need to cultivate and live a fasted life. We shouldn't engage the biblical fast only when we are in trouble or when we are faced with situations that we need solutions or directions on how to deal, but we should cultivate fasting as a lifestyle maybe weekly or even daily.

More often, our fast is reactionary, driven by desperation or prompted only on the announcement of a corporate fast. However, I encourage everyone to engage in prayer and fasting both individually and corporately, let us develop and build our spiritual capacity by engaging in personal biblical fast. Daniel's fast was personal while the fast in Nineveh was corporate involving a whole nation and both were effective because God averted looming disasters. God will do the same for us to save our lives, the lives of our loved ones and indeed, a whole nation, when we pray and fast. More importantly, like Anna, we can also worship God with the biblical fast. As we noted earlier in Chapter three, Anna engaged the biblical fast as a form of worship to God continuously until the Lord Jesus Christ was brought to the temple (**Luke 2:37; NKJV**). In other words, we should learn to **wait on God for God,** not necessarily because we want something from Him.

# CHAPTER EIGHT

# Does God hear and answer Prayers?

The answer to the question whether God answers prayers is a resounding 'YES'. God does hear and answers our prayers. The guarantee to answered prayers are encapsulated in these few verses:

> So I say to you, ask, and it will be given to you; seek, and you will find; knock, and it will be opened to you. [10] For everyone who asks receives, and he who seeks finds, and to him who knocks it will be opened. [11] If a son asks for bread from any father among you, will he give him a stone? Or if *he asks* for a fish, will he give him a serpent instead of a fish? [12] Or if he asks for an egg, will he offer him a scorpion? [13] If you then, being evil, know how to give good gifts to your children, how much more will *your* heavenly Father give the Holy Spirit to those who ask Him!" (**Luke 11:9-13**) (**NKJV**).

This scripture relates specifically to the guarantee of the release of the Holy Spirit upon us when we ask, it could also relate to other things, but there are instances where the physical manifestations of our requests/prayers take longer than we expect. There are few reasons why this is the case. Before we discuss the circumstances where there are seeming delays in answers to our prayers, let us discuss the prayer that God hears and answers.

## 8.1 What are the conditions for answers to our prayers?

God has already guaranteed in His word that His ears are inclined unto our prayers. He said before we call He will answer and while we yet speak He will hear (**Isaiah 65:24; NKJV**)). He said when we pray according to His will He will hear us and grant the petitions of our hearts. He also said that if His people which are called by His name will humble themselves, pray, seek His face and turn from our wicked ways, He will hear from heaven, forgive us and heal our land. There are several other scriptures that guarantees answers to our prayers and we can all testify that God does hear and answers prayers. Below are some things to remind us of the prerequisites to guaranteed answers to our prayers.

## 8.1.1 When we pray in the Name of Jesus

We established in the first part of this book that prayer is access to God our heavenly Father and what gives us legal access to God is the name and the blood of our Lord Jesus Christ. This is the very foundation of the Christian faith and it requires unpacking for complete understanding. The access we have to God is only through the finished redemptive work of our Lord Jesus Christ on Mount Calvary over two thousand years ago. Therefore during His earthly ministry, the Lord said in response to Thomas' question of how they could know the way that: **'I am the way the truth and the life no man cometh to the Father except through me'** (**John 14:6; NKJV**).

The point of emphasis in this scripture is the definite article **'the'**. Therefore, there were in ancient times and even in our day different ways that people have devised to know God and to reach Him, but they are all illegal, illegitimate, null and void. The only authentic way is through the Lord Jesus Christ; the express image of the invisible God, the one in whom all things consist and the one in whom all the God-Head dwelt bodily... (**Hebrews1:3, Colossians 1:15-18, 19; 2:9; NKJV**).

The Lord also said in the teachings leading to the end of his ministry that hitherto we have asked nothing, but now, He said we should ask and receive so that our joy can be full.

Until now you have asked nothing in My name. Ask, and you will receive, that your joy may be full. [25] "These things I have spoken to you in figurative language; but the time is coming when I will no longer speak to you in figurative language, but I will tell you plainly about the Father. [26] In that day you will ask in My name, and I do not say to you that I shall pray the Father for you (**John 16:24-26**) (**NKJV**).

When we pray in the name of the Lord Jesus Christ we are guaranteed answers to our prayers. This is a fundamental prerequisite to prayer. Nevertheless, it appears some people have made a cliché out of it. Yes indeed, the scripture says anything we ask in His name will be given to us (**John 14:13-14; John 15:7; Matthew 18:19-20; Matthew 21:22; Mark 11:24; NKJV**). However, what does this mean? Does it mean the literal name Jesus? This cannot be, because there were several other people who answer or bear the name 'Jesus' in ancient times and even in contemporary times. Therefore, the reference and instruction to pray in the name of Jesus carries a deeper spiritual connotation, power and authority than its literal meaning or just making a cliché out of it.

## 8.1.1.1 What does the name of our Lord Jesus Christ mean?

Every name carries with it a meaning and sometimes names reflect the settings, cultures and certain events in our lives. Likewise, the name **Jesus** means **our salvation** and **Christ** means **the messiah or the anointed one**, and it carries the mandate and culture of heaven. Thus, the name reflects the authority, character, sovereignty and power of God as revealed and given to save humanity. When we have this understanding, calling the name and praying in the name of Jesus can make tremendous miracle working power available to us.

In line with this understanding of the potency in the name of Jesus, some years ago at a Music/Worship Conference, one of my Pastors and mentors Rev Chuks Okonyia of blessed memory gave an exposition of the Name of Jesus and he said the Name of Jesus carries with it God's Sovereignty, His Character, His Rank, His Authority and His Majesty and he gave us the acronym SCRAM so we don't forget it. In other words, according to Rev Chuks, when we invoke the Name in prayer or worship we should have these attributes in mind and not engage in a religious calling of 'in the name of Jesus'. He also said that in relation to prayers, just like the word SCRAM means to vamoose, to bolt, to flee, to get out, that is the exact same way we should expect and see all unpleasant situation 'SCRAM' from our lives when we pray in the name. Therefore, SCRAM has a dual meaning (double-edged sword), first it is an acronym for God's sovereignty, character, rank, authority and majesty and second it is the weapon we release against every onslaught of the enemy in spiritual warfare.

What is more, certain scriptures come to mind regarding the power in the Name. The Lord Jesus said *'If you ask anything in My name I will do it'* (**John 14:14; NKJV**). Also, the Name of Jesus has been highly exalted above all other names... (**Philippians 2:9; NKJV**). Indeed, there is *dunamis* - dynamic, potent and miracle working power in the Name of our Lord Jesus Christ. Desiring progressive revelation means that we should continue to press for deeper revelation of the Name of the Lord Jesus Christ so we can constantly pray in the Name with deeper revelation and understanding rather than use it as a cliché.

## 8.1.1.2 Do we have to use the phrase 'In the Name of Jesus' or 'In Jesus' Name' to start and end all Prayers?

Notwithstanding the above discussion, when the Lord gave the command to pray in His name, I do not think He meant it literally. I do not think that every prayer must start and end with the use of the phrases *'in the name of Jesus' or 'in Jesus' name'*. It is not wrong to use the phrase, but we should guard against a religious practice of routine recitations and repetitions in prayers. Rather, we should get into greater understanding of what we say and why we use certain words and phrases when we pray. We do get answers when we pray using the phrases. However, there are times we just speak the word or even say some words to the Lord without necessary using the phrases or even thinking that we are praying in that serious sense and yet those appear to be the most powerful prayers that we have ever uttered.

In fact, there were some instances in scriptures where people prayed without adding the phrase; 'In the Name of Jesus' and yet their prayers were answered. Perhaps, this was why the Lord said hitherto you have not asked anything 'in My Name', because He had not yet died and resurrected, he had not paid the price that gave the name the potency and power. This is why predominantly, in the OT, because the Lord Jesus Christ had not come in flesh, and because the name hadn't been given, they couldn't pray in the name of Jesus. Therefore, for example, Elijah stopped rain for three and half years by his (Elijah's) word (**1 Kings 17:1; NKJV**), Daniel prayed as his custom was and his prayers invoked the power of God to shut the mouths of lions (**Daniel 6**), Joshua spoke to the sun and the moon to stand still in the battle at Gibeon against the five kings of the Amorites (**Joshua 10:12-14; NKJV**). Interestingly, there were no references to the Name of Jesus in these prayers. Conversely, in the NT, Bible records concerning the seven sons of Sceva who went casting out demons in the name of Jesus that Paul preached and we know the rest of the story (**Acts 19:11-17; NKJV**). Therefore, now that we have the Name of Jesus, which connotes authority and power, it is vital for us to get more intimate in our relationship with the Lord Jesus Christ so that we can have better understanding and deeper revelation of the sovereignty, character, rank, authority, majesty and the miracle working power and potency in the Name, rather than engage in religious rhetoric, repetition and recitations.

## 8.1.2 When we Pray the Word

God is bound by His word and the only thing that provokes His hand is His word. The Psalmist says God has magnified his word above all His name (**Psalms 138:2; NKJV**). Therefore, we must refrain from praying our problems. One thing that can give us the assurances of God hearing and answering us, is when we pray His word. He said 'put me in remembrance' of my word (**Isaiah 43:26; NKJV**). In **Isaiah 55:11 NKJV**, God said His word will not return to Him void but must accomplish the purpose for which it has been sent. Therefore, praying God's word is a sure guarantee to answers to our prayers.

An exception to this could be Hannah whom Bible records poured out her heart to God. Admittedly, there are times in which we pour out our hearts to God like Hannah did because at such times we cannot put words to our prayers. There have been different expositions on the story of Hannah and how she was in bitterness of soul because she was barren and added to that was the constant provocation by Peninnah. However, instead of being provoked to malice, bitterness and anger, she was propelled to pour out her heart to God. Indeed, some prayers may lack words, I am sure we can all relate to Hannah's situation because I have been in situations where I didn't have the words to say to the Lord in prayer other than my tears. God did come through for me because even in my tears I spoke His word to Him. Therefore, we cannot discount the fact that sometimes the most powerful prayers are the ones we couldn't and can't verbalise in words. Nevertheless, when we pray using the word of God, we are assured of answers to our prayers.

The emphasis here is for us to understand that the integrity of God is in His word. He said He is not a man to lie neither the son of man to repent or change His mind. This relates to God's blessing for us because concerning the Israelites, Balaam although hired by Barak to curse, couldn't release a curse because God already blessed them. God's word of blessing, peace, protection, preservation, prosperity and our total well-being is His covenant to us that cannot be revoked. He said, the words that goes from His mouth is like the rain and snow that comes down to water the earth, it will not return to Him void but it will accomplish all that it was set out to accomplish. He said heaven and earth will pass away but not an iota of His word will go unfulfilled. Forever oh Lord your word is settled in heaven. This is the assurance and confidence we have in Him that when we pray according to His will, not according to the intensity of our problems and desperation, but according to His will, He will hear us and grant the petitions that we desire of Him.[49] Well, the intensity, frustration and desperation of our situations should propel us to pray or pour out our hearts to God like Hannah did, but our prayer has to be in harmony with His will/word.

In addition, Apostle Paul admonished in his epistle to the Church at Ephesus to put on the whole armour of God and interestingly the last pieces of the

---

[49] See Numbers 23:19; Isaiah 55:10-11; Matthew 5:18, 24:35; Luke 21:33; Psalms 119:89; 1 John 5:14-15

armours he mentioned was the word of God which is the sword of the spirit. In other words, no matter how prepared a soldier is for battle, without the sword- the word- such a soldier is meat for the enemy.

## 8.1.3 When we stay Connected to the Word/Source

To enjoy the guarantee of answers to our prayers when we engage in prevailing prayer, we must stay connected to our source, which is the word. **John 15:7** says *if you abide in me and my word abide in you, then you will ask what you will and it will be given to you* (**NKJV**). Therefore, in addition to praying the word, we must remain in the word. This is important because to prevail in prayer includes constantly maintaining the atmosphere of the word of God. The life and sustenance we have flows directly from the tree - the vine - and hence as branches we cannot afford to be disconnected at any point. It may be difficult sometimes because we may be overwhelmed by our situations and the negative things happening around but we need to stay connected and focused on the word.

## 8.1.4 When we have Faith in God

Faith runs through our walk with God and it is the currency of the Kingdom of Heaven. Without faith it is impossible to approach an unseen God and to believe that He will be and do what He has promised in His word. Therefore, faith is the bedrock on which our relationship with God stands. Also, in relation to prayer, **Mark 11:24** says when we pray we should believe we have what we ask and we shall have them

> Therefore I say to you, whatever things you ask when you pray, believe that you receive *them,* and you will have *them* (**Mark 11:24**) (**NKJV**).

Faith gives us confidence in approaching God in prayer as well as helps us to receive and to continue in thanksgiving until we see the physical manifestation of what we asked for or prayed about. Some things might take long to manifest, but faith is required while we're waiting, patience is also required and we must not cast away our confidence which has great reward.

## 8.1.5 When our words (sayings) align with our Prayers

Faith is connected with what we say. Indeed, our faith is called 'profession', our declaration and our sayings. We believe and therefore we speak **2 Corinthians 4:13; (NKJV)**. The background to the requirement of faith and belief mentioned in **Mark 11**, the Lord had cursed the fig tree that didn't bear fruit and in response to the question by His disciples of how the tree had dried up, the Lord said have faith in God:

> So Jesus answered and said to them, "Have faith in God.
> [23] For assuredly, I say to you, whoever says to this mountain,
> 'Be removed and be cast into the sea,' and does not doubt in
> his heart, but believes that those things he says will be done,
> he will have whatever he says **(Mark 11:22-23) (NKJV)**.

The phrase 'have faith in God' in **Mark 11:22** in its original meaning is translated 'have the God kind of faith' and the God kind of faith can be found in the beginning. When God came on the scene and saw that the earth He created had become void, shapeless and formless, He didn't start grumbling, complaining and saying oh what happened, the earth is void, the beautiful earth we created has become void and without form, what shall we do now? Rather, Bible said and God said 'let there be light…' **(Genesis 1:3; NKJV)**. Therefore, the God kind of faith is declaring those things which be not as though they were **(Romans 4:17; KJV)**. We must learn to declare what we want not the unpleasant situations and negativities that we see.

Interestingly, **Mark 11:23** uses the word 'says' three times shortly after the Lord said 'have faith in God'. In other words, one way to demonstrate our faith in God or the God kind of faith is by what we say. This means that beyond what we say in the place of prayer, we must continue to maintain and affirm the same things we prayed as we carry on with our regular, daily lives. Whatever we say outside of the 'prayer time' must align with our prayers otherwise, we may negate the prayers and it is what we say that we will have not what we prayed. In **Numbers 14:28**, God said concerning the Israelites that whatever they have said to His hearing is what He will do to them (NKJV). We have what we say, we are ensnared by the words of our mouth, and life and death are in the power of the tongue... When what we say aligns with God's word and our prayers, we are sure to receive answers to our prayers.

## 8.1.6 When we Live Holy Lives

Our prayers are heard and answered by God when we are holy. God says to us; be ye holy just as I am holy (**1 Peter 1:15-16; NKJV**). We may occasionally fall into sin but we need to deal with sin whenever it occurs, we must not hide sin. The Psalmist says if I regard iniquity in my heart God will not hear me (**Psalms 66:18; NKJV**). Who shall ascend unto the hill of the Lord, who shall stand in his holy place? He that has clean hands and pure heart... (**Psalms 24:3-4; NKJV**).

As discussed in the first part of this book, the only prayer of a sinner (a person that has not received the Lord Jesus Christ into their heart and has no relationship with God) that God hears is the prayer of salvation. However, God is merciful and sovereign so He does show abundant mercy to everyone. For example, Cornelius was not saved yet his prayers, arms and good deeds were not only received but they were a memorial to God and this brought him the gift of salvation. Therefore, there are exceptions to what we know. However, as we discussed earlier, prayer is relationship, prayer is access to God and God is Holy therefore we must be holy in order for God to hear and answer our prayers. Being holy means living a life that is free of sin, a life that is patterned after Christ, a life that exudes the essence of scriptures.

## 8.1.7 When we are Conscious of our Righteous nature

Righteousness is the nature of God. Bible talks about the sceptre of God's kingdom being the sceptre of righteousness (**Psalms 45:6; Hebrews1:8; NKJV**). This is all that makes God right, just and fair in His judgement. Indeed, He is the God of faithfulness, without injustice, true, righteous and upright is He (**Deuteronomy 32:4; NKJV**)). God's righteous nature was given to us in Christ because He who knew no sin was made sin for us so that we might become the righteousness of God in Christ Jesus (**2 Corinthians 5:21; NKJV**).

Therefore, righteousness was imputed to us when we received the Lord Jesus Christ into our hearts. This is very important because although certain habits disappear by reason of the new birth, as new ones are formed by reason of our regular fellowship with the Lord, studying and meditating on the word, the new birth is nothing to do with the physical. However, the nature of God that we have is the regeneration of our spirits, whereby our spirits were recreated after God. Therefore, because it is not an outward thing, there is the tendency to think that we are still the old man of sin. By regeneration, the sin nature was taken away from us and the righteous nature of God was credited to us. I will use a little illustration to explain this.

Once, my daughter Lemmy called me from school and said she needed money to buy a few things. I immediately transferred some money to her bank account. However, she was busy throughout the day and didn't check her account and didn't realise I had credited her account with some money. Therefore, later that evening she sent another text message asking for the same thing, in fact this time, she said 'Mum, am feeling really low, nothing in my account…I really need that money I asked so I can buy a few things'. At this, I responded to her to check her account that I transferred some money earlier on when she first asked. Immediately she checked, she was aglow with excitement, which I felt in her voice when she called to say thank you. This excitement came as a result of her *consciousness* of what she has in her bank account. However, that money had been there a few hours earlier, yet because she was not conscious or aware of it, she was dull and unenthusiastic. This is the same thing with our consciousness of our righteous nature, which Jesus credited into our spiritual bank account by reason of the substitutionary work in His death, burial and resurrection. We became righteous when we received Him and all we need is to be constantly conscious of that righteous nature.

Remember, the righteous nature was purchased by the precious blood of the Lord Jesus Christ and so that will propel us to live holy lives in accordance with His word. Therefore, righteousness consciousness is not a licence to live in sin. Rather, it helps us to live out what is on the inside, our words, thoughts and conducts begin to align with and reflect the righteous nature. Since it is a nature, we do not grow in righteousness, but we can grow in our consciousness of our righteousness and hence in the place of prayer, a righteousness consciousness will change our prayer life. Rather than begging, we will be bold to approach the throne room of God. He said to us to come boldly to the throne to obtain mercy and find grace to help in time of need (**Hebrews 4:16; NKJV**).

Conversely, when we are sin conscious, we dwell in the natural, carnal and mundane realms and we're unable to approach God boldly. We must always remember that one of the strategies of the enemy is to accuse us day and night, he has a dossier of our wrongs, mistakes and weaknesses and so he keeps accusing us of sin, he specialises in bringing our weaknesses to us to discredit us and make us feel unworthy to approach God in prayer. But we must be conscious of the nature of righteousness that we have in Christ.

Righteousness consciousness is not a cloak to sin. Rather it is a call to a consciousness, an awareness of the nature/seed of God in us and Apostle John said because we have the seed of God in us we do not sin i.e. we do not make practice of sin or we do not habitually live in sin and we cannot sin (**1 John 3:9; NKJV**). However, we do make mistakes and fall into sin, and in such circumstances, he says we should not run away from God but we should come to Him, confess our sins and repent i.e. turn away from them because our God is faithful to forgive us and to cleanse us from all unrighteousness (**1 John 1:9; NKJV**). A righteousness consciousness will help us to come boldly before God in prayer not by our righteousness, which **Isaiah** likens to filthy rags **Isaiah 64:6**, but by the righteousness of the Lord Jesus Christ purchased for us through His precious blood (**Hebrews 10:19-20; 4:14-16; Romans 5:17; NKJV**). Such righteousness consciousness creates boldness, which then creates the confidence and guarantee that our prayers are and will be answered.

## 8.1.8 When we understand the Spiritual Realm

Earlier in part one we discussed the spirit realm. The main thing to reiterate here is that everything in the physical/earth realm is controlled from the spirit realm. The challenge is that we cannot see or perceive the spirit realm with our physical senses, but the fact that we cannot see something physically does not mean it doesn't exist. A practical example is the television channels. Sometime ago, at home, the TV in my room stopped working and on a particular day I had wanted to watch a programme on KICCTV channel, but simultaneously, my children were engrossed in a Disney programme on another channel. 'Mum please let us enjoy this episode, we will record your programme for you and you can watch it later' said my older son. Therefore, I allowed them to enjoy their programme, while they recorded mine. This became a regular occurrence for a while and it demonstrates that while we cannot access 2 or 3 different TV channels at the same time, the truth is those other channels run their programmes concurrently. The same is true with the spirit realm, the fact that we cannot see or feel that realm with our physical senses does not mean that it doesn't exist.

If the spirit realm exists and as we examined in chapter two, our blessings and all that Christ has made available to us are located there, then we cannot afford to be visitors to that realm, we ought to live in that realm concurrently by praying. This is why Apostle Paul said to us that the weapon of warfare are not carnal… in other words, we do not engage in a physical fight but spiritual. When we understand that the spirit realm controls the physical, we can add patience to our faith after prayers and also be in expectation because like Daniel, our answers may have been dispatched but maybe a 'prince of Persia' in the spirit realm is withholding our answers? Nevertheless, by the same spiritual reinforcement of a higher angelic assistance in Daniel's case, I decree divine speed, acceleration and unhindered physical manifestations to all our prayers in the Name of the Lord Jesus Christ.

### 8.1.8.1 Rules of Engagement in Spiritual Warfare

Like every warfare, there are rules of engagement in spiritual warfare. The first rule of engagement in spiritual warfare is that we must understand that there are no de-militarised zones. You must understand that just by being a human being, right from the day of birth you are born into a warfare. The consciousness of the warfare and the intensity of the opposition vary according to our purpose and assignment. Sometimes, the consciousness of spiritual warfare comes the moment we receive the Lord Jesus Christ and we become born again. One woman of God I admire so much Rev Funke

Felix-Adjumo says 'life is a battle, it is either you are fighting or someone is fighting for you'. This implies that whether we are aware of it or not, there is ongoing fight, and at some point, when the reality of the warfare dawns on us, we become more aware to the extent that we cannot stand aloof, we too have to start fighting for ourselves and also fight for others. Therefore, we must know where we belong in the ongoing fight.

The second rule of engagement is the understanding that we have a common enemy – Satan and its demons. We must understand that Satan and its demons are spirit beings who do not have the legal right to be on earth so one way they fight us and our loved ones physically is through other people, human beings who have yielded their bodies to be used. In **Romans 6:16**, Apostle Paul said whomever we yield ourselves (our bodies) we become servant to (NKJV). Although he was writing in relation to sin, but certain persons have yielded their bodies to be used by Satan and demon spirits. Nevertheless, we must understand that the people; our bosses, supervisors, colleagues, teachers, students, classmates, roommates, neighbours, families and friends and everyone that seems to be the cause of our problems are not the real enemy. They may have knowingly or unknowingly yielded themselves to be used by Satan, but the enemy is Satan, which is unseen. An understanding of the real enemy will help us to deal with issues spiritually from the root and not engage with symptoms in the peripheral or physical.

The third rule is that belligerents (persons or group of persons who engage in conflict or war) fight with a strategy. In addition to the understanding that we have a common enemy Satan and its fallen demons, we must also understand the strategies or weapon that Satan and his cohorts employ in fighting. This will help us to also deploy every spiritual and strategic biblical weapons to prevail against the enemy. Satan's *modus operandi* (mode of operation) or strategy, which Bible calls 'schemes' and 'devices' are deception, lies, fear, intimidation and accusations. We must not be ignorant of the devices of the enemy lest Satan should take advantage of us (**2 Corinthians 2:11; NKJV**). Also, **2 Chronicles 29: 11** says we must not be careless or negligent, because the fact that God has chosen us to serve, worship Him and burn the incense of prayer (NKJV), sometimes makes us targets for the schemes of the enemy.

A common denominator of all the schemes is falsehood, as Satan magnifies things to make them appear differently than they really are.

The fourth rule of engagement in spiritual warfare is that there is order and ranking in the realm. We rank higher and have greater authority in the spirit realm than Satan. Satan and its demon spirits are not only aware of our spiritual superiority over them, they respect spiritual order and ranking and therefore, they respect and kowtow to us. Therefore, where we are faced with demon spirits which manifest in spirit form or through other creatures, there is no need to fear, because Greater is He God the Holy Spirit that is in you than he that is in the world. Take your stance in the word and with the understanding of the higher authority you have in the realm of the spirit, all you need do is sometimes laugh or speak the word and they will be crushed, destroyed or vamoosed forever never to return. Glory to God for giving us such an awesome authority!

The above list is not exhaustive but the understanding of these rules, namely, no neutral grounds, we have a common enemy Satan, not our friends, family or colleagues, the enemy is illegal on earth but uses human vessels and devices, as well as recognising that the enemy knows and respects our superior authority will enhance our prevailing prayers. Understanding these rules, especially that the enemy is Satan and not the physical human beings will help us to deal with the root of problems in the spirit realm. It will also help us to be proportionate when we pray and not take things for granted, because the enemy is not gentle, he is strategic and brutal.

## 8.1.9 When we understand our Position and Authority in the Spirit Realm

The last point on the rules of engagement relating to order and ranking necessarily leads to our position and ranking in the realms of the spirit. We must understand that in all of God's creation man i.e. human beings are the only tripartite being created as spirit, having a soul and living in a physical body. Man is created after God's own image and likeness and this got Satan very jealous as the Psalmist began to reiterate that what is man that you are mindful of him and you have made him a little lower than the angel/

Elohim... **(Psalms 8:4-6; NKJV)**. Human beings also have the capacity to function both in the earth realm and in the spirit realm simultaneously.

This reality cannot be ignored, if we must prevail in spiritual warfare. I recall an incident narrated to me by a friend Debra. Debra was in Law School at the time and according to her this was the first and only time she ever experienced the activity of witchcraft spirit in her life practically. 'On a particular day during an informal tutorial class', Debra said, 'I had an argument with a classmate 'Madam' but I apologised, we laughed over it and I thought it was resolved'. Unfortunately, Debra said that madam sought to take revenge at night while they were asleep, with two other roommates in the hall of residence that night. While Debra was enjoying her sleep that night, the madam with whom she had altercations earlier in the day came to her desk, sat on her chair and placed her left hand on Debra's legs and began to apologise for what had happened. In what appeared to be a dream, Debra immediately told madam that the issue had been settled and she was fine. However madam persisted in placing her hand on Debra's legs around her knee and suddenly, Debra related, that that hand felt like a heavy weight of a truck or iron pole on her body. Debra said she struggled to get the hand off her body with all her strength but to no avail, she screamed but her voice couldn't be heard. I was full of goose bumps as Debra narrated her story. 'What did you do? How did you get out of that evil witchcraft oppression...?' I asked eagerly. 'Finally, I managed to scream JESUS!!!! And with that I woke up and sat up on my bed' said Debra. All that had happened to her wasn't as strange as the amazement and shock that Debra felt on waking up to find madam on the other side of the room on her bed fast asleep. 'This made fear to well up inside of me' said Debra 'I couldn't say a word...'. However, Debra narrated that suddenly, scriptures began to come to her mind...

> *The righteous is as bold as a lion, greater is He that is in you than he that is in the world. I have given you authority to trample on snakes and scorpions and upon all the powers of the enemy and nothing shall by any means harm you...* **(Proverbs 28:1; 1 John 4:4; Luke 10:19) (NKJV).**

'With these scriptures, boldness came and I stood up from my bed and began to pace the room praying and making declarations. At about 4.00am, I went to my friends; Michael and Rich and related the experience to them, they prayed with me and reinforced my declarations.' Debra narrated. 'They were "dangerous" declarations', said Debra, 'because Bible says suffer not the witch to live...' she added. 'Ah did you pray for her to die?' I queried curiously. Debra told me that they didn't pray for her to die, but that they decreed that the hand she had used would become useless, paralysed and she wouldn't be able to write the Bar exams and it was so. According to Debra, madam travelled for about two weeks and returned with the hand cast in a POP plaster application. 'She couldn't write the Bar exams that year, as she subsequently moved out of school for the rest of the session'. She may have sat for the Bar exams in the subsequent year' Debra concluded.

Debra's story buttresses the fact that we have been given authority as believers, the same power and authority that raised Jesus from the grave resides in us. The Holy Spirit that in-dwells us is the spirit of boldness, for God hasn't given us the spirit of fear but of love, power and sound mind. Thank God also for spiritual friends and prayer partners, Debra had great company two friends whom she ran to and who encouraged and prayed with her. We are never meant to be alone in spiritual warfare, look for people of the same or higher level of spiritual walk and let them encourage you in the place of prayers, two are better than one the Bible says. More significantly, in spiritual ranking, after the God-head, Almighty God the Father, the Son our Lord Jesus Christ and the Holy Ghost, believers in Christ come next. We rank higher than angels, because angels, Bible says, are ministering spirits, sent to minister to us, and it is written that we shall judge angels, if we have the capacity to judge angels, then it means we rank higher than them (**Hebrews 1:14; 1 Corinthians 6:3; NKJV**). Of course, Satan and its demon spirits are below us in ranking. They are under us, beneath our feet. Satan is a defeated foe!

*We must recognise our superior authority and fight from the stance of the victory we already have in Christ. Do not let your head and shoulders hang down, do not kowtow to the intimidations of the enemy, they are schemes and devices fashioned deliberately to make you lose heart and give up. Arise mighty man and woman of valour, greater is He that is in you than any mountain before you right now for who are thou oh great mountain before Zerubbabel thou shall become plain. They shall surely gather, but because their gathering is not of the Lord they shall fall for your sake. No weapon formed/fashion against you and your family shall be able to prosper. Victory is yours, you shall laugh for He that sits in the heavens shall laugh because the Lord shall have them in derision...Be strong in the Lord and in the power of His might...You are more than conqueror...*

An understanding of the superior authority we have in the realm of the spirit will help us to be bold when we engage in prevailing prayer. No doubt this is a powerful ingredient to answers to our prayers. As we said in the first part of the book, prayer is the mechanism or strategy God has given to us to enforce His will on earth and enforcement, needs a bit of force. That is why there is *force* in the middle of the word, 'en-*force*-ment'. We need to strategically apply force in the place of prayer to ensure that God's will is done on earth. We need to know that we have the legal authority to enforce God's will. Jesus left us here and He said to us to *occupy* till He comes. Although used in a different context, one of the ways we can occupy is to engage in prevailing prayer to ensure that God's standard, His original intent for creation is enforced and superimposed on earth.

## 8.10 When we pray in the Spirit/Tongues

Another very important prerequisite to answers to our prayers is praying in the spirit. This is so important because it is only by praying in the spirit that we do not pray amiss. Bible says, we do not know what we should pray for as we ought... in other words, not only do we not know what to pray for, we also do not know how. Therefore, even if we know what to pray for, say for example my child who is in a distant city studying at the University, but how do I pray and what do I pray? This is so huge and so important because, it highlights our limitations and weaknesses that the Bible says it is only by submitting to the Holy Spirit that groanings; effective prayers, which cannot be uttered can be made.

> Likewise the Spirit also helps in our weaknesses. For we do not know what we should pray for as we ought, but the Spirit Himself makes intercession for us with groanings which cannot be uttered. [27] Now He who searches the hearts knows what the mind of the Spirit *is,* because He makes intercession for the saints according to *the will of* God (**Romans 8:26-27**) (**NKJV**).

Prevailing prayer must start in the heart of God and it is only by the help of the Holy Spirit that the mind of God is revealed to us.

> But God has revealed *them* to us through His Spirit. For the Spirit searches all things, yes, the deep things of God. [11] For what man knows the things of a man except the spirit of the man which is in him? Even so no one knows the things of God except the Spirit of God. [12] Now we have received, not the spirit of the world, but the Spirit who is from God, that we might know the things that have been freely given to us by God (**1 Corinthians 2:10-12**) (**NKJV**).

Praying in the spirit is important for every child of God, and indeed, every believer in the Lord Jesus Christ.

## 8.2 What are the reasons for seeming delays in answers to our prayers?

There are several reasons why there could be delays to answers to our prayers. Due to space constraint we will highlight only a few. First, when we do not employ all of the ten prerequisites to answers to prayers we discussed above when we pray, then there may be no answers to our prayers or there may be delays. There could be more preconditions to answers to prayers but basically every other point could be subsumed in one or two of the points we have discussed.

Apart from failure to apply the ten prerequisites being a reason for delay to answers, a second reason could be found in Daniel, where there was delay due to territorial spirits withholding his answers.

> But the prince of the kingdom of Persia withstood me twenty-one days; and behold, Michael, one of the chief princes, came to help me, for I had been left alone there with the kings of Persia **(Daniel 10:13) (NKJV).**

The 'prince' of Persia referred to here is not a physical person, it is a spirit. Interestingly, while there was a physical king, King Cyrus who was in power and to whom everyone looked as the political leader, there were demonic spirits in control of the entire Kingdom of Persia. This is very instructive because in contemporary times, we must realise that those in positions of authority like Prime Ministers, Presidents, Members of Parliament, Judges, Counsellors, Mayors etc., may not actually be the ones in charge of affairs in relation to certain decisions, obnoxious laws and policies prevalent in our societies. Sometimes, they are only ceremonial heads because there may be higher spirits in charge either using them consciously or unconsciously or ruling side by side with them. To buttress this point, Bible records where Prophet Ezekiel was asked to prophesy judgment against certain nations and cities. He prophesied against the 'King' and the 'Prince' of Tyre in **Ezekiel 28**, indicative of a physical and a spiritual ruler over the city. Although this is debatable and a few Bible scholars have said the use of King and Prince refer to the same person,[50] I think they are different especially when we read in context from at least the two preceding chapters.

---

[50] See for example Biblical Hermeneutics at https://hermeneutics.stackexchange. com/questions/8985/who-is-the-prince-of-tyre>; Cooper, L. E. *The New American Commentary Vol. 17: Ezekiel*. In *Logos Bible Software*. Oak Harbor, WA: Logos Research Systems, Inc., 1994. Jamieson, R., Fausset, A. R., Brown, D. *A Commentary, Critical and Explanatory, on the Old and New Testaments*. In *Logos Bible Software*. Oak Harbor, WA: Logos Research Systems, Inc., 1997. See also Dr. Joseph R. Nally, 'Who is the Prince of Tyre?' Dr Nally is the Theological Editor at Third Millennium Ministries (IIIM). Available at http://thirdmill.org/answers/answer.asp/file/40519> (Accessed 16 October 2017).

The point is that beyond the physical human beings we have elected and appointed to rule and govern us, there are spirits governing and ruling nations and cities. They are called territorial spirits, whose influences and evil agendas are perpetuated through the leaders and people in positions of authority. This understanding should propel us to pray constantly for everyone in the position of authority as Apostle Paul admonishes in **1 Timothy 2: 1-4 (NKJV)**. The fact that there was a prince of Persia that withstood the angel for 21 days and prevented him from bringing down the answers that Daniel prayed for, suggests that the activities of territorial demonic spirits can sometimes stop or delay the physical manifestations or answers to our prayers. However, like Daniel, we must not give up, we need to keep up our faith and expectancy.

Third, there could be delays when the season and timing for what we want is not due. God will not give us anything that will destroy us. Much as we are His children and He delights to bless us, He loves us too much to allow His blessing to become a source of distractions and destructions to our lives. Therefore, He knows us and what we can handle per time. As a parent, a 10 year old child cannot ask you for a car and you give him even if you have fleet of cars. This is because, you know that the car will destroy the child. Therefore, God wants us to mature to become sons and then He will release His blessings in abundance. God makes all things beautiful in its time. It is true that God's promises are yes and in Him Amen, but we need to understand that all of God's promises are predicated upon certain conditions and timing. Therefore, we need to ensure that we have fulfilled the conditions attached to every of God's blessing because God is ready to avenge every disobedience when our obedience is complete or fulfilled (**2 Corinthians 10:6) (NKJV).**

In addition to maturing in Christ, understanding God's timing and fulfilling all conditions, another reason for delay may be that the people or person through whom or in whom our blessings have been wrapped may not be ready. A good example is the children of Israel, whom God already said would be in captivity in Egypt for 400 years (**Genesis 15:13; NKJV**). Nevertheless, they did not get physically delivered until after 430 years (**Exodus 12: 40-41; NKJV**). There may be other reasons but I believe the main reason for the delay and the additional 30 years the Israelites spent in Egypt, was because Moses was not ready. God had to prepare Moses to align him to His divine purpose. Similarly, sometimes our answers are tied to people who must be ready and align to God's divine mandate before we see the physical manifestations to our prayers.

## 8.3 When God is Silent

Is God silent sometimes? Yes! There are times when God is silent, but in His silence, there are answers sometimes. Most of the instances recorded in scriptures when God appeared silent, didn't demonstrate that God was far away neither did it mean that the people were in sin that was why God was silent. Practically, God can be silent in either of three situations. The first is when we are in sin and disobedient, the second is for character development; when the timing is not right and there are certain things we must learn by no other means but by going through the process. The third scenario in which God can be silent is when we are in His divine purpose for our lives and we must go through a specific process.

## 8.3.1 God is Silent when we are in Sin and in Disobedience

God was silent when Saul sinned and disobeyed in making sacrifices that He was not meant to make. For that reason even though he reigned over Israel for 42 years, God was with him only during the first two years of his reign. For the remaining forty years, Saul was only a ceremonial head, he remained King over Israel only for as long as David needed to complete and mature through the process that God wanted him to go through. King Saul's disobedience did not only result in God being silent over him, God anointed David as king over Israel while Saul was King. God is not the author of confusion, but He is sovereign, no man could and can question Him. Not only did God make David King over Israel while Saul remained king, indicating that Saul's generations will not be king over Israel, God also sent an evil spirit to torment King Saul. The consequences of sin and disobedience can be grave. (**1 Samuel 13:1-14; 15:10-23; 16:14; NKJV**).

The Psalmist declares, 'if I regard iniquity in my heart the Lord will not hear me' (**Psalms 66:18; NKJV**). There is a lot more to sin than we know. The Bible talks about sin, transgression, and iniquity. Sin is first a nature, a spirit that manifests in people's thoughts, words, and actions. For believers, we don't have the nature of sin anymore, because at the new birth, we were given a new nature; the nature of righteousness. However, the Psalmist says that when the thoughts of our hearts are not right, they constitute iniquity, lawlessness, and perverseness for which God will not hear us when we pray. No wonder the Psalmist goes on to say; 'Let the words of my mouth and the meditations of my heart be acceptable in Your sight O Lord...' (**Psalms 19:14; NKJV**), for nobody can know his fault, no one can understand his own errors. Therefore we pray for God to deliver us from secret faults, from presumptuous sin, and every sin of the heart (our thoughts) that is not manifested in actions. Also, there is the sin of omission, for the Bible says; to him who knows the right thing to do and fails or refuses to do it, to him is sin (**James 4:17; NKJV**). Therefore, sin is not only the act of commission, sin includes omission and wrong thoughts.

## 8.3.2 God can be Silent when we are in His Divine Will

There are three instances in which God was silent in scripture because the people concerned were at the pinpoint centre of God's will for their lives. There could be more, but for our purpose, we could discern in the trajectory of the lives of Joseph, David and the Lord Jesus Christ that even though they were in God's will, God was silent on them.

With Joseph, during his growing up years in his father's house divine visitations and revelations through dreams were regular occurrences in his life. Although eleventh out of Jacob's thirteen children (twelve sons and one daughter), it appeared there wasn't a day in which Joseph didn't have something to say to his parents and siblings about what God had revealed to him in a night vision. The statement from his brothers '...Behold, this dreamer cometh' (**Genesis 37:19; KJV**) and the envy and jealousy that his dreams provoked were proof of the streams of revelation that he had.

However, it appeared that God became silent when Joseph needed to hear God the most, at least to confirm the dreams he had earlier? This appears to be the case because after his brothers sold him and throughout his sojourn and transfer from one group of Ishmaelite traders to another and then to Potiphar's house, down to being put in prison unjustly, there was no record of when God spoke to him anymore. However, for our benefit, Bible records several times that God was with Joseph.

There are divergent views and expositions on the story of Joseph. Some perspectives say Joseph lacked wisdom, he shouldn't have told his dreams to his brothers. Nevertheless, I truly find solace in the trajectory of Joseph's life because it reassures me that it is not true that because I am in a 'pit or prison' experience that God has left me. The same thing goes for Prophet Jeremiah who was in prison when he wrote the book of Jeremiah and Apostle Paul who wrote more than half of the books in the NT while he was in prison.

**The fact that you are in a horrible situation right now does not mean that God has left you. The story of Joseph should give you some encouragement as it does me. God does not give details of how the process is going to be. He sees and declares the end from the beginning saying my counsel shall stand and I will do all of my pleasure - Isaiah 46:10. Therefore, in whatever situation you are going through right now, just hold on even if everyone thinks and it seems God has left you. In fact the very fact that God is silent should tell you that you are at the pinpoint centre of God's will for your life. I encourage you to pray for sustaining grace to enable you to continue and not to truncate the process. Interestingly, Joseph's father Jacob and his brothers who sold him concluded that Joseph was dead, yet God was aligning Joseph to fulfil the revelation/dreams and to cause His divine will to come into full manifestation. All things will work together for your good and to the glory of God, everything will fall in line and work in accordance with God's divine purpose for your life. Nothing, no**

**situation lasts forever, it will pass, this present mess will become a message and all your tests and trials will turn to testimonies. Do not give up... Hold on to God and His word...continue in prayer until you prevail!**

Similarly, David was the last of Jesse's eight sons. He was faithful in keeping watch over his father's sheep and on the day God was to promote him to be king, he was not present. David didn't look like a candidate for the throne so there was no need to bring him to the gathering. Yet, God had ordained him and Samuel said, nothing could be done until David was fetched from the bush where he was tending sheep as usual. Despite God anointing David, and God declaring that He found in David a man after His own heart, hiding in caves, fighting terrible wars against the Philistines and being alienated from his family became the trajectory of David's life. One would have thought that after being anointed king, things will begin to fall in line. On the contrary, the anointing triggered several troubles and challenges for David. The question is; where was God while Saul threatened to kill David, where was God when David had to hide in caves, it appeared God was silent because David was at the centre of God's will for his life? Could this be the exact same situation you have found yourself right now? Rejoice because, while men may think that your life is upside down, you may actually be in God's will and in due season, the process will end and you will be enthroned.

With regards to the Lord Jesus Christ, in fact the Lord said constantly during His earthly ministry that He is in the Father and the Father is in Him; what I see my Father do is what I do; I thank You because You hear me always... yet when it was time for Him to step into His divine purpose, the same God who was always with Him became silent.

> [36] Then Jesus came with them to a place called Gethsemane, and said to the disciples, "Sit here while I go and pray over there." [37] And He took with Him Peter and the two sons of Zebedee, and He began to be sorrowful and deeply distressed. [38] Then He said to them, "My soul is exceedingly sorrowful, even to death. Stay here and watch with Me." [39] He went a little farther and fell on His face, and prayed,

saying, "O My Father, if it is possible, let this cup pass from Me; nevertheless, not as I will, but as You *will*." [40] Then He came to the disciples and found them sleeping, and said to Peter, "What! Could you not watch with Me one hour? [41] Watch and pray, lest you enter into temptation. The spirit indeed *is* willing, but the flesh *is* weak." [42] Again, a second time, He went away and prayed, saying, "O My Father, if this cup cannot pass away from Me unless[a] I drink it, Your will be done." [43] And He came and found them asleep again, for their eyes were heavy. [44] *So He left them, went away again, and prayed the third time, saying the same words.* [45] Then He came to His disciples and said to them, "Are *you* still sleeping and resting? Behold, the hour is at hand, and the Son of Man is being betrayed into the hands of sinners. [46] Rise, let us be going. See, My betrayer is at hand (**Matthew 26:36-46((NKJV).**

Interestingly, the Lord warned against *vain repetitions* in prayers, and certain people have interpreted this to mean that we must not repeat when we pray. However, this is not what Jesus was saying, He actually warned against **vain**, otiose, futile, empty and idle and not just repetition because on this occasion, the Lord Jesus Christ repeated the prayer thrice because in *verse 44* above, Bible records that *he went away again the third time and prayed the same words.* Despite the repetition and the agony that the Lord Jesus Christ went through on this occasion, God was silent. I believe the reason God couldn't answer Jesus was because this is the whole purpose of the Lord's coming to earth - to die for the sin of humanity. Therefore, at that critical moment even though it would have been expected that God would remind Him and say this is what we agreed and this is what you have to go through, God chose to remain silent because He had absolute confidence that the Lord Jesus Christ will not truncate the process and that He will submit to the most shameful, excruciating and humiliating process – death on the cross.

If God could be silent on the Lord Jesus Christ, you can be encouraged when He is silent on you right now. Be encouraged that through it all He has absolute confidence in you that you will not fail, you will not fumble, fall or falter. God has absolute trust and confidence in you that you will be able to bear it, and that you will go through the process and not truncate it. The beauty is that the process has an expiration and there is glory, victory, and joy ahead of you. For the Lord Jesus Christ, Bible records that for the joy that was set before Him, He endured the cross despising the shame (**Hebrews 12:2b; NKJV**). All you need to do right now is to begin to see the joy ahead of you. Glory to God! Create a picture of the other side!!! Better is the end of every matter than the beginning or any part thereof (**Ecclesiastes 7:8; NKJV**).

## Conclusion

God does answer prayers. I believe in our individual lives, we can testify to the fact that He does. God said, He is not a man to lie, neither the son of man to repent. He said that when we call he will answer and when we speak He will hear us. Let us not be weary in prayer, let us not faint. When we study and understand the ten prerequisites to answers to our prayers we've discussed and reasons why there might be delays sometimes, we will be encouraged to continue in prevailing prayers, because our God hears and answers prayers. However, when there are seeming delays, we should ensure we are not in sin or walking in disobedience, if we are, then we need to repent and turn from our wicked ways. He promised to hear from Heaven, forgive, heal us and our land; He is faithful and just to forgive us and cleanse us from all unrighteousness. We should also recall that God's perfect timing may be different from our expectations.

> For My thoughts are not your thoughts, Nor are your ways My ways, says the Lord. For as the heavens are higher than the earth, So are My ways higher than your ways and My thoughts than your thoughts (**Isaiah 55:8-9**) (**NKJV**).

We have also established that God can be silent sometimes. Therefore, when God is or appears silent, we can take solace in the lives of Joseph, David and our Lord Jesus Christ that God's silence does not mean that He has left us. In fact, He might be bragging about us like He did Job. Do not give up and do not truncate the process. There is victory, glory and beauty ahead. I would like to add that there are times when God does not answer our prayers at all. In fact, we should be grateful for unanswered prayers sometimes, because when we look back at some seasons of our lives and see why we didn't get what we prayed for, we can only thank God who in His sovereignty and loving kindness towards us, knows what is best for us and decides to withhold certain things from us for our good. Glory to God for unanswered prayers!

CHAPTER NINE

# Prevailing Prayer, Praise and the Prophetic

There was an avalanche of the 'P' words in this season all connected to prevailing prayers and I noted them down as the Lord impressed the words in my heart. Interestingly, there is a place where prayer and praise intermingle, therefore, we cannot totally separate the two. When we separate prayer from praise, it is only because there are only a few aspects or types of prayer that we are conversant with and these are the prayer of faith, the prayer of petition or supplication and the prayer of intercession in which we ask, make requests and entreaties for ourselves and for other people. Of course there is nothing wrong with asking because the Lord Himself says to us to 'ask, seek and knock' (**Matthew 7:7; NKJV**). However, as already discussed in the first part of this book, there are other kinds of prayer all of which are biblical and equally important.

## 9.1 Prayer and Praise Equals the Prophetic

Our discussions on the types of prayer in Chapter 3, includes the prayer of worship/praise. If we recall the instances where this kind of prayer was mentioned in scriptures, we would see that there is a fine line between the prayer (request) and the praise (worship). For example, in **Acts 13**, Bible says that while the apostles, prophets and teachers prayed, fasted and **ministered** to the Lord, the Holy Ghost spoke to them. We said earlier that the word minister is the same as **worship.** So in this instance, we cannot really differentiate between when they prayed and when they worshiped but we can infer that they engaged all three spiritual act, they prayed, fasted and they worshiped. Also, the Syrophoenician woman came to the Lord Jesus Christ to ask i.e. pray for healing for her daughter and because she was not a Jew, she did not, and neither did her daughter qualify to receive the healing she asked for. However, at a point in her prayer she fell down and worshiped. From these two examples, we can infer that worship is an integral part of prayer. In fact, there is hardly any prayer that does not start and end in worship or praise. This means that prayer and praise cannot be totally separated from each other and engaging them simultaneously can provoke the prophetic.

## 9.2 What is the prophetic?

Simply put, the prophetic is the open declaration of the mind of God for a person or people, in a season and regarding a specific situation.[51] It is a

---

[51] There are at least three dimensions of the prophetic that we must understand. First, there is the office of the prophet, which is one of the five-fold ministry gifts given to some as recorded in **Ephesians 4:11**. Second, there is the gift of prophecy, which is one of the nine gifts (manifestations) of the Holy Spirit expanded by Apostle Paul in **1 Corinthians 12**. The third is the ability to prophesy that every believer can exercise themselves in by the help of the Holy Spirit. With the office of the prophet, when we associate with those who have been called into that office, there is a rob-off of some of the dimensions of the prophetic in our lives but that does not make us prophets. The fact that you have been in the company of prophets and you are able to operate in the prophetic does not make you a prophet. Example is King Saul in the Bible, after being anointed by Samuel one of the signs given to him was that he was going to get into the company of prophets and that he was going to prophesy, which did happen. Although those moments of prophesying came, the fact of prophesying alone didn't make Saul a prophet. Also, Joel declaring prophetically concerning when the Holy Spirit would be poured out in the later days, said '...your sons and daughters shall prophesy...' the fact of the ability to prophesy doesn't come with an automatic call into the office of a prophet. Regarding the gift of prophecy, it is one of the ways that the Holy Spirit can manifest or express Himself to edify the Church. Therefore, in a service, the Holy Spirit can move through anyone as He wills to speak a word (word of knowledge or wisdom) that will comfort, build and edify the Church. The ability to prophesy is given to us all and it is the ability to speak an inspired word. Prophesying is giving a word or message that is inspired by the Holy Spirit. The motivational gift of prophecy mentioned in **Romans 12** among 6 other motivational gifts are different from the gift of prophecy discussed in **1 Corinthians 12**.

*'knowing'* that is triggered by the Holy Spirit. The prophetic was what the apostles experienced in **Acts 13**. They had previously been engaged in the work of the ministry, yet, on that occasion, it was recorded that the mind of God was revealed specifically for Paul and Barnabas and the instruction was to separate them for further ministry (a new phase). In other words, the prophetic brings direction and it comes with specificity, precision and clarity. If this did not occur, we may have lost out of the progressive revelation brought by Apostle Paul's ministry and we may never have received much light because we would have been denied all of his epistles, which were actually birthed on this occasion. The physical manifestations occurred as Paul took the steps of obedience to go on his missionary journeys planting churches in every city and subsequently writing to encourage, correct, and to strengthen them. For us to experience the prophetic in our lives as believers and as we pray, we must develop the ability to hear God.

The prophetic may be expressed by prophesying. A prophesy is an inspired word, a word inspired by the Holy Spirit and hence every believer ought to be able to prophesy as recorded by Prophet Joel (**Joel 2:28; NKJV**). It does not necessarily have to be a long sermon. It could be, as well as it could be a word or phrase like the Lord saying to us 'I love you', or 'repent', or 'forgive' etc. It could be a new song and it could be a word of encouragement for the Body (Church). Recall my earlier testimony about the 'Mummy' I prayed for regarding healing and how the Holy Spirit inspired the word 'bitterness' in my heart and how we addressed the issues of unforgiveness, resentments, malice, and bitterness in her heart before we prayed? This is the prophetic. It brought direction as the reason for the condition, precision, and specificity as to what we were to do to ensure her healing and ultimately it brought encouragement, as she did receive her healing after we obeyed the instructions of the Holy Spirit, first: forgive and then pray. No wonder Apostle Paul admonished that the expression or manifestations of the Holy Spirit is for our profit/benefit (**1 Corinthians 12:7; NKJV**). The most important thing in our prayer is not what we say but what the Holy Spirit tells us to do, we should give the Holy Spirit full expression because we know the mind of God through Him.

Previously, we mentioned that God's will is His word and *vice versa*. However, in addition, God's will can be found in Him; in His mouth. Therefore, as we prioritise the place of prayer, God is surely going to help us know His specific will by speaking back to us. When this happens, we progress from praying based on the general will which is scriptural and very important, to praying prophetically. I will give this example very briefly. There was a season when I began praying for an American preacher whom I have never met physically. I began praying for 'them' because the Lord prompted me to by showing me 'their' picture. But as I prayed, the Lord by the Holy Spirit helped me to progress in my prayer by giving me an understanding that I should pray against a particular ailment that was going to plague this American preacher in the future.

Until this understanding came to me, I only prayed according to the word of God in scriptures and what I thought should be prayed for. I prayed that God would make this American preacher's ministry to prosper, blossom, and to have greater impact: 'Lord as "they" traverse the lengths and breadths of cities and the nations of the world, please accompany Your word in their mouth with miracles, signs and wonders, do not let their words fall to the ground, let Your power and presence bring about supernatural interventions and positive impacts in people's lives. Lord, let men, women, young people, and children be saved and delivered as "they" preach Your word…' No doubt, this is praying according to God's will, because everything I mentioned in my prayer was scriptural. However, when the Lord gave me specific instructions on what to pray about, I made a shift and progressed in prayers. By the help of the Holy Spirit, I began to pray prophetically, by first rebuking every spirit of infirmity and then declaring God's healing and deliverance for this American preacher. How often do our anointed preachers and pastors keep on doing the work of ministry preaching everywhere and yet sometimes they are under attacks, or imminent danger is looming over them or their family members?

## 9.2.1 Listening to and Hearing the Lord in Prayer

This is a distinctive feature of our prayer as children of God. Although we said earlier that everyone prays because prayer is spiritual communication, the difference between other people's prayer and ours is that when we pray, we speak to our Heavenly Father who is 'Spirit Speaking God' and who speaks back to us. Other gods are not alive, they don't have mouths and can't speak back. Communication is incomplete unless the receiver responds with a feedback. Therefore, we are confident that God speaks back to us when we speak to Him in prayers.

In line with the above, a common definition of prayer is that *prayer is talking to God and God talking back to us.* However, in reality, we engage the first limb of the definition more than the second. We hardly engage in listening to and hearing God when we pray. For some people, prayer has almost become a ritual, a routine, and a mere recitation of some written codes. Sometimes we say the words without engaging with them mentally let alone spiritually. Therefore, sometimes, we do not expect that God would speak back to us.

The Bible says in **Deuteronomy 8:3** and **Matthew 4:4** that man must not live by bread alone but by every word that proceeds from the mouth of God (NKJV). This is literally saying to us to daily desire to hear from God a fresh word just the same way we have our daily meals. It also refers to the 'give us this day our daily bread' in the Lord's Prayer we discussed earlier. 'Daily bread' not being literal food only, but also and more importantly, God's word for our daily sustenance. Job said; 'I have not departed from the commandment of His lips, I have treasured the words of His mouth more than my necessary food' (**Job 23:12; NKJV**). Isaiah says '…My words which I have put in your mouth, shall not depart from your mouth, from the mouth of your descendants, nor from the mouth of your descendants' descendants…' (**Isaiah 59:21; NKJV**). Furthermore, in **John 10:27**, Bible says My sheep **hear My voice**, I know them, and they follow me. We cannot pray i.e. talk to God and not expect God to talk back to us. In fact the discussions in the preceding chapter relating to the question whether God answers prayers can be seen here, because sometimes God answers with instructions. He tells us what to do and it is in obeying His instructions that we receive the answers to our prayers. Therefore, if we lack the ability to hear Him, we will think that He has not heard and answered our prayers.

Whilst one of the primary ways God speaks to us is through the instrumentality of His word, God does speak expressly and specifically to us when we pray, and we should expect to know the mind of God and hear His voice when we pray. It could be by the still small voice, it could be in a vision or any form, but we should anticipate and create the right atmosphere and quietness to be able to hear Him speak to us. Peter wrote about a gentle and quiet spirit that is very precious in the sight of God (**1 Peter 3:4; NKJV**).

## 9.2.2 Examples of Ananias and Zacharias

I like the example of Ananias in the Bible a lot because without him we wouldn't have had the privilege and opportunity of Apostle Paul's ministry and epistles. The Lord spoke to Ananias to go to the street called Straight to the house of Judas and enquire of Saul. He did and through that supernatural occurrence and ability to listen to, and hear the Lord and obey His voice, Saul was converted and baptised. Bible records that it was in a vision (**Acts 9:10-19; NKJV**), this means that there are dimensions of visions, revelations and other supernatural visitations that we should expect to come into when we pray. There should be some progression in our prayer life. It may well be that the visitation and conversation took place while Ananias was praying, it could also be that the Lord moved in His sovereignty to visit Ananias not necessarily at the time of prayers, it could be that Ananias had prioritised the place of prayer previously and had hitherto been obedient? Any of these and other conjectures may well be the case, but what we can confidently say is that Ananias had the ability to hear the Lord. Otherwise, with his knowledge of the antecedents of Saul (Paul) and from the conversational prayer he had with the Lord, Ananias could have rejected the assignment and instructions.

But thank God he heard God and obeyed. I think that Ananias may have been one of Saul's target for arrest and imprisonment in his mission to Damascus? We should never ever imagine that we would be exempt from calamities when they occur in distant places and therefore be detached, dispassionate and disconnected from them and not pray about them, because sooner, the very far away issues come knocking on our door steps. Amos says woe to them who are at ease in Zion (**Amos 6:1; NKJV**). Sometimes, answers to our prayers is in hearing what the Lord is saying and obeying His instructions promptly. This cannot be overemphasised.

What the Lord is saying now is that we need to pray more than we've been praying, we need to pray with more understanding, pray strategically and with discernment. More importantly, we need to learn to hear His voice and obey promptly what the Holy Spirit lays in our hearts when we pray. I imagine that Damascus Christians may have been in fear since they may have heard that Saul was on his way to the City to kill and destroy every one of them? But despite being in fear, Ananias may have supposedly continued in prevailing prayers? Can you imagine what could have happened to Ananias and the Christians in Damascus at the time and even to the body of Christ generally had he failed to hear and obey the Lord? God could have in His sovereignty sent someone else, but that may have taken longer or could it even be that Ananias was the only disciple who engaged in prayers in the right way at the time i.e. listening to God as a vital part of prayer? We cannot but see that the impact of prayer, listening to and hearing God speak to us and promptly obeying Him is generational. I can't recall any other place in scripture where this particular Ananias was mentioned, and I wonder, could this be the only assignment God had for him?

In contrast, Zacharias was in the temple burning incense and angel Gabriel visited him and brought him good news of what he had prayed for all his life, yet he did not believe. How so often we are in the house of God and in His very presence yet we are not expectant and because there is no expectation, He speaks most times, but we discount His voice and we don't realise He is speaking to us? Sometimes we grieve and quench the presence of the Holy Spirit by our irreverent attitudes? May the Lord help us all! Angel Gabriel continued his message to Zacharias and at an age when he and his wife Elizabeth thought it was impossible, God answered and granted their request for a child. (**Luke 1:5-23; NKJV**).

I make bold to say that listening to and hearing the Lord is the most important aspect of prayer. Otherwise, how do we know what the 'Kingdom' entails in 'Your Kingdom come, Your will be done'. This cannot be referring to only the *logos* i.e. the written word which is the Bible? The word that proceeds from God's mouth regularly is part of what makes up His Kingdom that we must enforce on earth. In prayer, what can help us progress from the *logos* (general) to the *rhema* (revealed/specific) word, is when we hear God speak. One of the ways we can cultivate this art of hearing God is to anticipate and be in expectation that the Lord will speak to us. Let's anticipate the inevitable interventions and supernatural moves of God in our lives, which could be manifest in any way including in dreams, visions, the still small voice, as well as in the scriptures. Let's learn to be open, expectant, worship and wait on God and not come with our own agenda and long list of requests.

In addition to the need to listen to and hear the Lord when we pray, there is a blend, an intermingling of prayer and praise that can sharpen our ability to hear the Lord. Bible says that God inhabits the praises of His people **(Psalms 22:3; NKJV)**, therefore, one way to activate His presence and hear Him speak to us is when we add praise to our prayers. Praise and prayer intermingle and there are dimensions of the prophetic that we can never come into until we have this understanding that in corporate worship services, our sessions of praise and prayers do not compete but complement and complete each other.

As we engage in prevailing prayers, we should be conscious of the fact that we are actually making deposits in our spiritual bank accounts. One of my pastors, Pastor Funmi Obembe whiles coordinating prayers usually says 'if you think you do not need the specific prayers right now "bank" it', whenever she speaks of banking prayers this phrase 'deposits in our spiritual bank account' comes to my mind.

## 9.3 Prevailing Prayer: Deposits in our Spiritual Bank Accounts

In addition to the discussion in the preceding chapter about the question of whether God answers prayers, it is interesting to note that whether we believe that God has answered us or not, our prayers are actually being saved or banked in the heavenlies.

> Now when He had taken the scroll, the four living creatures and the twenty-four elders fell down before the Lamb, each having a *harp*, and golden bowls full of incense, which are *the prayers of the saints* (**Revelation 5:8**) (**NKJV**).

It may appear like taking scriptures out of context but this scripture tells us that each of the 24 elders have a harp and a golden bowl full of incense, which are the prayers of the saints. It is interesting that the golden bowl did not contain the preaching, sermon, giving and faith of the saints. What it contained was the *prayer* of the saints. This implies that when we pray, our prayers actually ascend to heaven as sweet smelling savour and they come to the heavenlies as incense stored in the golden bowls.

This revelation thrilled me so much because it means there is no prayer that is wasted. Whether we think we have answers or we do not have the physical manifestations of what we pray for, our prayers are actually being deposited in our spiritual bank accounts. We now know that our prayers ascend to God as incense, now let us see what happens to the incense.

> Then another angel, having a golden censer, came and stood at the altar. He was given much incense that he should offer it **with the prayers of all the saints upon** the golden altar which was before the throne. [4] *And the smoke of the incense, with the prayers of the saints, ascended before God from the angel's hand.* [5] Then the angel took the censer, filled it with fire from the altar, and threw *it* to the earth. And there were noises, thunderings, lightnings, and an earthquake. (**Revelation 8:3-5**) (**NKJV**).

In these few passages, the phrase *'the prayers of all the saints'* was repeated twice. The incense and our prayers are mixed together as they ascend before God from the angel's hand. This is very reassuring; that our prayers are mingled with incense and are offered to God. This is an encouragement to all who are weary because of the feeling of seemingly unanswered prayers.

## 9.3.1 The intermingling of our Prayers and Praise/Worship

In addition, the use of the phrase *'the prayers of all the saints'* include the different kinds of prayers we discussed in Chapter 3, especially the prayer of worship/praise. This is so because in **Revelation 5:8** above we see that each of the 24 elders had a *harp* and the golden bowls full of incense.

The *Harp* is an instrument of music of the stringed kind, of a triangular figure, held upright and commonly touched with the fingers.[52] It is a symbol that represents music, instruments, joy and worship. In ancient times, it was used as an accompaniment to songs of cheerfulness as well as of praise to God.[53] The harp was the national instrument of the Hebrews that had ten strings and was played on with the plectrum.[54] This implies that in addition to our prayers (prayers of the saints), worship is part of the incense in the golden bowl. No wonder, Apostle Paul admonished us to *pray all kinds of prayer with all perseverance...* **(Ephesians 6:18; NKJV).**

This means that we cannot separate prayers from praise/worship. We have discussed this earlier but the main understanding here is that when we engage in prayer and worship, we need to understand that there is a synergy in the spirit. Both prayer and praise/worship are deposits in our spiritual bank account into the golden bowls in heaven. Indeed, the most powerful prayer sessions I have attended were the ones in which the synergy between prayer and praise were harmonised and the Holy Spirit given full expression. If we have this understanding the seeming tensions between prayer and worship sessions would be better managed. Essentially, the coordinators of the sessions should take a cue from each other and not abruptly end the session because of the haste or need to move on. Although balance is needed, we need to truly *minster* to the Lord and learn to listen to what He will say to us. What completes prayer and praise is the prophetic i.e. the Lord speaking to us.

---

[52] KJV Dictionary Definition: Harp. Available at http://av1611.com/kjbp/kjv-dictionary/harp.html> (Accessed 17 October 2017).

[53] Harp. Available at http://www.biblestudytools.com/dictionary/harp/>

[54] Harp. *Smith's Bible Dictionary.* Available at http://biblehub.com/topical/h/harp.htm

## 9.3.2 What happens after the incense are offered to God?

**Revelations 8:5** says what happens after the incense are offered to God. *Then the angel took the censer, filled it with fire from the altar, and threw it to the earth. And there were noises, thunderings, lightnings, and an earthquake.* This implies that as the golden bowls become full with our prayers offered to God by the angel, the result is that the fire of God comes down in response to our prayers. Therefore, the impact of 'thunderings, lightnings and earthquakes' is the indignation of God upon the oppressions and injustices against His people. In other words, they represent answers to our prayers. Could this imply that perhaps one of the reasons there are no answers to our prayers is that there is nothing in our spiritual bank account or that the golden bowl is not yet full? I am persuaded that this may be the case because in the physical, we only go to the cash point/ATM or to the bank to withdraw cash because we have deposited some money there previously or someone has done so on our behalf. What happens when we go to cash points is we first try to find out what balance there is in the account. We carry on with further transactions to withdraw or transfer only if there is sufficient funds in the account. Similarly, when we have not prayed and praised and made sufficient deposits in our spiritual account, there could be nothing to draw on. The fire of God will not pour out to deal with all the injustices that we have prayed against. Thus, the continuity and persistence required in prevailing prayer is to ensure that we don't leave our spiritual bank account empty or half full, as we continue in prevailing prayers our spiritual bank accounts get full to overflowing...

## Conclusion

Prevailing prayer and praise are inseparable. Although in some kind of prayers, a distinction can be made between when we commune with God, and when we address the devil and enforce God's will on earth, especially with the prayers of intercession and supplication, both prayer and praise involve spiritual communication with God. Therefore, when we engage prayer and praise we should expect God to speak to us, which is prophetically making the mind of God known in our situation, what we pray about and also giving us instructions and directions in our prayers.

Does the prophetic differ from hearing from God or God speaking to us? I think they are both related. To the extent that the Lord speaks, and we listen to and hear Him, both hearing God and the prophetic are the same. Significantly, most of the time a prophetic word confirms what the Lord may have spoken to us previously and what He is speaking at that moment either privately or publicly. In this sense, hearing from God and the prophetic are related in that the latter confirms the former. The slight difference is that the prophetic is spontaneous and happens mostly in corporate meetings. For example, although Apostle Paul already knew what was going to befall him, a certain prophet Agabus at a gathering spontaneously picked Paul's belt, tied his own hands and feet and declared that Paul was going to be bound in Jerusalem, thereby confirming what Paul already knew. (**Acts 21:10-12; NKJV).**

There are times the Holy Spirit is present and yet we do not know what to do with His tangible presence. However, when we are sensitive at such times to inquire what the Lord would want to do, then we can, by the help of the Holy Spirit, speak His mind right there and then either through the word of knowledge, word of wisdom or word of prophecy. (The word of knowledge relates to supernatural knowing about the past and present, the word of wisdom relates to supernatural knowing about the future and word of prophecy is Holy Spirit inspired word that brings direction and edification to the body. All are expressions or manifestations of the Holy Spirit for our benefit.) This is so critical because once we miss the moment, we may not be able to get that 'flow and presence' anymore. Therefore, some church services are too structured, we seem to have structured out the person of the Holy Spirit, yet we keep praying; 'Holy spirit have Your way...' We need order and balance, but sometimes we seem to go to the other extreme of shutting down the flow of His presence because the service/meeting must close at designated times.

The spontaneity of the prophetic is something that we need to learn and yield to. We cannot box the Holy Spirit. It is to our detriment when we do. Therefore, while we need order and structure, we also need to be open and be yielded, because the Lord may want to heal and deliver someone at the point of benediction in our meetings. Can we allow Him to interrupt us sometimes? Most notable miracles by the Lord Jesus Christ recorded in scriptures happened because the people broke protocols like the paralytic man whose four friends blew the roof opened to get their friend to Jesus. Interestingly, after the paralytic was healed, nothing was said about the roof that was destroyed. This is not encouraging disorderliness. God is a God of order, but can we take a cue from scriptures and allow full expression of the Holy Spirit sometimes?

Prayers don't die. Our prayers remain potent long after we are gone. This is the place of the spiritual deposits in our spiritual bank account. The Lord did admonish that we should lay up treasures in heaven, where neither moth nor rust destroys... **(Matthew 6:20; NKJV)**. One way we can lay up treasures in heaven is by our prayers and praise. We can enrich our spiritual bank account with prayers and praise that can positively impact generations yet unborn. This is the core of prevailing prayer lifestyle. In other words, regardless of whether we get instant answers to our prayers, we must continue to engage in prevailing prayer as long as we have breath because we are confident that our prayers are safely banked in heaven.

# CHAPTER TEN

# The 7 'P' Words in Prevailing Prayers

The impression of prevailing prayer came with a few questions and I suspect that some of us may have been waiting to see a huge testimony in this book of how I prevailed in prayers? I hope no one feels disappointed because there is no such testimony. Rather, the instruction I got and which I think I have conveyed hopefully in the course of the book and I will reiterate here is that God is calling every one of us His children back into the place of prayer. You might respond like I did, 'but we've been praying'!!! This was my exact response to the Lord when He impressed the instructions in my heart.

Sincerely, I think I have not prayed as much as I have in this season in my entire life. Except for the season in 2001 while I was pregnant with my second child, this period specifically from 2016 through to 2017 have been a season I have prayed the most at least in my estimation. Yet, the Lord said to get back to the place of prayer. As I began to spend time with the Lord, the Holy Spirit impressed the word 'prevailing' in my heart, with some other 'P' words that are linked to prevailing prayers. They include *place, prioritise, precision, persistence, purposeful, posture and proportionality*. Although we have mentioned these words in Chapter 5 when we used Daniel as a case study, in this last chapter, we will highlight these words in more detail.

## 10.1 The Place of Prayer

For a while, it appears everyone talks about prayer than do the actual praying? Therefore, the Holy Spirit says, it is time to get back to the place of prayer. What is this place of prayer? The place of prayer includes a physical place, as well as maintaining an attitude and atmosphere of continuously praying without ceasing. As an individual, the Holy Spirit says to get a place of prayer, whether on your bed, on a sofa in your bed room, in your study or your kitchen, toilet area or living room, wherever! For Daniel, his place of prayer was his upper room. As we discussed earlier, so many things happened in the **upper room** in scripture, both positives and negatives. Therefore, if when we are meant to pray we sleep and do all other things but pray, we can be sure what the consequences might be.

As a congregation, as a family and prayer groups, we need to get into the place of prayer and take it more seriously. As we have identified, the place includes an attitude and atmosphere. We must not quench the spirit by our lukewarm and irreverent attitudes. None of us will miss an appointment with or get distracted when talking with our bosses at work, presidents or prime ministers of our countries. Yet, when it is prayer time we make all kinds of excuses. Legitimate as some of our excuses may appear, they are not in God's sight because like the dignitaries invited to the wedding banquet, no one is indispensable (**Matthew 22:1-14; NKJV**), but may that not be our portion. For some people who are present at prayer meetings/times, we are sometimes too complacent, careless, casual, and lethargic because we allow distractions with our mobile phones. The Lord is saying that the destinies of children, generations yet unborn and the greatness of cities and nations are determined in the place of prayer.

Therefore, this is an encouragement for everyone to continue in the place of prayer; both real and virtual (online). God is calling us all to the place of prayer wherever that place might be. As already emphasised, the 'place' of prayer is not necessarily circumscribed to a particular geographic or physical location. In addition to having a location, it is important to pray ceaselessly and to ensure that our thoughts, our words, our attitudes and the atmosphere we create are in alignment with the word of God. The days are evil and rather than allow ourselves to be provoked to anger by on-going unsavoury situations, we should be propelled to take our place of prayer. Better still, if we are provoked, let the provocation be a holy indignation that will propel us to pray and not to engage in physical altercations, arguments or pointless reactions in the flesh.

## 10.2 Prioritise Prayer

Prioritising prayer means we should put prayer first. **Matthew 6:33** says we should seek first the Kingdom of God and His righteousness (NKJV). One of the ways to seek God's Kingdom first is to pray first. In everything and with everything, we need to pray first. This is what prioritising prayer is all about. It means asking and seeking God's mind about things first before we take any other action. But beyond that, prioritising prayer is being proactive in prayer and not waiting for unpleasant happenings to occur before we pray. The key to prioritising prayer is having an understanding that 'Your kingdom come Your will be done on earth as it is in heaven' actually gives us a mandate to enforce God's intent on earth. Therefore, rather than wait for when things go wrong, we should be proactive to enforce God's will and make the news instead of allowing the news to dictate when and what we pray about and sometimes the intensity of our prayers.

Being prompted to pray by the news is not wrong. We need to be propelled to priorities prayer when we hear about the negative things happening around the world, rather than complain or be complacent about them or even allow fear to well up in our hearts. Therefore, prioritising prayer includes making prayer our first reaction when we hear or read about unpleasant situations in the news. It also means that we can depend on the Holy Spirit to help us to pray proactively with discernment before things happen or to avert them entirely. Certain things happen and most times we get angry, we complain, moan, grumble and we try to do everything but pray about them. However, like Daniel, when bad situations get worse, the best thing to do is not to react in the flesh but to pray. Also, despite being a Queen, Esther prioritised prayer when a death sentence hung over her, over her Uncle Mordecai and over the entire Jewish people. Sermons are replete with Esther's beauty, her wisdom and the favour she enjoyed. These are great, as they made the way for her to become Queen. However, becoming a Queen didn't exempt her from the death penalty. Nevertheless, she didn't forget her identity and therefore when the need arose, she prioritised prayer by calling for a 3 day fasting and prayer, which she and her maids engaged in amidst affluence in the Shushan Palace. **(Esther 4:16; NKJV).**

We must realise that the earth realm is the place where things manifest physically, but before they do, they already exist in the spirit realm. Therefore, if there is anything in our lives that we do not like and specifically things that do not align with the word of God for our lives, then we must change them in the realm of the spirit by making prayer a priority.

## 10.3 Precision in Prayer

To be precise means to be exact, to be accurate and to be on point. Precision in prayer entails exactitude and accuracy with God's word. Whilst it is good to present our situation before God, we must learn to locate the scripture that speaks of the situation and speak that word in prayer to God. This is because God is only bound by His word. Again, Daniel was precise in his prayer. Although the content of his prayer was not recorded, we were told that this was what he did previously, noting '…as his custom was from early days.'**(Daniel 6:10; NKJV).** Therefore, we could infer that his prayer was precise and not laced with unnecessary or vain repetitions. As surmised earlier, Daniel may have told God about the decree, and he may have asked for God's protection, vindication and intervention. Three ways by which we can ensure precision in prayers is when we pray God's word, when we pray in the spirit and when we engage the prayer of thanksgiving and praise.

## 10.4 Persistence in Prayer

For a while, it appears weariness is wearing our prayer life out? It appears some of us have been battle-weary and like Elijah, we seem to have thrown in the towel or about to do so thinking that we are alone and no one else is praying? I would rather we are enlisted among the end-time prayer warriors. To persist means to continue, to persevere, to insist, to endure, to stick, to carry on… This is apt in relation to prevailing prayer because it carries with it the notion of continuity. Indeed, prayer is *ad-infinitum*, a continuum and as long as we have breath and we remain in the earth realm, prayer must be in our hearts and on our lips.

Elijah had prophesied that there would be abundance of rain after three and half years of drought. The fact of a prophecy didn't just make it to happen. Rather, Elijah went and tucked his head between his knees and began to pray. In line with the command to watch and pray, Elijah sent his servant to go out and check if the rain had started pouring.

> Then Elijah said to Ahab, "Go up, eat and drink; for *there is* the sound of abundance of rain." [42] So Ahab went up to eat and drink. And Elijah went up to the top of Carmel; then he bowed down on the ground, and put his face between his knees, [43] and said to his servant, "Go up now, look toward the sea." So he went up and looked, and said, "*There is* nothing." And seven times he said, "Go again." [44] Then it came to pass the seventh *time*, that he said, "There is a cloud, as small as a man's hand, rising out of the sea!" So he said, "Go up, say to Ahab, 'Prepare *your chariot*, and go down before the rain stops you.'" [45] Now it happened in the meantime that the sky became black with clouds and wind, and there was a heavy rain… (**1 Kings 18: 41-45**) (**NKJV**).

Elijah kept his servant going back and forth to check until the 7th time when he came with some good news about seeing 'a cloud as small as a man's hand'. What could have happened if Elijah stopped praying after the 3rd or 4th time of checking? There is no substitute to persistence in prayer especially when a word of prophecy has gone forth. The fact that God said something doesn't mean it would automatically come to pass because the enemy is constantly fighting to ensure that the word doesn't come to fruition. No wonder Apostle Paul instructed Timothy that by means of the word of prophecy that had been said over him, he should wage a good warfare. (**1 Timothy 1:18; NKJV**). This is why the trial, test, tribulations and temptation we go through are not necessarily about us but because of the word (**Matthew**

**13:21; NKJV).** We need to enforce God's word in the place of persistent prayer.

Another example of persistence in prayer was reflected in the parable of the widow and the unjust judge in **Luke 18**. Most people refer to this as a type of prayer, namely, the prayer of importunity. I decided not to classify importunity as a type of prayer in Chapter 3 because importunity means persistence and I believe every prayer should carry some element of persistence until we get what we want. Even the prayer of faith which I noted earlier should ideally be prayed once, we are meant to accompany it with the prayer of thanksgiving; specific and general. For the purpose of persistence in prayers and as analysed in the previous chapter, even if we do not receive answers, the realisation that our prayers are being banked spiritually should be sufficient impetus for us to be persistent. **Luke 18** opens with the sentence that *'...men ought always to pray and not faint...'* **(KJV).** Therefore, although in the parable the judge was wicked and unjust, did not fear God neither did he regard man, nevertheless, because of the persistence of the widow, the judge granted her request.

In contrast, the Lord said, if a wicked judge can grant the widow her desires by reason of her persistence, God is able to do much more for us when we persist in prayers.

> Then the Lord said, "Hear what the unjust judge said. [7]And shall God not avenge His own elect who cry out day and night to Him, though He bears long with them? [8]I tell you that He will avenge them speedily... **(Luke 18:6-8) (NKJV).**

It is important to note that by this parable, the Lord wasn't making a comparison but a contrast. First, the judge is wicked, our God is loving and kind. Second, the judge responds from the place of weariness our God responds from the place of abundance, generosity and compassion. Therefore, He says that if a wicked judge can respond at all, how much more Him, our loving Father.

I recommend a read of the entire Chapter 18 of Luke gospel because the Lord went on to give a parable of the prayer of the Pharisee and the Tax Collector telling us how we need to humble ourselves when we pray. He said to us that the things which seem impossible to men are possible with God when we humble ourselves in the place of persistent prayer. The chapter ends with the healing of Blind Bartimeous who had been blind from birth. Interestingly, it was his persistence that attracted the Lord Jesus, because people around had hushed him, but Bible records that he cried all the more. And in the midst of several other people who may have needed healing and a touch from the Lord on that day, only Blind Bartimeous was singled out because of his persistence **(Luke 18:35-42; NKJV)**. Whatever or whoever is telling you to be quiet must invoke a louder cry from you to the Lord in prayer. Let nothing and no one stop you! When we are persistent in our cry to the Lord, He hears and answers us speedily.

## 10.5 Purposeful in Prayer

To be purposeful means to be focussed, to be determined, deliberate and resolute. What is the purpose of our prayer? When we pray what is our motivation. Our motivation will help us to be purposeful. As we said earlier, prayer is access to God meaning prayer establishes a relationship, communion and intimacy with God. We go to God in prayer because He is our Father/Source. Therefore, prayer links or connects us to our source. Prayer becomes a lifeline without which we are empty or dead spiritually. This makes us to be focused, strategic and deliberate because we know that what the enemy does is to get us to shift focus from praying to complaining, to being careless and complacent. However, when we realise that prayer is actually our lifeline, then we will do all we can to remain focused, determined, deliberate and purposeful in prayer.

## 10.6 Posture in Prayer

Posture is everything. Posture means position, pose and carriage. It also means stance, demeanour, deportment and attitude. Is there an appropriate posture for prayer? The answer is yes, the appropriate posture for prayer is kneeling down. In her Bible Study series on Gideon, the great American preacher who is also a voice to this generation and beyond, Priscilla Shirer declared; 'begin the battle on your knees'.[55] Indeed, when we do, we are not only sure of victories over the challenges that confront us daily, we will also not kowtow to the lies, fears and intimidations of the enemy. This was demonstrated by Daniel, who even though was above 80 years old at the time, knelt down while he prayed. Also, Bible records regarding King Solomon at the dedication of the temple that '...when Solomon had finished praying all this prayer and supplication to the LORD, that he arose from before the altar of the LORD, *from kneeling on his knees* with his hands spread up to heaven' (**1 Kings 8:54; NKJV**). Apostle Paul in his epistle to the Church in Ephesus said '...for this reason I *bow my knees*', obviously in prayers, for the Church 'to be strengthened with might...' (**Ephesians 3:14-16; NKJV**). If Daniel at over 80 years, King Solomon who is recorded as the wisest and wealthiest King that ever lived and Apostle Paul who wrote more than half of the New Testament could kneel down in prayers, I don't see any reason why we shouldn't. As discussed earlier, regardless of our position and status in society, kneeling reflects submission, total surrender to and humility before God.

Whilst kneeling down is the right posture in prayer, we must also guard against a religious practice of kneeling down because others are doing it and because we do not want to be criticised for not doing it. Rather, when we kneel, let it be a reflection of total submission and reverence to God genuinely from the heart. There are other postures for prayers recorded in scriptures, such as 'Standing before the Lord' – Abraham in **Genesis 18:22; 19:27; NKJV** 'Prostrating before the Lord' – Moses in **Deuteronomy 9:25; NKJV** and 'Bowing with face tucked between the knees' – Elijah in **1 Kings 18:42; NKJV.**

**However, in addition to the physical postures, our heart posture is equally important.** We don't have to kneel down physically when we pray in public. In other words, physical kneeling is good but it may not be practicable sometimes due to the places we may find ourselves at specific times, for example when we are in public places such as schools, hospitals, public

---

[55] Priscilla Shirer, 'Begin the Battle on Your Knees' Available at https://www.youtube.com/watch?v=FTulnDFuhds> (Accessed 4 April 2017).

transport buses, while driving, on the train and aircrafts, at work places or other public places. Therefore, the physical **postures** should reflect our heart posture and attitude of submission, surrender and reverence to God when we pray.

Heart posture includes demeanour, deportment, attitude and stance. Demeanour speaks of our manner, our conduct, our character and our appearance when we pray. Therefore, while we encourage kneeling down as the appropriate posture for prayers, a religious or outward display of kneeling that is not genuinely from our heart should be jettisoned. We should also be mindful of our attitude and general demeanour and disposition, because it may be easy for us to say the Lord sees our heart posture which is more important, and then appear in whatever way we like. But we cannot afford to be casual when we approach God in prayer. Our God is loving and kind and we must come before Him in awe and with reverential fear. Our God is a God of Knowledge and by Him actions are weighed. As noted above, in addition to kneeling in public places being unrealistic, it may also be impracticable for some people to kneel down due to some medical reasons. Therefore, posture carries dual equally important connotations; the physical kneeling down where we are able to and our heart attitude, which should show respect, humility and deep awe for God.

## 10.7 Proportionality in Prayer

In law, the principle of proportionality is the idea that an action should not be more severe than is necessary, especially in a war or when punishing someone for a crime.[56] It is the idea that a punishment for a particular crime must relate to how serious the crime is.[57] Proportionality therefore relates to the quality of corresponding in size or amount to something else. In relation to prevailing prayer, it means our prayers must be equal, should correspond and should be commensurate with the force of the opposition. As discussed earlier, we have a common enemy – Satan and its demons. We also identified

---

[56] Definition of proportionality. Available at https://www.collinsdictionary.com/dictionary/english/proportionality> (Accessed 20 January 2017)

[57] What is proportionality? Available at https://dictionary.cambridge.org/dictionary/english/proportionality>

that spirits are illegal on the earth realm without a body. Therefore, one of the ways Satan perpetrate evils most times is through human beings who give their bodies to be used by demonic spirits.

Therefore, the source of all evil is Satan. Satan forms the opposition and the opposition is not gentle. Have you been in a situation before and you think you are almost getting out and then another one rears its head and then another and another? It's as if everywhere you turn, you are surrounded by calamities and heart-breaking situations? It is the work of Satan, its ministry is to 'steal, kill and destroy' (**John 10:10; NKJV**) and to accomplish the three fold mission statement, Bible says it runs to and fro the earth. Curiously, on the two occasions in which the sons of God gathered in the spirit realm, Satan was there and on both occasions, God had to ask Satan, 'From where do you come?'. Satan's response was the same *'going to and fro on the earth…'* (**Job 1:7; 2:2 NKJV**). In **1 Peter 5:8** Bible adds the objective of the 'to and fro' movement, which is to **seek whom he may devour.** Therefore, while in Daniel's dispensation the lions were confined in a den, in our day, the devil is roaring like a lion and it's on a rampage, but Glory to God that we have the 'Lion of the Tribe of Judah' on our inside (**Revelation 5:5; NKJV**). Therefore, greater is He that is in us than he that is in the world. We do not see Satan on the earth as a physical fact. This means that the destructions, sadness and sorrows that we see are caused by him. It means that spiritual forces are more real than the physical because there are so many things we don't see with our physical eyes, we do see the effects and impacts but we do not see the force behind them. It also means that Satan's mission to 'steal, kill and destroy' is continuing relentlessly and with force.

The essence of proportionality in prayer is that we must realise that the opposition, which is Satan, is not gentle. Therefore, we need to apply proportionate or equal force in the place of prayer. In **Zechariah 1**, the prophet was shown a vision of four horns that were sent to scatter Israel, Judah and Jerusalem to the extent that people were unable to lift their heads. In proportion to the four horns, God sent four carpenters/craftsmen to terrorise the four horns.

> Then I raised my eyes and looked, and there *were* four horns. [19] And I said to the angel who talked with me, "What *are* these?" So he answered me, "These *are* the horns that have scattered Judah, Israel, and Jerusalem." [20] Then the LORD showed me four craftsmen. [21] And I said, "What are these coming to do?" So he said, "These *are* the horns that scattered Judah, so that no one could lift up his head; but the craftsmen[a] are coming to terrify them, to cast out the horns of the nations that lifted up *their* horn against the land of Judah to scatter it. (**Zechariah 1:18-21**) (**NKJV**).

Why didn't God send one craftsman/carpenter in response to the four horns? Power must match power, there must be fire for fire! Therefore, when we engage in prevailing prayer and depending on what we are dealing with in prayer, we must not be lethargic! While it is not expected that we use a gun to kill an ant, it will amount to foolishness to attempt to use a broomstick to kill a snake.

I would use the example of Hannah's prayer to conclude on proportionality. As mentioned in previous chapters, the story of Hannah has been sermonised severally to show how we should pour out our heart to God in prayer. Indeed, Hannah was driven by desperation, she was provoked by Peninnah but propelled to pray. A critical point that people don't talk about in Hannah's story is that God was the source of her problem, because Bible says '... although the Lord had closed her womb' (**1 Samuel 1:5b; NKJV**). This is an exception to the general rule that Satan is the source of all troubles. Indeed, we can see in scriptures that God allowed Satan to bring calamities to Job, God allowed Joseph's brother's to sell him to the Ishmaelite traders, God allowed Daniel to be hated to the point that a law was promulgated and he was eventually thrown into the lions' den...God allowed the early Church to be persecuted so the gospel could spread from Jerusalem to Judea, Samaria and to the uttermost part of the earth as He originally intended. So there are instances where we are in trouble that are seemingly being entrenched by Satan but God may have allowed them. Hannah's situation was one of such situations where God was the source of her problem but it was for a reason.

In Hannah's story we could see the wickedness or the 'ungentleness' of the opposition. It was bad enough that Hannah was barren, it was bad enough that in the sharing of meat at Shiloh she could only have a large portion while Peninnah was given portions in proportion to the number of children she had. Despite the pains and deprivation she already suffered, Bible records that Hannah was provoked severely by Peninnah (**1 Samuel 1:6; NKJV**). We must realise that the opposition is not gentle.

Hannah responded to her provocation in pain, in tears and in fasting. Bible says, **'...therefore, she wept and did not eat'** (**1 Samuel 1:7b; NKJV**). Have we been in situations where there is plenty, and yet we are unable to eat? You are so provoked that there is no space for anything, your situations kind of fill you up that there is no appetite for even your favourite meal or drink? Hannah was in that exact situation. What was her further response? It is instructive that Hannah did not only weep and refrain from eating, she also did not allow any pity-party by her loving husband. Rather, Hannah took her prayer to the next level.

> So Hannah arose after they had finished eating and drinking in Shiloh… And she *was* in bitterness of soul, and prayed to the LORD and wept in anguish. [11] Then she made a vow and said, "O LORD of hosts, if You will indeed look on the affliction of Your maidservant and remember me, and not forget Your maidservant, but will give Your maidservant a male child, then I will give him to the LORD all the days of his life, and no razor shall come upon his head." [12] And it happened, as she continued praying before the LORD, that Eli watched her mouth. [13] Now Hannah spoke in her heart; only her lips moved, but her voice was not heard. Therefore Eli thought she was drunk. [14] So Eli said to her, "How long will you be drunk? Put your wine away from you!" [15] But Hannah answered and said, "No, my lord, I *am* a woman of sorrowful spirit. I have drunk neither wine nor intoxicating drink, but have poured out my soul before the LORD. [16] "Do not consider your maidservant a wicked woman for out of the abundance of my complaint

and grief I have spoken until now." <sup>17</sup> Then Eli answered and said, "Go in peace, and the God of Israel grant your petition which you have asked of Him." <sup>18</sup> And she said, "Let your maidservant find favor in your sight." So the woman went her way and ate, and her face was no longer *sad*. (**1 Samuel 1:9-18**) (**NKJV**).

There isn't space here to unpack the steps Hannah took in proportion to the opposition. However, the first thing she did was to **arise.** We need to arise from the situation we are in, we don't have to bury our heads in shame and in pain. No matter how protracted and no matter how despicable we may appear before the people around us because of our situation, we must arise! Despite ongoing widespread persecution, the Church needs to arise for this is also the hour when people will troop to the Church to seek solution, solace and succour. Arise Church!

Second, Hannah didn't engage in altercation with Peninnah, she didn't allow the sweet words of her husband to stop her, neither did she get carried away by the feasting. There comes a time when some things must come to an end. This is not the first time Hannah came to Shiloh, we do not know how many times they had been previously, but Bible records that Elkanah and his family went to Shiloh yearly. Apparently, this was also not the first time she may have been provoked by Peninnah, and maybe on previous occasions, she may have responded and reacted in the flesh by engaging in altercations with Peninnah.

However, on this occasion, the third thing we observe that Hannah did was that she was provoked to engage proportionality in prayer because she realised that the source of her problem and the only one who has the solution was God.

> But to Hannah he would give a double portion, for he loved Hannah, although *the LORD had closed her womb*. <sup>6</sup> And her rival also provoked her severely, to make her miserable, because *the LORD had closed her womb*. (**1 Samuel 1:5-6**) (**NKJV**).

There are a lot more to glean from Hannah's story, but the fact that God was the source of her problem makes me think that in God's sovereignty, God already saw into the future that Eli's sons Hophni and Phinehas were not going to be upright so God made Hannah to be barren until such a year, when she would be provoked to the point when she would run to and pour out her heart to Him? The reason I think this way is because God gave us a will, Hannah may have prayed, poured out her heart but may not have made the vow, or she may have made the vow but not fulfil it. However, because everything was God orchestrated or God ordained, she made a vow and fulfilled it whereby she met God's need for a Priest and Prophet in Israel at that time in history. Perhaps the reason for this protracted situation, the reason for this severe provocation from the enemy is because God wants you to run to Him and He wants you and your story or testimony to fill a void and meet a need for His eternal purpose and plan? Do not give up!

Also concerning the early Church, it appeared they were going to become complacent, turning a movement (the outpouring of the Holy Spirit) into a monument by remaining in Jerusalem? It appeared that contrary to the instruction of the Lord Jesus Christ that they were going to be happy and comfortable with spreading the gospel around their comfort, convenient zones? However, God's will was for them to make a start in Jerusalem but then spread to Judea, Samaria and to the ends of the earth, therefore, the Lord who is Almighty, all-knowing, omnipotent, omnipresent and omniscient saw into the future and decided to allow persecution so that His original intent for the spread of the gospel to the entire world was accomplished. Could this relate to the Church in contemporary times? Of course we recognise that the ongoing persecutions are signs of the end time, but could it also be something that God has allowed so His Church could wake up? Be bold Church! You are the end time army of the Most High, be strong and be courageous!

Hannah was very careful and humble in her response when Eli thought that she was drunk. (The tension between pastors and prayer and praise/worship coordinators most of which stems from the lack of discernment didn't start today). Therefore, we should learn that with proportionality, it was not only Hannah's prayer, pouring out her heart to God and vow, but her humility, ability to walk in love together with her respect and submission to authority, all worked together to bring her miracle. She agreed with Eli's prayer, she went, ate and began to be merry, she was no longer sad. Even though she hasn't seen the physical manifestation of her prayer, she thanked God in advance (the specific prayer of thanksgiving) because she believed in her heart that the matter was already settled. Proportionality includes walking in love and being in submission to authority. We may be doing everything right but that one thing that is wrong and uncorrected can hinder our prayers.

Therefore, with proportionality in prayer, not only are we to arise out of the dire situations we find ourselves, not only are we to disregard pity-parties, and not only are we to submit to authority, we must also know the source of our problem and then apply proportionate and persistent force. Hannah did not resign to fate and say 'what's gonna be, gonna be'. Rather, she ran to God who is the source of her barrenness, because all good and perfect gifts come from God and He promised that none shall be barren. Similarly, when the source of our problem is the devil, we need to apply proportionate force to rebuke him first and then superimpose God's will in our lives. Jeremiah was first asked to root out, pull down, destroy and throw down, before he was to build and plant (**Jeremiah 1:10; NKJV**).

## Conclusion

As I noted at the introductory part of this book, it is evident that persecution is upon the Church, as promised in scriptures and as happened with Daniel and the early Church. Everyone who is against the Church do not only think they are enthroning justice but that they are also doing God a great service, as some of them continue to twist (misinterpret) scriptures to suit their purpose. But the devil is a lair. We have been forewarned in scriptures and we cannot be deceived. Simultaneously, Bible also records that people will come to the Church and ask for help, for solution, for direction, for salvation and deliverance. What will prepare the Church for the forthcoming influx is when we engage the 7 P words in prayer, we must continue to maintain the right *posture* as we *prioritise* the *place* of prayer, and we must also be *precise, purposeful, persistent and proportionate* in prayers.

The 7 'P' words are cumulative and they all relate to how we must engage in prevailing prayer. The need to have a specific location, *place* of prayer in these times cannot be overemphasised. In addition to the specific place, we need to maintain an attitude and atmosphere of prayer. We also need to *prioritise* prayer. We can't afford to respond any other way than by prayers. Let our default position be prayers because we can never go wrong when we pray. Furthermore, prayer is communication with our Heavenly Father, therefore our *posture* when we pray is important. We must not be casual, careless or complacent; engaging in pleasantries, and chatting on social media while we pray. Rather, we must show reverence both in our heart and outwardly. We must be *precise* in prayers. We can avoid vagueness when we have knowledge of God's word. We must be *purposeful* in prayers. The purpose for coming to God is first because He loves us and we love Him. He is our Father and we belong to Him thus, our purpose must first be to have intimacy with Him. Purposeful prayer is also to enforce God's will on earth. We must also be *persistent* and *proportionate* in prayer.

With Hannah, one may ask; what did God respond to? Was it her pouring out her heart, was it her vow or was it Eli's prayer? I think all worked together and most importantly she did not harbour bitterness or resentment. She humbled herself, submitted to authority and declared an 'Amen' to Eli's prayer by saying 'let your maidservant find favour in your sight' despite Eli's earlier perception of her as a drunk. She then went afterwards to eat and thank God even when she hadn't received the physical manifestation. When we engage in prevailing prayers, we must also learn to engage in specific prayer of thanksgiving and we should learn to rejoice in advance.

# Conclusion
# Proof of Prevailing Prayer

The proof of prevailing may be found in the answers to our prayers. Thank God we serve a God who is a prayer answering Father. We already discussed these in Chapter 8, but also, in **Psalms 65:2** Bible says, *'O You who hear prayers, to You all flesh will come'*. Further in verse 5, the Psalmist says *'By terrible things in righteousness wilt thou answer us...'* (**KJV**) and he began to list some of the terrible ways in which God answers us. In other words, God does not answer in the exact way and time we expect because His ways and thoughts are higher than ours.

Daniel was used as case study in the first part of this book. He had a place of prayer, he prioritised prayer, he had the appropriate posture, he was precise, purposeful, persistent and he was proportionate in his prayers and yet in our estimation, it would appear that there was no proof, because God did not answer his prayers. This is so because the obvious expectation would have been for God to cause the laws to be reversed or repealed immediately so that Daniel wouldn't be in breach and be made to face the consequences of being thrown into the den of lions. Nevertheless, despite Daniel's prayers he was thrown into the lions' den. His answers came when God sealed up the mouths of the lions that they could not touch or harm him. I think this is one of the 'terrible' ways God answers us? No wonder the Psalmist says, *'...the Lord Most High is terrible; He is a great king over all the earth'.* (**Psalms 47:2; KJV**).

'Terrible' in the sense that sometimes we get into very precarious situations in which we give up, because if God was going to answer and save us, he could have done it earlier? It appears things have gone progressively worse and there is no hope anymore?[58] Nevertheless, when God shows up, it is usually without controversy. God preserved Daniel in the lions' den and yet his adversaries didn't survive, they were torn into shreds and feasted upon by the lions within seconds of being thrown into the same den. God demonstrated His might and power to the king and everyone in Babylon and especially to Daniel that He is God who is terrible and who answers in defence of His people in terrible ways.

Whilst we acknowledge that God hears and answers us and this is a vital proof of our prayers, the thrust of this book is not to engage prevailing prayer only because we expect proof in the form of answers. Rather, the thrust is to encourage us to engage in prevailing prayer as a lifestyle whether we see immediate answers or not. Therefore, whilst the proof of prevailing prayers, which is answers to our prayers is good impetus, we must continue to engage in prevailing prayers even when we don't seem to get the answers that we desire for the following reasons.

First, prayers don't die, like we said in chapter two, words spoken by a spirit don't die, they must find points of entry and come into physical manifestation no matter how long it takes unless they are reversed by words of a superior spirit. We know that in the spiritual hierarchy we are next to the God-Head, therefore we have higher authority and no other spiritual force can stop our words from coming into manifestations. In this sense, we must not give up or speak contrary words to negate our prayers. No matter how long it takes,

---

[58] This scenario is replete in the Bible; recall the other three Hebrew children Shadrach, Meshach and Abednego and how the fire was heated seven times more when they prayed? God allowed them to heat up the fire 7 times more and allowed these three boys to be thrown in. But guess what; our 'Terrible God' shows up as a fourth man in the fire. Although the people who threw the three boys into the fire got burnt to death, these three youths didn't even have a smell of smoke on them let alone be burnt by the fire. What an awesome God we serve! Recall also Lazarus that while he was sick, there was hope and therefore message was sent to the Lord Jesus who was in a nearby city? Recall how Bible records that the Lord delayed another 3 days before he came to the scene? In fact by the time He arrived Lazarus was already dead and buried, now in the tomb for four days? Nevertheless, the Lord called him forth out of the grave...We serve a 'Terrible God' who answers us in terrible ways.

answers to our prayers are sure to come. It may not be in our lifetime, it may be in the next generation if the Lord tarries.

Second, sometimes, answers to some of the prayers we engage in are meant to manifest in the next generation and generations yet unborn. A typical example was Jacob when he prevailed over the angel he wrestled with. Recall that the outcome of that wrestling was not only a physical deformity, as Jacob's thigh was out of joint, but also more importantly, the wrestling resulted in the birth of the nation of Israel. A nation is not born at once but 'as soon as Zion travails she brought forth her children' (**Isaiah 66:8b; KJV**). When we take the posture of travailing in prayer then we are ready to birth the next generation. Prevailing prayer will result in the birthing of nations and shaping of destinies that we may not live long enough to see. Therefore, if the Lord tarries, engaging in prevailing prayer is a great opportunity to leave a legacy of prayer for the next generation.

The third reason why we should engage in prevailing prayers regardless of answers is because prayer connects us to God. Prayer establishes our relationship with God, in which we have access to our Heavenly Father, through the Lord Jesus Christ. Prevailing prayer is a lifeline that connects us with our source without which we are dead spiritually. Therefore, prayer is where we commune with the Father, where we are energised, revitalised and most importantly, we become one with the Father.

Fourth, as we discussed in the book, there is a place where prayer and praise mix and our prayers are collected in golden bowls and offered together with incense unto God. Therefore, prevailing prayer lifestyle helps us to make deposits in our spiritual bank accounts. What an honour that it is our prayers in golden bowls that the twenty-four elders and the four living creatures hold whiles they sang the new song... (**Revelation 5:8**). Also, as stated in **Revelation 8:3-4**, the angel had the golden censer with much incense to offer together with the prayers of the saint. What an honour that heaven is waiting on our prayers!

We cannot overemphasise the fact that God hears and answers our prayer and that the proof of prevailing prayers is the answers and physical manifestations we receive. Nevertheless, the danger of looking for proof of prevailing prayer is that some people might stop praying as soon as they get answers, some might not even pray at all until or unless they have problems for which they need answers and solutions. The worse danger is that the devil also has answers and solutions, but these are always inferior and perverse compared to the overall great and divine package and purpose of God for our lives. We short-change ourselves when we settle for lesser options. Therefore, if the only reason we pray is because we want answers and solutions as proof of our prayers, the enemy might take advantage to give us what we want so we can stop praying? God forbid!

The angels, the four living creatures and the twenty-four elders are waiting on our prayers to offer with incense unto God. We cannot fail in this awesome privilege to provide prayers and ensure the golden bowls are constantly full. What an encouragement, because whatever we deposit in our spiritual bank account are treasures that cannot be stolen or broken into and which can be available to our children and generations yet unborn. This makes prevailing prayer a lifelong relationship and therefore a lifestyle.

## What is the Lifestyle?

Throughout the book, we have discussed the meaning of prevailing prayer being spiritual communication orchestrated by God or in line with God's divine mandate and fervently enforced on earth on a continuous basis. We have discussed the different types of prayer and the categorisation of prayer whether made in public or private by individuals or groups, the essential ingredients of faith and agreement underlying every prayer. Using Daniel as a case study, we have also discussed how the Church must prioritise the place of prayer, continue in intimate *relationship*, which will result in receiving *revelation* and then culminate in the continued *relevance* of the Church on earth despite ongoing obnoxious laws and persecutions.

## The Lifestyle of Love

In addition, it is important to understand that certain lifestyles are needed to engage in prevailing prayer. The first is the lifestyle of *love, love and love (triple love)*. Our love for God will drive us to the place of prayer. Our ability and decision to prioritise the place of prayer is directly proportionate to the extent of our love for God. The Bible says to love the Lord our God with all our hearts, soul, might, mind and strength **(Deuteronomy 6:5; Matthew 22:37; Mark 12:30; Luke 10:27; NKJV)**. When we love the Lord, we will prioritise spending more time with Him in the place of prayer, including the prayer of worship, ministering to and worshiping Him with fasting and prayers like Anna did even at over 80 years old **(Luke 2:37; NKJV)**. At those times of intimacy and communion, God reveals His mind to us and we are able to enforce His mandate here on earth.

We also need to be driven by love for ourselves. Love for self is scarcely talked about and misunderstood, yet it is vital. We need to love ourselves and see ourselves the way God sees us. There is a divine purpose for all of God's creation and especially those who have become part of God's family. The Psalmist declares that we are fearfully and wonderfully made and that before we were formed in our mothers' wombs God knew us and our days have been written down in His book. **(Psalms 139:14-16; NKJV).** In other words, God has a divine purpose for our lives long before we were conceived and we have been chosen and predestined to be part of God's family even before the foundations of the world. Unfortunately, Satan's mission is to derail some of us from fulfilling the divine purpose. Therefore, loving ourselves will drive us to prioritise the place of prayers to discover and fulfil God's divine purpose for our lives and our children regardless of the devices and schemes of the enemy. Nevertheless, we shouldn't be self-centred, our prayers shouldn't be laced with 'me, I, myself, my family...' alone. We need to extend the same love God has given to us to others.

Therefore, the last love in the triple love is love for our neighbours. Everyone we come in contact with is a neighbour. God desires, not only that we should love our neighbours as ourselves, but that all men should be saved hence the Lord Jesus Christ left us with the ministry of reconciliation. It is difficult to pray for someone you abhor. The Bible instructs us to love our enemies, pray for those who persecute us and do good to our enemies. **(Matthew 5:44; Proverbs 25:21-22; Romans 12:20; NKJV)**. Therefore, we need to love so we can pray for the people around us. The word says the love of Christ has been shared abroad our heart by the Holy Ghost (**Romans 5:5b; NKJV**) and so it is possible to love others with the love of God. Also, **2 Corinthians 5:14** says the love of God constrains or compels us (NKJV). Let love propel and compel us to pray for other people, our communities, cities and nations of the world and also pray for people who occupy positions of authority. The preconditions of *selflessness, identification, persistence and discernment* to effective prayer of intercession and supplication discussed in Chapter 3 are summed up in our love for others. When we love other people, we will be able to lay down our lives selflessly and sacrificially, we will be able to identify with their situation and not be judgmental and we will be able to persist in prayers for them.

We must also realise that Satan is the god of this world and he has blinded the minds of people and hence they cannot see the love, peace and power of the glorious gospel of the Lord Jesus Christ. Evangelism must be backed by prayers and fuelled by the Holy Spirit. The early Church were locked up in the upper room in obedience to the Lord's instruction to tarry until they were endued with power on the Day of Pentecost. It was the force of Pentecost that brought boldness to the Apostles and the daily addition to the Church was a consequence of the manifestation of God's power in the preaching of the gospel and the demonstration of love in the communal and selfless living of the apostles that the people saw.

Closely linked to love is forgiveness. We need to forgive those who hurt us and let God avenge for us. In addition to preaching, one vital tool to reconciling the world back to God is through the instrumentality of prevailing prayers. We need to continue to intercede for the dying world. Loving God, loving ourselves and loving our neighbour is a command from God. We must be at peace with all men and walk in love towards all men.

## A life in the Word and in the Spirit

In addition to love, which is multidimensional, another lifestyle to cultivate to enhance prevailing prayers is to be saturated with God's word. We need to constantly study, meditate and confess the word of God. The Bible is God's manual for His creation because it is God's will and His original intent for creation. Therefore, to engage in prevailing prayers as we have discussed in this book, we should be acquainted with the manual to which we need God's creation to conform. This is vital because enforcement can only be according to law i.e. according to what has been legislated. Do we know what has been written in the manual? We need to search and find where it has been written and then carry out enforcement according to what has been written. In addition to 'Your Kingdom come Your will be done…' that gives us enforcement power, **1 John 5:14-15** says when we pray according to His will, He hears and answers. God's will is His word. We need to be full of the word because our being full of the word is directly proportional to our ability to prioritise the place of prayer, our understanding of the need to pray with the right posture, to be precise, purposeful, persistent and proportionate in prayer. Of course, as noted earlier, knowledge of the word of God includes both the *logos* written and the *rhema* spoken/revealed word.

A life in the Spirit is also vital in engaging in prevailing prayer. The Bible describes believers as experiencing a new birth at the point of receiving Jesus Christ as Lord and personal saviour. More often than not, this new birth is not talked about, is not taught, not nurtured, not accurately understood and not developed, but the starting point is as declared in **John 3:6 'That which is born of the flesh is flesh and that which is born of the Spirit is spirit.' (NKJV).** This implies that a new spirit life is born at the new birth. How to grow and cultivate this new life, is hardly taught. Therefore, individual believers are left to themselves. However, the Holy Spirit was promised and given to us on the Day of Pentecost. He is with us and abides in us continually to help, teach and guide us into all truth. He is our helper. Our *paracletos* (one called alongside to help: helper, comforter, teacher, guide, intercessor, advocate, enabler and standby), Therefore, a life in the Spirit includes recognising that we have a helper-the Holy Spirit- and engaging Him in our daily lives, including in the area of prayer. This is important because Apostle Paul says we do not know what to pray for as we ought because of our weaknesses, shortcomings, limitations or inadequacies, but that the Holy Spirit knows, not only what we should pray for, but can actually help us to pray accurately, precisely and effectively.

Therefore, a lifestyle in God's word that can help us in prevailing prayers is not limited to the Bible, but it also includes knowing what the Holy Spirit is speaking to us; hearing a prophetic word. A life in the spirit is enhanced by our intimacy with the Holy Spirit, which includes reverencing Him, learning to hear Him, being sensitive, totally yielded to and promptly obeying Him. Therefore, these lifestyles of love, life in the word and in the spirit are cumulative. We must love as Christ has commanded us to, Jesus was moved by compassion to perform most of the miracles recorded in scriptures. Likewise, compassion should make us to deepen our intimacy with God our Father and it should also propel us to pray for others, especially people and situations that we may never be acquainted with in our lifetime.

Some people might say a lifestyle of holiness, sin-free living, righteousness and obedience are more important than what I have listed above. Yes; these are equally important, but I think very strongly that they all come under the lifestyle of *Love* because we naturally gravitate towards the people we love, we like to spend time with them and as we do, there is usually a rob-off of their character and mannerisms in our lives. This is the same with God, our love for God is demonstrated in the time we spend with Him in prayer and as we do, we become more like Him. Moses spent so much time with God that he didn't realise how much of God's glory that had robbed-off on him in the process, so much so that Aaron and the entire camp of the children of Israel were frightened and couldn't come near him. He had to put a veil on his face to shroud the glory whenever he spoke with them (**Exodus 34:28-35; NKJV**). As we behold Him, as in a mirror, we are transformed into the same image, Christ is formed in us as we spend time with God in prayer.

Similarly, when we love God and spend time with Him in prayer, sin will not only be far from us, but we will also continue to exude God's glory. His righteous nature and holiness in our daily living becomes our default position. Also, our love for God will make us obedient to His word and His commandments. When we love somebody, the last thing we want to do is make them sad, disobey or disappoint them. Our love for them will always propel us to follow their instructions, to refrain from what will displease them and to do only those things that would make them proud. This is the exact same thing with God. No wonder the Lord Jesus Christ said love is the fulfilment of the law. Sometimes we sermonise on the subject of sin too often that it leaves us more sin conscious than the consciousness of the righteous nature we possessed at the new birth. The best way to get out a dirt from a glass of clean water is to keep pouring more clean water into the glass.

## Prevailing Prayer: Unfinished Business

Are there instances where and when I engaged in prevailing prayers? How did God come through for me? Obviously, I believe we've all engaged in prevailing prayers and we continue to do so, as God continues to come through for us in diverse ways. Your testimonies are great and vital to the process of persistence in prevailing prayer. Therefore, we must not discount or forget our testimonies. In most instances when I think I engaged in prevailing prayers, I was clueless as to what I was doing. However, in hindsight, I realised God came through for me not necessarily because I prayed but because of His love, mercy and grace, which enabled me to engage all spiritual principles, especially walking in love with all men while I prayed.

An instance that occurred sometime in 2001, was one in which despite all the unsavoury situations, I chose to walk in love. I mentioned the situation briefly earlier in the book. I had a medical condition which made it impossible for me to be pregnant after my first child. I sought help from different medical experts, but the result was the same, namely, that I will be unable to conceive. During this period there were persistent provocations from the enemy, but purposefully, I focused on God and His word in prayers. Finally, I met my doctor who carried out several ultrasound scan tests with the results that there were ovarian cyst and fibroids in my womb. My doctor later advised that if I ever wanted to be pregnant again, it would be necessary for me to undergo a surgery to remove them, because according to him, the cyst is large and the fibroids are many leaving no space for a baby to stay. 'Even if you got pregnant, there is 99% chances of miscarriage' my doctor concluded.

Consequently, my doctor, my husband and I, agreed a date in December 2000 to have the surgery done. However, on the agreed date I refused to show up at the hospital. I recall that my spiritual Dad Rev Efe Obuke had flown in to Lagos to see me and to pray with me on the Sunday preceding the Monday of the scheduled surgery. On arrival at my house, he was surprised to hear that I had gone to the saloon to make my hair. When I returned and we discussed, I told him that I am not having a surgery because I have prayed, but the Lord has not given me a go-ahead. Therefore, regardless of medical report and advice, I wouldn't go for a surgery.[59] My spiritual Dad is also a medical doctor therefore, he was aware of my condition. Nevertheless, he said, to me to follow my heart and if I haven't heard from the Lord then I should wait to know the direction the Holy Spirit would have me take. He has taught me/us the life in the Spirit and so he was pleased to hear my decision and the reason for my decision.

A few things happened, but I kept praying and declaring God's word that says *'...Himself took my infirmities and diseases...' 'by His stripe I was healed'* (Isaiah 53:4-5; Matthew 8:17; 1 Peter 2:24; NKJV). We had a programme in my local church in Lagos then, at which a guest minster preached and specifically prayed for me. That prayer was to me the seed/word that I needed. Nevertheless, my situation remained. However, there was a shift in my prayer afterwards, as my attitude and general disposition changed. Instead of praying and asking for healing, I began to thank God for my twin boys, because that was what the guest preacher prayed for. He specifically mentioned a boy but I said in my heart I wanted two boys; twins.[60] In retrospect, I now know this was a specific prayer of thanksgiving i.e. thanking God while we wait for the physical manifestation of what we prayed about.

Sometime in May 2001, my husband and I decided to see my doctor because I noticed a few changes in my body. With some trepidation, we saw my doctor. He was very upset because he had lost his Dad and being the first

---

[59] Please this is a specific and personal walk I had with the Lord at that time. Taking medication is not wrong, neither does following medical advice to go for a surgery mean you are not walking in faith. God can and does work with medicine to bring us our healing and deliverance therefore we must not discount medical advice.

[60] I didn't have twins, but I had my boys in quick succession. The Lord revealed to me in a vision why I wouldn't be able to have twins and the consequences if I insisted. That is another story, but I am grateful to God for how merciful He is, that He does not give us what we ask and pray for sometimes. I am indeed grateful.

son, he had postponed the funeral, so he could be present to carry out the surgery as we agreed. Unfortunately, I failed to show up for the surgery and I didn't even send a word to cancel the appointment. Thus, meeting with my doctor, was really difficult. We eventually did, and I apologised profusely for not turning up for the surgery.

After the preliminary exchange of pleasantries, I told my doctor my suspicion and his first reaction was 'oh you did the surgery elsewhere?' 'No I didn't' I responded. 'But there is no way you can be pregnant with those things in your womb. It is impossible!' Replied my doctor. He examined me and didn't see any scar in my lower abdomen indicative of surgery, but he also noticed the movements and the largeness of my tommy. He recommended a scan immediately which confirmed that I was about 3 months pregnant. While I was giggling with excitement, thanking God and holding my hubby's hands, the doctors weren't at all. There was such a concern on both their faces.

The complexity that the medical team had to deal with was that the cyst and fibroids were still in my womb. Accordingly they thought removing my baby at some point might be better. My pregnancy became a case study for how to manage the foetus in the midst of cyst and fibroids. At 4 months, I looked like I was ready to have my baby because at every point I presented like multiple pregnancy because of the presence of the cyst and fibroids.

I still didn't have any indication from the Holy Spirit to undergo a surgery so the suggestion to remove my baby at 6 months was never presented to me a second time. My doctor had to manage the medical team and explained to them my stance. Sometimes in our walk with God we need to take a stance and heaven will back us up. Miraculously, I carried my pregnancy to term and it was at the point of delivery that my doctor said he is breached and therefore only a caesarean section (C-Section) could bring my baby out. Of course, at this point, there was a go-ahead signal to undergo a C-Section. I immediately told my doctor that this is the right time to do a surgery and told him to try and remove those things – cyst and fibroids as well. 'It is not that easy and straightforward' said my doctor. 'This procedure is usually very bloody and so the first priority is to save your life first and then your baby's' he noted further. At this point fear gripped me but I kept speaking the word. I was given anaesthesia and told to breathe normally whilst one of the doctors engaged me in some conversation until I faded away...

I was on a long journey in a tunnel initially being driven by a 'Being'. He told me I would be fine but that he was a messenger that was told to pick me. At his reassurances I became calm. However, the journey went on and on and I became curious; 'where are we going? This journey is getting too long', 'when are we going to arrive at our destination?' I asked several questions in desperation but didn't get any response. Rather, the speed at which we travelled doubled...

At this point, I began to say Lord have mercy. In my subconscious, I continued to make confessions and declarations, most of which I had made during my pregnancy... ***I shall not die but live, I shall live to declare the goodness of God. The end for me is peace.*** At some point, I didn't know where I was any more, but I realised I was still on the journey but couldn't see the 'Being' that carried me. All I could see was clouds all around me. After a while, we came to a place full of people, with so many activities going on and everyone very busy. You couldn't stop anyone to ask a question. Everything was happening very fast beyond my comprehension. So, in my subconscious, I asked where on earth do you have things move this fast...?

At that moment, I found myself standing in front of another 'Being' different from the one who carried me earlier. I looked like an ant compared to the size of this being as I found myself all alone with clouds all around. And in a flash, while I stood before this Being, like the speed of lightning, everything about my life came to me in a picture. With each flash I saw the words 'unfinished business'. My husband flashed...unfinished business, my only child then Oyarelemi (Lemmy) flashed ...unfinished business, my job flashed... unfinished business my local church flashed.... unfinished business. Everything I was engaged in all my life up to that particular season flashed and with every picture came the words 'unfinished business'. Suddenly, the Being before whom I stood pushed me back and said, 'this one has unfinished businesses, she is not meant to be here yet'. And with that push, I woke up...

I saw my little sister Emily Gbinigie beside my bed and a nurse on the other side of the bed. I asked them where I was and as they began to explain to me that I was in the hospital and that I had a baby boy, I fell into subconscious again. This time I found myself right in front of the 'Being' who pushed me the first time. He looked at me and smiled and pushed me a second time, this time with a greater force and I woke up again with Emily and the nurse still beside me. I began to say; 'yes, I knew it, I know I cannot die now because I have unfinished business!' My sister was very happy to see me conscious and talking, but she wondered about what I was saying. The nurse tried to get me to calm down and to stop me from talking but she couldn't. I went on repeatedly saying 'I have unfinished business, unfinished business, unfinished business, unfinished business....' and then I began to throw-up and finally came back to full consciousness.

I was later told that I had been given a second dosage of anaesthesia to keep me sleeping because although my child was brought out within the first 5 to 10 mins after I was wheeled into the theatre, it took over an hour before I was wheeled out. The doctors began taking out the cyst and fibroids after they removed my baby and since it was taking long and it was almost time for the first anaesthesia to wear out, they had to give me a second dose to keep me sleeping so they could finish. They wheeled me to the recovery room and applied all the recovery techniques on me, but I was on my long journey. According to the nurse, although I didn't respond to recovery techniques, they wheeled me to my hospital room only after I resumed breathing. Previously, I didn't show any signs of life. Apparently, I had slept for almost 2 days and they had begun feeding my baby with milk.

This is an experience in which I think God showed me mercy. In my subconscious, I kept muttering those words *'I shall not die, I shall live, the expectation of the righteous shall not be cut short, I am the righteousness of God in Christ Jesus therefore my expectations shall not be cut short, my end is peace, I shall live...'* these words were in my subconscious mind rolling over and over whilst I was on the long journey. Although I prayed like I never did in all my life during the 9 months of pregnancy, the burden to pray never left me even after delivery. After I was discharged from the hospital, it was as though the battle had only just began and I continued to pray...

While I prepared for the prayer weekend in my local Church AGP in 2017, the Lord impressed in my heart that for now and eternity prevailing prayer remains **UNFINISHED BUSINESS**...*ad-infinitum...*, a *continuum...* Therefore, while I prayed to God to help me 'finish my assignment' at the start of this book, it appears there is one assignment that I and we cannot finish – prevailing prayer. I am more surprised than anyone else that I have written this book. It is actually a message for me and I continue to pray; 'Lord, teach me how to pray, help me to *prioritise* the *place* of prayer, teach me how to maintain appropriate *posture,* how to be *purposeful, precise, persistent and proportionate* in prayers'. The Holy Spirit is my/our helper.

# References

- Cambridge Dictionary available at http://dictionary.cambridge.org/dictionary/english/prevail> (Assessed 7 October 2017).

- Carn, B., 'Getting to the Next Level of your Life' https://www.youtube.com/watch?v=aR27VWe4IEg> (Assessed 20 May 2017).

- Cooper, L. E., *The New American Commentary Vol. 17:* (Biblical Hermeneutics) at https://hermeneutics.stackexchange.com/questions/8985/who-is-the-prince-of-tyre>

- David M, 'Does God Answer Prayers?' Being message preached at Liberty Square Ministries (LSM) Church Gwarinpa, Abuja Nigeria on Sunday 18 June 2017.

- English Oxford Living Dictionaries. Available at http://scriptoriumdaily.com/every-spiritual-blessing/> (Accessed 12 July 2017).

- First United Methodist Church Shreveport, 'Standing in the Gap'. Available at http://firstshreveport.org/2014/09/19/standing-in-the-gap/> also at http://www.myredeemerlives.com/intercession.html> (Assessed 18 March 2017).

- Hagin, K.E, 'The Believer's Authority 02 Exercising Our Authority 110188' (between the 10 to 20th minutes of the message. Available at https://www.youtube.com/watch?v=NUvGz0hMezA> (Assessed 20 October 2017).

- Harbor, W.A., *Logos Bible Software*. Logos Research Systems, Inc., 1994.

- Imoedemhe O., '**Workers: Refreshed or Burning Out?**' Unpublished message at a worker's retreat held in Leicester UK November 2015. (Personal notes referred).

- Imoedemhe, O., '**Worship: The Essence of Man**' (forthcoming), Unpublished manuscript refers

- Israel Meaning' *Abarim Publications*. Available at http://www.abarim-publications.com/Meaning/Israel.html#.WeCYGz93GUk> (Assessed 2 April 2017).

- Jamieson, R., Fausset, A. R., Brown, D. *A Commentary, Critical and Explanatory, on the Old and New Testaments*. 1997.

- Liardon, R., *God's Generals: Why They Succeeded and Why Some Failed* (Whitaker House).

- Munroe, M., 'How to Pray and Fast Effectively' Available at https://www.youtube.com/watch?v=l3kKSsUwUOI> (Accessed 20 January 2017)

- Nally, J.R., 'Who is the Prince of Tyre?' Dr Nally is the Theological Editor at Third Millennium Ministries (IIIM). Available at http://thirdmill.org/answers/answer.asp/file/40519> (Accessed 16 October 2017).

- Obuke, E., *School of the Spirit: Functioning in the Spirit* (Towdah Publications Benin City Nigeria 2013).

- Shirer, P., 'Stand in Victory' https://www.youtube.com/watch?v=xv9dncEL00k> (Assessed 20 November 2017).

- Shirer, P., 'Begin the Battle on Your Knees' Available at https://www.youtube.com/watch?v=FTulnDFuhds> (Accessed 4 April 2017).

- Torrey, R.A., 'Every Spiritual Blessing: From God, in Christ, By the Spirit' *The Scriptorium Daily* 10 April 2014.

- White, P., 'The Power of Fasting' https://www.youtube.com/watch?v=QJWCOG-Zb9g&t=855s> (Assessed 7 October 2017).

Printed in the United States
By Bookmasters